The Onward Workbook

The Onward Workbook

Daily Activities to Cultivate Your Emotional Resilience and Thrive

Elena Aguilar

JOSSEY-BASS™

A Wiley Brand

Published by Jossey-Bass
A Wiley Brand
One Montgomery Street, Suite 1000, San Francisco, CA 94104-4594—www.josseybass.com

Jossey-Bass books and products are available through most bookstores. To contact Jossey-Bass directly call our Customer Care Department within the U.S. at 800-956-7739, outside the U.S. at 317-572-3986, or fax 317-572-4002.

Wiley publishes in a variety of print and electronic formats and by print-on-demand. Some material included with standard print versions of this book may not be included in e-books or in print-on-demand. If this book refers to media such as a CD or DVD that is not included in the version you purchased, you may download this material at http://booksupport.wiley.com. For more information about Wiley products, visit www.wiley.com.

ISBN 9781119367383 (Paperback)
ISBN 9781119367277 (ePDF)
ISBN 9781119366973 (ePub)

Cover image: © Erick Joyner / EyeEm / Getty Images
Cover design by Wiley

Printed in the United States of America

FIRST EDITION

PB printing

SKY10031608_112321

CONTENTS

2 *Understand Emotions*   75

Reflecting on Regrets 103
Invite Your Emotions to Tea 104
Lessons About Strong Emotions 105
Thanking Your Emotions 107
Thanks, but No Thanks 109
Exploring Moments of Emotional Intensity 112
How to Breathe 114
RAIN: Dealing with Uncomfortable Emotions 116
Noticing Physical Cues 118
Assessing Your Stress 119
Quick Calm: Grounding 120
Recognizing Cognitive Distortions 121
A Letter to Anger 124
Artistic Depictions of Anger 125
Destination Postcard: Understand Emotions 126
Chapter Reflection 127

3 Tell Empowering Stories 129

Tell Empowering Stories: Resilience Self-Assessment 130
Three Good Things 132
Intention Setting 136
Start a New Habit 140
Reflect on Thoughts 141
What Einstein Says About Stories 149
Exploring the Impact of Cognitive Distortions 150
Catch That Distorted Thought 154
Visually Depicting a Life Story 156
Affirmations 158
Authoring Your Life 159
Take Apart That Thought 160
Try This Thought 164
Optimism: Choices 165
Challenge That Thought 166
Interrupting Distorted Thoughts 172
Problematic Core Beliefs 174
Rilke on Love 178
Challenge That Core Belief 179
"The Optimism of Uncertainty" 181
River and Rut Stories 182

4   *Build Community*   205

5   *Be Here Now*   267

8   Cultivate Compassion   413

9 Be a Learner   467

10 Play and Create   507

11   Ride the Waves of Change   549

12 Celebrate and Appreciate   591

Conclusion   629

PREFACE

Welcome to your workbook.

This is a place for you to explore the ideas I've described in *Onward* and to engage in practices that might shift your thinking, feeling, and behaviors. Resilience is cultivated with intentional action, and I hope that action might start in the pages of this book. I hope you'll allow me to guide you along some of the paths that can boost your resilience.

This book is me as a coach. It contains the questions I'd ask you if I were coaching you or facilitating your team's weekly meetings; it contains the activities I'd suggest that you try. You always have choice, and you don't have to do any activity that you don't want to do. But if we met in person, you'd hear the encouragement in my tone of voice and the gentle nudge in my words, "Just try it!" I'd encourage you to try every activity in this book, even the ones you'd like to turn away from.

Here are some of the ways I envision you using this workbook: I see you waking early on Monday, having slept a full eight hours, but up in time to crack this book open before heading off to school. I see you drinking a cup of coffee or tea, flipping through the chapter of the month, and spending 15 minutes on an exercise before going to school. In another scene, you're using this book with a group of colleagues, reflecting on one of the activities and talking to each other about your insights and connections. Sometimes I see you in the evening, jotting down a short reflection on one of the activities you'd tried that day. Finally, I envision you on a weekend afternoon, sitting under a tree or somewhere comfortable and digging into one of the activities that'll take a little longer, or going through a series of activities.

I hope you will integrate this workbook and its activities into your daily life. Toss it into your school bag on occasion, even only so that it serves as a reminder of what you're learning and practicing. You will cultivate your resilience if you engage in these activities regularly. You're about to build some mighty resilience muscles—and those need daily strengthening.

How This Workbook Is Organized

Each chapter contains enough activities for you to do one each day for a month—that's how I've envisioned that this workbook (and *Onward,* the book) will be consumed. However, there are many activities that you'll want to try more than once. You'll need to transform these activities into mental and physical habits in order to truly cultivate your resilience. It's the equivalent of wanting to have big biceps; you know that you'll need to do more than one set of biceps curls on one day if you're going to change your body shape. Of course, I don't assume that you'll be able to do every one of these exercises every day. That's why you need to try them all—so that you can figure out which ones work best for you and which ones most benefit your mind.

The order of activities in each chapter is somewhat random. The first activities introduce the habit, and the final activities guide you to reflect on your learnings from the chapter. I've organized the activities in between to offer variety in the kinds of activities and the topics they explore. You might go through them in order, but you are also welcome to jump around to the ones that most interest you.

Each chapter offers a few recurring exercises in which the structure is the same, but the topic is different. For example, I invite you in every chapter to explore an emotion (such as love, envy, or anger) through visual art. Each month, I also invite you to write a letter to an emotion as a way to understand that emotional experience for yourself. I close each chapter with an activity to help you reflect on the learnings in the chapter and also concretize a vision for yourself of a more resilient you. One of those activities is called "Destination Postcard" (a term adopted from the Heath brothers' brilliant book *Switch*). That's an activity for which I hope you'll consider sketching, collaging, or doing anything that makes that vision more vivid and meaningful to you.

Some of these activities will be best engaged in before or after school, or when you have more time. The following icons clarify which activities will be best during what time of day.

 An activity for morning

 An activity for evening

 An activity for when you have a little time and perhaps a reflective, relaxing space to sit

How to Make the Most of This Book

This is your workbook, and to make the most of it you'll need to do what feels right for you. You'll also need to stretch yourself.

Where to Start?

You might want to go through this book in the order it's written. Or you could engage in the activities according to the month they are aligned to. In Appendix A of *Onward,* there's a reflective tool to help you identify which habits and dispositions you might want to focus on. Or you might just jump around this book in random order. It's up to you! It's your book.

Try Everything

I'll introduce dozens of resilience-boosting strategies in this book. I encourage you to try them all! Some will resonate more; some you'll want to repeat; others will feel uncomfortable. For example, I'm very visual, and if I draw something (even with my scribbly stick figures), the ideas are more likely to stick in my long-term memory. But this may not work for you. Try everything and be open to what happens, but also know that you don't have to repeat activities that feel too awkward.

That said, do try the drawing prompts. If you suffer from fear of art or believe that you're "bad at art," the easiest advice I have for you is this: Shove that fear and anxiety into a box and take it out at the end of the year. It's an old fear, it won't help you here, and it's only going to impede your ability to cultivate your resilience. You might also consider a detour adventure into the land of sketching and sketch notes, starting here: rohdesign .com. You'll be amazed at what you can pick up in just a couple of hours and how these sketching strategies can deepen your self-knowledge and understanding—and, ultimately, your resilience. Don't let your insecurities about drawing or art prevent you from messing around with images, crayons, collage, and stick figures. No one will judge your art except you. So just don't.

As you try the activities, it's essential to preserve time for reflection. You will miss important insights if you plow through the exercises without pausing to think, write, and talk about your learning. I hope that by the end of the book and, ideally, after a year exploring these strategies, you'll know which ones work best for you. This is an individual discovery; the things that I do when I'm feeling emotionally depleted may be different from what works best for you or for your colleagues. So try everything!

Write and Talk

Your learning and application will be more profound and permanent if you talk about this experience with others—which is why in my wild fantasies, you're going through this learning with friends, colleagues, and teammates. And your conversations with them might lead to closer interpersonal connections, which adds another layer of resilience. The process of putting experience into words also happens when you write, so don't skip the writing prompts.

Supplies and Materials

You don't need much for this workbook, but an excuse for a few extra office and art supplies makes some of us very happy. Find a few pens that you like to write with, ones that run smoothly and fluidly. Maybe get a special pen or two. Keep a pencil nearby, and perhaps a set of thin markers. Find what works for you and what you enjoy using.

There will be sections in this workbook where you may want to add additional pages of writing, images from magazines, and photos. Keep a glue stick and roll of tape handy. I can't read anything without using stacks of sticky notes—that's how I flag pages and ideas to return to—so consider this an invitation to expand your collection of sticky notes. It's also possible that you might want a blank journal. Although I've provided space for you to write in this book, you may need more journal space if you're like me and find writing cathartic.

Find a Friend

Although I am confident that you'll get a lot out of these activities if you engage in them alone, I encourage you to find another person or a group with whom you might undertake this learning. Perhaps your department or grade level can incorporate this learning into team meetings during the year; maybe you could start a book study with other teachers in the district. If you're a principal, perhaps you could make a study of this book an option for a strand of professional development. Although being with others in person is ideal, you can also find a community of educators engaging in this learning online through the website, www.onwardthebook.com.

This workbook, as well as *Onward*, invites vulnerability. If you read this book with colleagues, I encourage you to establish agreements for your conversations. Here are some examples:

- Observe deep confidentiality
- Listen to understand
- Speak your truth, without blame or judgment

If you engage in these practices together, two things could happen: You might experience discomfort, and you might create deeper, more meaningful connections with colleagues. In other words, it will be well worth the discomfort.

Here's my fantasy: In schools across the world, on a Wednesday afternoon—or perhaps a Friday morning (a much better time for educators to engage in serious and focused learning), groups will gather to learn about and cultivate emotional resilience. We'll start with exploring our own resilience, and there'll be time for reading and writing, talking and practicing the strategies in this book. Sometimes there'll be markers and snacks and even musical instruments on the tables.

There'll often be laughter and maybe a hug, and even a tear or two. And then there'll be conversations about how to shed ourselves of biases so that we can see our kids' full humanity and potential and how to cultivate resilience in our students. We'll have conversations about how to build our students' social and academic skills, so that they can do whatever they want to do with their wild and precious lives. We'll listen to each other's heartbreak and hope, and we'll talk about despair and fatigue, and we'll tell stories about our ancestors and stories of survival and resistance. When the meeting ends, we'll practically bounce out of our chairs feeling energized and alive and connected to each other, and we'll leave the room saying, "I can't wait until our next meeting! This is the best PD I've ever had!"

Please visit www.onwardthebook.com for more resources and videos, to download tools, for guided meditations, and to engage in community discussions on these topics.

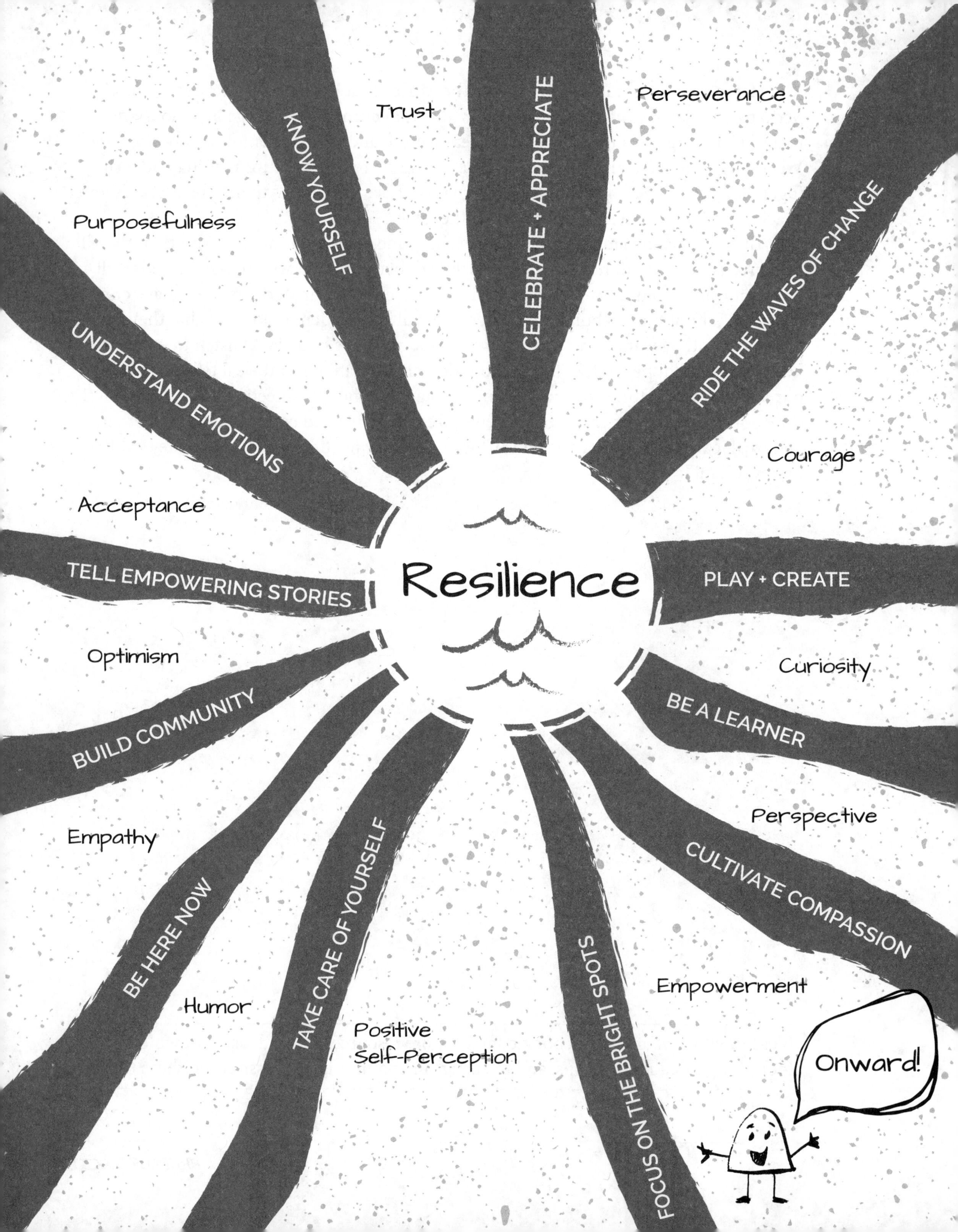
Resilience
KNOW YOURSELF
CELEBRATE + APPRECIATE
RIDE THE WAVES OF CHANGE
UNDERSTAND EMOTIONS
TELL EMPOWERING STORIES
PLAY + CREATE
BUILD COMMUNITY
BE A LEARNER
BE HERE NOW
TAKE CARE OF YOURSELF
FOCUS ON THE BRIGHT SPOTS
CULTIVATE COMPASSION
Trust
Perseverance
Purposefulness
Courage
Acceptance
Optimism
Curiosity
Empathy
Perspective
Humor
Positive Self-Perception
Empowerment
Onward!

INTRODUCTION

Consider engaging in the activities in this chapter after reading *Onward*'s introduction. You'll be introduced to some of the key ideas in this book, and you'll also muster your commitment to practicing the habits of a resilient educator.

Put On Your Hiking Boots

Onward describes the journey to cultivate resilience. I've offered the metaphor of an internal wellspring of water to represent the resilience that lies within all of us, which we can journey to, tend to, and fill through many actions. Those actions are the 12 habits of a resilient educator, and I think of them as paths we travel down as we make our way to that inner pool. Along the way, we pass through the terrain of the 12 dispositions of a resilient educator, and as we explore those, we cultivate more resilience.

I'm so glad you're taking this journey. It's time to put on your hiking boots and get started. In the space provided at the top of the next page, draw a picture of the boots you'll wear, with your legs sticking out of them. Because this is your journey, your boots can look however you'd like: Worn and broken in or brand new and covered in sequins and glitter. This is your journey and your book, so you don't need to wear hiking boots at all! If you'd be more comfortable traveling in flip-flops, by all means wear those. Or if you're more confident in heels, put them on! Alright, let's get going!

What's brought you to this book? Why are you interested in resilience? Why do you want to develop your own resilience?

What do you want to be true when you've finished reading *Onward* and engaging in these exercises? How do you want to feel?

From The Onward Workbook: Daily Activities to Cultivate Your Emotional Resilience and Thrive by Elena Aguilar. Copyright © 2018 by Elena Aguilar. Reproduced by permission.

Current Challenges

What are the challenges you feel you face currently in your work? List as many as you can.

Now go down your list and code them as big (B) challenges, medium (M) challenges, or small (S) challenges. What do you notice about your list?

What's in Your Toolbox?

Which strategies do you currently use to manage the stresses and challenges you face at work? For example, if you have a colleague who drives you crazy, what are your coping mechanisms? Imagine that you have a toolbox for dealing with adversity and stress. What's in it right now? You could list your strategies here, or if you'd like you could also sketch a toolbox and label the implements within.

Create a Treasure Chest, or Just a Pocket

As you go through this workbook, I'm going to encourage you to collect artifacts of your experience as you build your resilience. These might include photos you take, books or journals, cards you receive from students, sticky notes, or even lesson plans! Yes, these could become artifacts of the resilience you cultivate. You'll need a place to store these artifacts. You might need only a file or a pocket in this workbook or a journal, or you might need a chest.

To create a pocket: You could affix this pocket to the front or back cover of this workbook, so that it will always be accessible, or to a journal you're also using. Find a piece of study paper or a file folder and cut it into the shape you want. Tape or glue it into place, leaving one side of the rectangle open. Duct tape works especially well to keep it secured. Decorate the front if you want. Then, so your pocket isn't lonely, find something to put in it. A leaf. The stub from a movie that inspired you. A copy of your student roster. Your class photo.

If you're excited by the treasure chest idea, go for it. Make it beautiful and inviting.

Resilience

Trust

Perseverance

KNOW YOURSELF
Purposefulness

CELEBRATE + APPRECIATE

RIDE THE WAVES OF CHANGE

UNDERSTAND EMOTIONS

Courage

Acceptance

PLAY + CREATE

TELL EMPOWERING STORIES

Curiosity

Optimism

BE A LEARNER

BUILD COMMUNITY

Perspective

Empathy

CULTIVATE COMPASSION

BE HERE NOW

TAKE CARE OF YOURSELF

FOCUS ON THE BRIGHT SPOTS

Humor

Empowerment

Positive
Self-Perception

CHAPTER 1

Know Yourself

When you know yourself well—when you understand your emotions, social identities, core values, and personality—you gain clarity on your purpose in life and in work. Being anchored in purpose makes you able to deal with setbacks and challenges.

June: This habit is foundational for all the others. In June you can reflect on last year, transition into summer, and contemplate next year while gaining deeper self-understanding.

Know Yourself: Resilience Self-Assessment

The purpose of this self-assessment is to help you gauge the level of your resilience reservoir and to explore what might be draining or what could replenish it. The exercises that follow and the information in the corresponding chapter of *Onward* can boost your resilience by helping you better understand yourself and by connecting with a deeper sense of purpose.

Imagine each circle here as a little *cenote* or reservoir within you, and fill it up according to how much each statement reflects a source of resilience. If you need something more concrete, imagine marks at ¼, ½, and ¾ full.

Before you start the exercises in this chapter, take this self-assessment and fill in the date. At the end of the month, take the assessment again. (You might even cover up your original markings with a strip of paper.) Is your resilience reservoir a little more full? If so, which practices do you want to keep up? If not, what else do you want to try?

Statement	Date:	Date:
I am clear on my core values and how they guide my behaviors.	◯	◯
I know how my personality affects me at work.	◯	◯
I know what I'm good at; I'm clear about my strengths.	◯	◯
At least for some part of my day, I do what I'm good at.	◯	◯

From *The Onward Workbook: Daily Activities to Cultivate Your Emotional Resilience and Thrive* by Elena Aguilar. Copyright © 2018 by Elena Aguilar. Reproduced by permission.

I'm aware of the connections between my sociopolitical identity and how I experience my work.	◯	◯
I recognize how messages from dominant culture affect how I think and feel about myself.	◯	◯
I have strategies to mitigate how dominant culture makes me feel about myself.	◯	◯
I know what makes me feel vulnerable, and I'm aware of when I feel vulnerable.	◯	◯
I feel very clear about my purpose in life. I know what I'm here on earth to do.	◯	◯
The knowledge I have of myself helps me manage challenges at work; it serves as a guidepost when I have to make decisions.	◯	◯

How Well Do I Know Myself?

Our "self" comprises the five elements here.

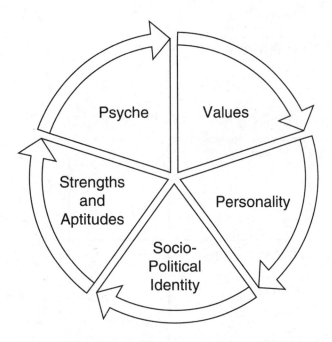

You're the judge of how well you know yourself. On a 1–10 scale, how well do you feel you understand these elements of who you are?

Element of Self	Description	Rating (1–10)	Thoughts, Reflections, Evidence
Beliefs	I know my core values and see how they guide my behavior. I am aware of when I'm operating from my values, and I make decisions that align with them.		

Personality	I am aware of my personality tendencies and the impact they have on my life and work. I can make decisions about what I do and how I work that play to my personality.		
Strengths and Aptitudes	I know what I'm good at and what my strengths and skills are. I make choices that allow me to play to my strengths and to develop areas in which I'm not strong.		
Sociopolitical Identity	I understand who I am sociopolitically, and I am aware of how this construction impacts me in a professional context.		
Psyche	I am aware of my emotions, and I understand them. I have healthy strategies to respond to and express my emotions that work for me.		

In which area do you feel most confident? How do you think you came to know yourself in this area?

In which area do you most want to do further learning? How might you benefit from doing more learning in that area?

The Wise Words of Martha Graham

There is a vitality, a life force, a quickening that is translated through you into action, and there is only one of you in all time, this expression is unique. And if you block it, it will never exist through any other medium, and it will be lost. The world will not have it. It is not your business to determine how good it is, not how it compares with other expression. It is your business to keep it yours clearly and directly, to keep the channel open. You do not even have to believe in yourself or your work. You have to keep open and aware directly to the urges that motivate you. Keep the channel open.

MARTHA GRAHAM

What do these words mean to you?

How do Martha Graham's words help you think about your purpose in life?

What actions, if any, do these words lead you to consider taking?

From The Onward Workbook: Daily Activities to Cultivate Your Emotional Resilience and Thrive by Elena Aguilar. Copyright © 2018 by Elena Aguilar. Reproduced by permission.

Whom Do You Know Who Knows Who They Are?

Whom do you know who really knows who she is? This person could be real or fictional (for example, Wonder Woman).

What does this person say or do that makes you feel that she knows who she is? How do you see this self-knowledge expressed?

What connection can you make between how you feel about this person (whether you like her or not) and the sense of self she has?

Draw a little picture here (stick figures are great!) of this self-aware person you know. Add details, captions, or thought bubbles.

I Am

Set a timer for five minutes and make a list all about *you*. Let your mind free-associate, and jot down anything and everything. This is just for you. Include things that you identify with, that resonate, that you love or care about; include adjectives and nouns and places and people. Some of the things on my list include cacao and corn and coffee, the East End of London, my mother's daughter, a redwood tree, and a lotus flower. Let your mind go where it takes you. After the timer goes off, read back through your list and star the ones that feel most important.

Purpose: Why I'm Doing This

Why did you get into teaching? Free-write in response to this question. Set a timer and write for three minutes without stopping. Don't edit yourself, and be honest.

Myers-Briggs Personality Types: Part 1

A good MBTI assessment shows your results on a continuum. Most people have shades of all of these aspects, but have a dominance in one tendency. Here's a quick overview of the four personality elements according to the MBTI and an opportunity for you to predict what you are before taking the test (which is a part of the following exercise).

1. Energy: Whether you draw energy from the outer or inner world.	
Extraversion (E)	Extroverts • Enjoy being in large groups of people and meeting lots of new people; they walk away from a daylong conference feeling energized and ready to socialize in the evening • Have a strong desire to form teams and can work well in teams • Appreciate a lot of time to talk and work through their thoughts using verbal processing • Tend to have many friends and associates
Introversion (I)	Introverts • Are drained by large groups of people and prefer interacting with one other person or a small group; they walk away from a daylong conference feeling exhausted and wanting to be alone or perhaps with one other person in the evening • Need planning time and thrive when they have it • Need quiet processing time before being asked to speak about something • Tend to have a small group of close friends, or a best friend • Enjoy being alone

Place an X where you believe you fall:

←——————————————————————————————————→

Introversion   **Extroversion**

I think I fall here because . . .

(*continued*)

Important to Know
Our tendency toward introversion or extroversion has nothing to do with shyness, social awkwardness, fear of public speaking, or ability to make friends. This is the personality type that is most likely to change as you get older. Most people become more introverted as they age, so if you were an extrovert in high school, it's possible that by your 40s, you might be an introvert. It's also likely, psychologists say, that these results may change as you get older because when you were a young adult, if you took a personality test, you may have answered the questions according to what you *thought* you should say—for example, when asked what you prefer to do on a Saturday night: go to a party or stay at home and watch a movie, you may have felt socially compelled to say party.

2. Perception of Information: Your tendency to focus on factual information or to interpret and add meaning to information

Sensing (S)	Sensors • Rely mainly on concrete, actual information • Value data (and might be driven by data) • Focus on what is realistic in relation to current constraints • Can struggle to step back and determine a path to success, especially when resources are scarce and tasks are overwhelming • Can be overwhelmed by details and may have a hard time seeing possibilities for new approaches
Intuition (N)	Intuitives • Rely on their conception about things based on their understanding of the world • Are always looking at the big picture and prefer to backward-plan • Want to know why something isn't working when there are problems, before moving ahead • Plan for long-term success and aren't tempted by short-term tasks • Delegate responsibility for implementing big projects

Place an X where you believe you fall:

←——————————————————————————————→

Sensing   **Intuition**

I think I fall here because . . .

From *The Onward Workbook: Daily Activities to Cultivate Your Emotional Resilience and Thrive* by Elena Aguilar. Copyright © 2018 by Elena Aguilar. Reproduced by permission.

3. Decision Making: How you process information: Whether you first look at logic and consistency or at people and circumstances

Thinking (T)	Thinkers • Make decisions based on logical reasoning and are less affected by feelings and emotions • Can be objective in the face of emotionally charged issues • Are able to look at and analyze data and enjoy it • Are less concerned with wanting to be liked and more focused on enduring results • Can be insensitive to others and can create conflict
Feeling (F)	Feelers • Base decisions in emotions • Are relationship oriented • Cultivate a positive climate in the classroom or school • Can struggle to hold people accountable because they worry about damaging relationships

Important to Know
Thinkers do have emotions, and feelers do use their cognitive capacities as well.

Place an X where you believe you fall:

← ——— →

Thinking   **Feeling**

I think I fall here because . . .

(continued)

4. External Structure: How you like to live your outer life: Whether you prefer things to be decided or to stay open and flexible

Judging (J)	Judgers • Are outcome oriented and decisive • Choose a plan of action and stay focused • Like to develop and execute plans • Are deadline oriented • Find changes to plans disruptive
Perceiving (P)	Perceivers • Are creative problem solvers always looking for new ideas and innovations • Like to keep options open • Often have new ideas and get overwhelmed with the number of things that could be tried • Can find change exciting

Important to Know

J or P preference only tells which preference people express in their outside world. Perceiving people may feel very orderly or structured on the inside, yet their outer life looks spontaneous and adaptable. Judging people may feel very curious and open ended in their inner world, yet their outer life looks more structured. Also, this type has nothing to do with how people organize their material world—both types can be a disheveled mess or supremely organized.

Place an X where you believe you fall:

←—————————————————————————————————→

Judging   **Perceiving**

I think I fall here because . . .

Take the free, online test at www.16personalities.com or http://www.humanmetrics.com (or you can take both and compare your results).

Write your four-letter personality type here:

Respond to the following questions:

Given your personality type, what really resonated? Were there any descriptions that felt particularly "like you"?

What were you surprised by in your results?

Were there any results that didn't feel accurate?

From The Onward Workbook: Daily Activities to Cultivate Your Emotional Resilience and Thrive by Elena Aguilar. Copyright © 2018 by Elena Aguilar. Reproduced by permission.

What are the implications of knowing these personality tendencies? Are there implications for what kind of work you do, where you work, whom you work with, and what you might be able to do?

Who are a few famous people who have shared your personality type?

Read about other types. Which types do you suspect are hardest for you to work with?

Pablo Neruda and Purpose

Something ignited in my soul . . . And I went my own way,
deciphering that burning fire.
PABLO NERUDA, POET

In the course of your life, what has ignited your soul?

If you've pursued what felt like a calling in your life, like a burning fire, where did it take you?

What did you decipher in that burning fire?

How might you connect with what ignites your soul?

What Motivates Me When I Speak?

Today, inquire into your motivations behind what you say. When you're about to say something, ask yourself:

- What's my intention in saying this?
- What emotions are below what I'm about to say? (Am I frustrated? Curious? Sad? Excited? Resentful?)

As many times as possible today, before you speak, ask yourself these questions. This can be hard to remember, so think of a cue that can jog your mind: Write something on your hand! Post a note above your whiteboard! If you can ask yourself these questions even a couple of times before you speak, you'll benefit.

How will you remember to ask yourself about the motivations behind your speech?

At the end of the day, capture your reflections here. What did you discover about what motivated you to speak? What did you learn about yourself?

From The Onward Workbook: Daily Activities to Cultivate Your Emotional Resilience and Thrive by Elena Aguilar. Copyright © 2018 by Elena Aguilar. Reproduced by permission.

Core Values

We all have core values, but often we're not aware of what those are. This activity will help you identify your core values. It's a useful one to do every year and to reflect on how they change—or don't change.

Process

1. Read through the list of values located at the end of this exercise and circle 10 that you feel are most important to you.

2. Cross off five of those values, leaving you with the five that are most important to you.

3. Now, from your list of five values, cross off two, leaving you with the *three* values that are most important to you. These are your core values.

Reflect

How does it feel to read your list of values? What did it feel like to do this activity?

One year ago, what do you suspect your core values might have been? Ten years ago, what do you think they might have been?

Consider how your actions reflect your core values. Which values show up more often in your actions at work? At home? In social circles? With family?

What are some ways in which your actions reflect your core values? Think of one example of how actions you take reflect your core values.

From The Onward Workbook: Daily Activities to Cultivate Your Emotional Resilience and Thrive by Elena Aguilar. Copyright © 2018 by Elena Aguilar. Reproduced by permission.

Can you think of a time—or two—when your actions conflicted with a core value? How does it feel to remember those moments when there was a discrepancy between a value and your actions?

Write your three core values on a piece of paper and post them somewhere prominent. Reflect on them for a few months. See if they still feel like "core" values.

Suggestions for Sharing Your Core Values

Sharing your core values with colleagues is a powerful way to connect and learn about each other. I often offer groups these discussion prompts:

- What do your core values mean to you?
- Describe the elimination process you went through to arrive at your three core values. How are the ones that you crossed off reflected in your top three?
- Share a time when you acted on your core values.
- Which of your core values feels easiest to uphold? Which feels hardest?
- Find someone with the same value as you have, and explore how you experience the value similarly and differently—one value can mean different things to different people.

Values

The following values apply to work and personal life. This is not an exhaustive list—you're welcome to add your own.

Acceptance	Appreciation	Belonging
Achievement	Arts	Caring
Advancement	Authenticity	Celebration
Adventure	Authority	Challenge
Affection	Autonomy	Choice
Altruism	Balance	Collaboration
Ambition	Beauty	Commitment

From The Onward Workbook: Daily Activities to Cultivate Your Emotional Resilience and Thrive by Elena Aguilar. Copyright © 2018 by Elena Aguilar. Reproduced by permission.

Communication	Harmony	Power
Community	Health	Pride
Compassion	Helping others	Privacy
Competition	High expectations	Productivity
Connection	Honesty	Recognition
Contribution	Hope	Reflection
Cooperation	Humor	Reputation
Creativity	Imagination	Respect
Democracy	Independence	Responsibility
Effectiveness	Influence	Results
Efficiency	Initiative	Risk taking
Empathy	Integrity	Romance
Equality	Interdependence	Routine
Equity	Intuition	Self-expression
Excellence	Justice	Self-respect
Excitement	Kindness	Service
Expertise	Knowledge	Sharing
Fairness	Leadership	Solitude
Faith	Loyalty	Spirituality
Fame	Making a difference	Success
Family	Meaningful work	Support
Flexibility	Mindfulness	Teamwork
Focus	Nature	Time
Forgiveness	Nurturing	Togetherness
Freedom	Order	Tolerance
Friendship	Passion	Tradition
Fun	Peace	Travel
Generosity	Perseverance	Trust
Goals	Personal development	Truth
Gratitude	Personal growth	Unity
Growth	Pleasure	Variety
Happiness	Positive attitude	Zest

From *The Onward Workbook: Daily Activities to Cultivate Your Emotional Resilience and Thrive* by Elena Aguilar. Copyright © 2018 by Elena Aguilar. Reproduced by permission.

Purpose: My Legacy

List 10 hopes you have as a teacher or leader:

Now put a star by the three that are most important. Is there one that is of top importance? Circle it.

    For teachers: What do you want students to say about you 15 years after they leave your classroom?

    For others: What do want the people you lead/coach/support to say about you 15 years after working with you?

    Write this as if someone were speaking about you in the third person.

Who do you hope will speak at your retirement party?

What do you hope this person will say? Script as much of the speech as you can here.

Crafting a Mission Statement

A mission statement is a declaration of your purpose. It has a dual audience: You and others. It helps you establish priorities and guides your decisions. You may want to create a mission statement that speaks to your purpose as an educator, or to a broader purpose in life.

Step 1

- Draft a few mission statements on 3-by-5 index cards. Don't worry about the wording, and don't show them to anyone. These prompts can help you generate ideas for your statement:
  - What do you hope will be true as a result of your work?
  - What impact do you want to have on others or the world?
  - Which values drive you to do what you do?
- Carry these index cards around in your pocket for a week.
- Pull them out occasionally and read them. Notice how you feel reading them. Is there one that feels more empowering? Closer to the truth? Are there elements in each one that if combined might reflect your sense of purpose?

Capture your reflections on your first round of mission statements here:

From *The Onward Workbook: Daily Activities to Cultivate Your Emotional Resilience and Thrive* by Elena Aguilar. Copyright © 2018 by Elena Aguilar. Reproduced by permission.

Step 2

After a week of carrying your drafts, write one mission statement that draws from them. Of course, you can write something entirely new if you want. Use words that feel like you. They don't have to be fancy—they need to feel authentic. Write your statement in the box here.

My Mission:

Reflect

How does it feel to see your mission statement?

Read it aloud. How does it feel to hear yourself proclaim it?

Share it with someone else. How does it feel to share? What was the person's response?

I feel very uncomfortable when I share my mission with others. Sharing makes me feel vulnerable and exposed. But I do it anyway. Here's mine:

My mission is to heal and transform the world. I help educators discover ways of being and working that are joyful and rewarding, that bring communities together, and that result in positive outcomes for children. I help people find their own power and empower others so that we can transform our education system, our society, and our world.

Step 3

- Write your mission statement in large letters and post it in your classroom or office where you'll see it regularly. Use color or decorate it if you want.
- When you're having a hard day, read it and notice how you feel.
- When you have a good day, reflect on how you acted on your sense of purpose. Often what contributes to our good days is that our actions were aligned to our mission.

I Am a Leopard, or a . . .

Leopards are noble, courageous, and confident. Eagles have grace and perspective. Owls are symbols of wisdom and equanimity. Bobcats are tenacious. Hummingbirds are pollinators.

Reflect on the animal that you'd like to be at work or in your life. Perhaps one comes to mind immediately. Or perhaps you could do some research and reading on characteristics of animals and then decide on one. Allow this thinking and exploration to be a reflection on who you are and who you want to be.

After some reflection, draw your animal here, or paste in a photo of it. Add some words to name the qualities of the animal that reflect aspects of yourself or who you want to be.

Part 1: Outside of Work

When you were a child, what were you good at?

When you were a child, what did you love doing? What did you want to be when you grew up?

Outside of your current work, what do you love doing? What do you feel good at? What do you feel good at and love doing that also feels easy to do?

Looking at your answers to these questions, what strengths, skills, or talents do you have to draw on in your daily work?

From *The Onward Workbook: Daily Activities to Cultivate Your Emotional Resilience and Thrive* by Elena Aguilar. Copyright © 2018 by Elena Aguilar. Reproduced by permission.

Part 2: At Work

As they relate to your professional role, list your aptitudes and interests. Let yourself free-associate and don't judge yourself for what comes up. In Exhibit 1.1 at the end of this section, you can see my reflection as a teacher.

Aptitudes *What are you good at? What natural talents do you have? What learned abilities do you have?*	Interests *What do you like doing?*
Which aptitudes do you wish you had or would you like to cultivate?	**What are you not interested in? What don't you like doing?**

From *The Onward Workbook: Daily Activities to Cultivate Your Emotional Resilience and Thrive* by Elena Aguilar. Copyright © 2018 by Elena Aguilar. Reproduced by permission.

Reflect

What insights did you gain from this activity? Do you see any patterns or trends?

What connections do you see between your aptitudes and interests?

Of the aptitudes or interests you feel you're missing, which ones do you think you could develop? Are there any that you're not willing to develop?

What implications are there for you from this reflection?

From The Onward Workbook: Daily Activities to Cultivate Your Emotional Resilience and Thrive by Elena Aguilar. Copyright © 2018 by Elena Aguilar. Reproduced by permission.

Exhibit 1.1: Elena's Reflection as a Teacher

Aptitudes *What are you good at? What natural talents do you have? What learned abilities do you have? What capacities to acquire a skill do you have?*	**Interests** *What do you like doing?*
• Planning units: I love researching and organizing units. • Making the content relevant to kids. • Integrating art activities.	• Taking kids on field trips. • Beginning units. • Sharing literature that I love with kids. • Being spontaneous and responding to things that kids are interested in or things going on in the world.
Which aptitudes do you wish you had or would you like to cultivate?	*What are you not interested in?* *What don't you like doing?*
• Assessments: Creating them, using them, analyzing them. • Coordinating big projects: I get lost in the details, and things fall through the cracks. • Creating structure and routine in the classroom.	• Assessments. • Report cards. • Maintaining structure and routine in the classrooms. I like to change things often.

From *The Onward Workbook: Daily Activities to Cultivate Your Emotional Resilience and Thrive* by Elena Aguilar. Copyright © 2018 by Elena Aguilar. Reproduced by permission.

Part 3: Where Worlds Intersect

Reference parts 1 and 2 and jot down some key phrases in the Venn diagram here that represent your skills, passions, and interests inside and outside of work.

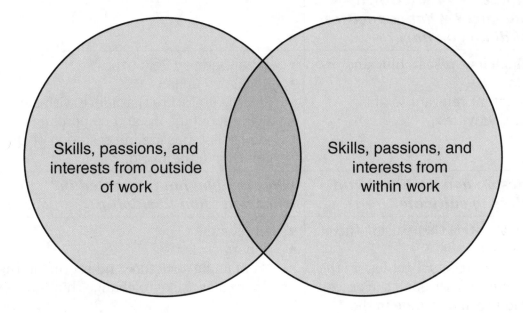

Skills, passions, and interests from outside of work

Skills, passions, and interests from within work

What insights into yourself do you get after filling in this Venn diagram? What does it raise for you?

Look at your list of aptitudes and what you love doing. Imagine a workday in which 85% of what you do draws on these lists. Describe that day.

What other kinds of roles, both within education as well as outside of it, require the aptitudes that you've identified? Are there any other roles that you want to learn more about that might be a good match for your skills and abilities?

Aptitudes: An Inquiry Experience

1. Identify 2–4 people who know you well within your world of work, and 2–4 people who know you well outside of it. (These lists can overlap.)

2. Ask these people what they think your strengths, unique talents, and aptitudes are. If you can do this in person, it will be more powerful.

3. When they say nice things about you, don't downplay those, disagree, or negate them. Simply say, "Thank you," and take notes.

4. Then ask if there are any other roles inside or outside of education in which they could see you thriving.

5. Write down what they say in the boxes here.

Friends and Colleagues from Work Life		
Name:	My strengths and aptitudes	
	Other roles or jobs?	
Name:	My strengths and aptitudes	
	Other roles or jobs?	

From *The Onward Workbook: Daily Activities to Cultivate Your Emotional Resilience and Thrive* by Elena Aguilar. Copyright © 2018 by Elena Aguilar. Reproduced by permission.

Name:	My strengths and aptitudes	
	Other roles or jobs?	
Name:	My strengths and aptitudes	
	Other roles or jobs?	

Friends and Colleagues from Personal Life		
Name:	My strengths and aptitudes	
	Other roles or jobs?	

(continued)

Name:	My strengths and aptitudes	
	Other roles or jobs?	
Name:	My strengths and aptitudes	
	Other roles or jobs?	
Name:	My strengths and aptitudes	
	Other roles or jobs?	

From *The Onward Workbook: Daily Activities to Cultivate Your Emotional Resilience and Thrive* by Elena Aguilar. Copyright © 2018 by Elena Aguilar. Reproduced by permission.

Friends and Colleagues from Both Work and Personal Life		
Name:	My strengths and aptitudes	
	Other roles or jobs?	
Name:	My strengths and aptitudes	
	Other roles or jobs?	

Reflect

What was it like to engage in this activity?

How did it feel hearing other people's perceptions of your aptitudes?

From The Onward Workbook: Daily Activities to Cultivate Your Emotional Resilience and Thrive by Elena Aguilar. Copyright © 2018 by Elena Aguilar. Reproduced by permission.

Did anything someone shared particularly resonate or feel particularly off?

What new insights did you gain into yourself?

What new ideas did you get about other roles or jobs to explore?

Spiritual and Mental Ancestors

The anthropologist Margaret Mead extolled the value of "spiritual and mental ancestors" in how we form our identity. These are the people to whom we aren't related but whose values we try to cultivate in ourselves. They are role models we seek out not from our immediate genetic pool but from the pool of culture, past and present, that surrounds us.

Who are your spiritual and mental ancestors? Who are the people from your past and present who are your role models?

The Paths We've Taken

Throughout life, we make choices about what to do, where to go, and which paths to take. Earlier in my life, I was on a path to becoming a journalist, then an anthropologist, and then a teacher. Sketch a graphic that represents the paths you've explored and that shows how you ended up where you are now. Feel free to include the paths you abandoned. Start and end wherever you want.

From *The Onward Workbook: Daily Activities to Cultivate Your Emotional Resilience and Thrive* by Elena Aguilar. Copyright © 2018 by Elena Aguilar. Reproduced by permission.

Reflect

Of the paths you didn't pursue, is there one that still calls to you? That you're still curious about?

How do you feel about the paths you didn't take? Is there sadness? Relief? Regret?

What insights can you glean from the alternate paths you've explored? What do those interests tell you about yourself?

Of the paths you wish you'd taken, how might you satisfy your interest in those areas or incorporate them onto the path you're on now?

Values: At School

As they relate to education, list your values. Some examples could be *relevance, meaningful curriculum, kids having choice about what they do,* or *creating class agreements together.* Also see if you can identify what you *don't* value, such as following rules because they are rules, standardized curriculum, testing, and so on. Let yourself free-associate and don't judge what comes up.

What I Value	What I Don't Value

From *The Onward Workbook: Daily Activities to Cultivate Your Emotional Resilience and Thrive* by Elena Aguilar. Copyright © 2018 by Elena Aguilar. Reproduced by permission.

Reflect

Did anything surprise you about your values?

How many of your values do you feel you are able to act on, regularly, in your work?

Of the things you don't value, how many do you feel you're asked to do regularly?

What do you see as the connection between your aptitudes and interests and your values?

What implications for action are there, if any, from this awareness about your values? Is there anything you might want to start or stop doing?

Sociopolitical Identities

	Star eight that feel very important to you	Star three that feel the most important to you	Put an exclamation point (!) next to three elements that you feel most aware of on a daily basis
Ability			
Age			
Education			
Ethnicity			
Family status			
Gender			
Geographical location			
Immigrant status			
Language			
Marital status			
Nationality			
Physical appearance			
Race			
Religion			
Sexual orientation			
Socioeconomic status			
Other:			

From *The Onward Workbook: Daily Activities to Cultivate Your Emotional Resilience and Thrive* by Elena Aguilar. Copyright © 2018 by Elena Aguilar. Reproduced by permission.

Reflect

What insights into yourself did you glean from this activity?

Were you surprised by any of your reflections?

What role do you think your sociopolitical identity plays in your daily work life?

What do you wish that others understood about your sociopolitical identity?

From The Onward Workbook: Daily Activities to Cultivate Your Emotional Resilience and Thrive by Elena Aguilar. Copyright © 2018 by Elena Aguilar. Reproduced by permission.

Signature Strengths

Take the Signature Strengths survey: http://www.viacharacter.org. Then reflect on your experience taking the survey and your results.

How easily were you able to answer the questions? Did you hesitate to answer any of them? If so, what might that hesitation reveal about yourself?

What was your initial reaction to the first two or three strengths listed in your results? What feelings came up for you? Does the list ring true? Does anything feel "off"?

Try to recall a situation in which one or more of your top five strengths shined. What happened? What was the result?

Scrolling to the bottom of your report, read the strengths least evident in your profile. What reaction do you have to reading this list?

Looking across all 24 strengths, are there any you wish to cultivate? What difference would it make in your life if you increased some of the strengths that weren't at the top?

Make a Values Jar

For many people, most of the values listed in the "Core Values" activity resonate in some way. It may have been hard to select your top 10 or top 3. For this activity, go back to the top 10 values that you identified and write each one on a small piece of card stock or heavy paper—maybe a piece around a half inch by two. If there were some other values that also really resonate, write those down too. You can have as many as you'd like.

Find a jar to put them in. This could be a special jar that you decorate, an old spaghetti sauce jar, or even just a mug.

For the next couple of weeks, before you go to school every day, draw one word from the jar. Let this be your value of the day. As you go through your day, notice moments when you demonstrate that value. Find opportunities to act on it. Ask others what the value means to them. Share what it means to you. If you'd like, at the end of the day, record your reflections in a journal.

This activity will help you gain insight into how your values play out in your daily life, and will give you more appreciation for them.

From *The Onward Workbook: Daily Activities to Cultivate Your Emotional Resilience and Thrive* by Elena Aguilar. Copyright © 2018 by Elena Aguilar. Reproduced by permission.

Astrology, Enneagrams, and More!

In our quest for self-knowledge, we've devised many ways to describe and understand ourselves. For example, we may find meaning or resonance with the description of our astrological sign because it gives us insight into who we are and why we do what we do. I like to attribute my insatiable passion for travel to being a Sagittarius, and my focus and persistence to my Chinese astrological sign, which is a rooster.

Going back to Socrates, and probably long before, humans have wanted to know and categorize themselves. In recent years, there's been a proliferation of online tests that claim to help you understand yourself based on which character you like the most on a TV show, your favorite snack, and so on. Astrology, Enneagrams, color personality categorization, and the like are metaphors for elements of ourselves and allow us to gain insight in new ways.

Of the symbols and metaphors for self-understanding, which ones resonate with you? Why?

Now could be a fun time to explore your Chinese astrological sign or to learn about Enneagrams. (This is a personality model with nine types that include the Helper, the Achiever, the Loyalist, and the Challenger. A resource to learn more about this model is www.enneagraminstitute.com.)

Take the results of whatever you find with a grain of salt. Or take them as truth. You get to decide this.

Behavioral Change: In the Past

Identify four distinct periods of your life. In each section, illustrate that stage with symbols or sketches, and/or add a few words, to reflect what you were like at that age. As much as possible, use drawing, color, and symbols. No one else needs to see what you've done, so these are representations only you need to understand.

Age	Time Period 1 (for example, 8 years old)	Time Period 2 (for example, 16 years old)	Time Period 3 (for example, 21 years old)	Time Period 4 (for example, 30 years old)
Recurring thoughts				
Physical behaviors I engaged in				
Relationships *What kinds? Quality?*				

From *The Onward Workbook: Daily Activities to Cultivate Your Emotional Resilience and Thrive* by Elena Aguilar. Copyright © 2018 by Elena Aguilar. Reproduced by permission.

Reflect

What was easy or challenging about this activity?

What did you learn about yourself from doing this activity?

Did anything surprise you?

Where do you see the biggest change from one stage to another? Were they changes that you made intentionally and consciously or not?

What does this activity tell you about yourself and change?

Who Am I? Who Do I Want to Be?

Other people's perceptions play a huge role in how we view ourselves. In 1902, the sociologist Charles Cooley wrote: "I am not what I think I am; I am not what you think I am; I am what I think you think I am."

What does this quote raise for you?

How true does it feel to you?

Can you think of a specific incident in which this felt most true to you?

Who Do I Want to Be?

There are many ways to gain insight into your values, what you stand for, and who you want to be. One way to discover these is to ask yourself which behaviors in others really bother you—which qualities do you find most off-putting? Which behaviors or ways of being do you feel are intolerable?

Your responses to these reflections will give you insight into what you truly value. For example, if arrogance really bothers you, it may be that you place a high value on humility. Or if you are offended by stinginess, generosity might be a core value.

Behaviors I Can't Stand in Others	What This Might Mean About My Values

The Role of Dominant Culture

In what ways do you feel you fit into dominant culture? Which of your identities, characteristics, values, or behaviors reflect dominant culture?

In what ways do you feel you may not fit into dominant culture? Which identities, characteristics, values, or behaviors aren't reflected in dominant culture?

When are you most aware of the ways in which you fit into dominant culture?

When are you most aware of the ways in which you don't fit into dominant culture?

Behavioral Change: Reflections on Past Experiences

Part 1

Brainstorm some behavioral changes you've made in your life, ones that you've felt good about and that you've sustained. These could be really big changes (such as quitting drinking or starting a healthy exercise regime) or little changes (such as checking Facebook less frequently or going to bed earlier). These could be related to work life, or not. Use the sentence stems here to describe these changes.

Example:
I used to: *Skip lunch, and by 4:00 I was famished and I'd eat a whole bag of potato chips.*

And now I: *Buy frozen burritos so I can always take one to school with me, and I also keep a bag of trail mix in my desk just in case.*

I used to:

And now I:

I used to:

And now I:

I used to:

And now I:

I used to:

And now I:

I used to:

And now I:

From *The Onward Workbook: Daily Activities to Cultivate Your Emotional Resilience and Thrive* by Elena Aguilar. Copyright © 2018 by Elena Aguilar. Reproduced by permission.

Select one of those behavioral changes to reflect on.

What led you to make a change? What motivated you?

What was challenging about stopping an old behavior? What did you have to give up by stopping a behavior?

What was challenging about starting a new behavior? What did you need to do or learn so that you could enact the new behavior?

How do you feel recognizing the change you've made? In retrospect, did it seem harder or easier than you'd anticipated to make the change?

Part 2

Now identify a few changes that you've tried to make, but didn't sustain (such as getting up early to exercise or quitting fast food). Select those that you wish you had sustained.

Example:
I tried: *Lesson planning for the following week for two hours on Fridays after school.*

Because: *Otherwise I spent the weekend dreading Sunday afternoon, when I'd need to plan, or leaving it until Sunday night when I didn't want to do it.*

But I didn't maintain this behavior because: *I was so tired by Friday afternoon that I couldn't muster the mental or physical energy, and I just wanted to leave school.*

I tried:

Because:

But I didn't maintain this behavior because:

I tried:

Because:

But I didn't maintain this behavior because:

I tried:

Because:

But I didn't maintain this behavior because:

Reflect on this question:

Looking at this history, what can you learn about yourself when it comes to making changes?

Behavioral Change: Identifying Grain Size

When it comes to making behavioral changes, a common mistake is to choose a goal that is so big that we quickly fail. Finding the right grain size is somewhat personal—what's right for you might be miniscule for someone else, so it takes some messing around to find that right size. As you're playing with size, ask yourself, Is this *really* doable? It's better to go with too small than too big. Make it manageable to set yourself up for success; later you can add another goal or make the first one bigger. Most of us are overambitious when it comes to setting goals, and there's far more danger that we'll feel defeated by a big goal than that we'll accomplish a small one too easily. Go for small. Accomplish it, then add another.

Here are some behavioral changes of a good grain size that I've coached educators to make or that I've made myself. They are high-leverage behavioral changes to make, given our work. Put a star by those you already do, and a check by some that you feel would be valuable for you to make.

- Sleeping eight hours a night
- Exercising a few times a week
- Eating a healthy lunch
- Reducing coffee or soda intake
- Having a date night with a partner once a month
- Doing 10 minutes of meditation every morning
- Doing yoga once a week
- Attending a religious service a couple times a month
- Reading inspirational texts in the evening
- Taking a class just for fun
- Reducing TV time
- Turning off the TV an hour before bedtime
- Journaling a few times a week
- Keeping a gratitude journal
- Looking at social media only on the weekend
- Not checking email upon waking
- Checking email only during two specific time blocks (for example, 7:00–7:30 a.m. and 5:00–5:30 p.m.)
- Cooking food on Sunday to eat throughout the week
- Doing all laundry and ironing Sunday afternoon
- Finishing school work by 5:00 p.m. and not taking work home three nights a week

From *The Onward Workbook: Daily Activities to Cultivate Your Emotional Resilience and Thrive* by Elena Aguilar. Copyright © 2018 by Elena Aguilar. Reproduced by permission.

- Cleaning up the classroom right after school
- Doing lesson plans for the next week on Thursday afternoon
- Prepping the next week's lesson materials on Friday afternoon
- Grading tests within two days of administering them
- Making one positive phone call home to a student's parent every day
- Responding to email within 24 hours
- Taking the entire weekend off once a month

Now list 3–5 behavioral changes that you'd like to make, and make sure the grain size is manageable.

There are two ways to go about choosing a change to make:

1. Select the change that you feel most excited to work on, the one that you know would make a big difference in your life.

or

2. Sequence these changes in a way that makes sense. For example, if you reduced your TV time and checked social media only on the weekend, you'd have time to write in a journal, which might allow you to go to sleep earlier and get eight hours of sleep, which might allow you to wake up early enough to exercise before school, and so on. With this approach, you would start with the first behavior you've identified.

The following activity will help you take this desire and put it into action. But first: Write the behavioral change you want to make:

Making Plans for Behavioral Change

Some of us love to make plans. (Personalities of the Judging type are most inclined to do this.) Whether or not you love making plans, creating a change plan can help you understand the change process. Appendix B in *Onward* describes this process, and now you get to try it.

Which behavior change did you identify in the previous exercise that you most want to make? Write it here:

1. Start at the end: Sit back, close your eyes, and spend a minute visualizing yourself doing the behavior. Then capture your reflection: How did it feel to see yourself doing it?

2. Backward-plan: What might you need to learn or know how to do in order to adopt this habit? Is there someone you know who does this well from whom you can get some tips?

3. Make little tweaks: Is the change you want to make a manageable grain size? Is there a way you can break your behavioral change goal into smaller components and then take one element at a time? Can you identify what those components might be?

4. Fire up emotions: What emotion could help you make this change? Write it here and reflect on how it could help.

5. Watch your mindset: Is this a change you believe you can make? What's your internal dialogue saying about making this change? Write down some of those phrases.

6. Activate autonomy: Create a few "want to" or "get to" statements about this change (for example, "I get to meditate every morning" or "I want to eat a salad for lunch three times a week").

7. Identify choice points: Which are the points at which you'll need to choose to do something different in order to enact this behavior? What are a few things you can do to set up those choice points to direct you to do the behavior?

8. Piggyback behaviors: Is there a habit that you already do onto which you can latch this new habit?

9. Make a precommitment: What might be obstacles to getting you to do this behavior? Create a few "if-then" statements to problem-solve the obstacles. For example, "If I wake up late and don't have time to meditate, then I'll meditate at lunch for five minutes and I'll also check my alarm clock to make sure it's set for tomorrow."

10. Soak in the satisfaction: After you do the behavior the first time, reflect on how it felt—even doing it just once. Jot down those reflections here.

Aligning Values to Actions

For many of us, our values are aspirational. We want to uphold our values—to be kind, creative, faithful, committed to community, and the like (see the list of values in the "Core Values" activity). Yet there are times when we fall short of demonstrating these values as we intend.

In the first column, list your top three to five values. In the second column, identify some moments when you have missed the opportunity to act on each value. In the third column, set clear and concrete intentions for acting on each value. These missed opportunities or intentions don't need to be an exhaustive list—just come up with a handful to get your mind making the connection between your values and actions.

Value	Missed Opportunity	Intention
Example: Kindness	When Xavier came into class late and disrupted the lesson. When I noticed that another teacher looked upset, and I didn't ask him if he was okay.	When a student comes in late, I'll take a breath and in a low voice ask him or her to quickly sit and get settled into the lesson. When I notice someone looking upset, I'll talk to him or her at that time, or as soon as I can.

(continued)

From *The Onward Workbook: Daily Activities to Cultivate Your Emotional Resilience and Thrive* by Elena Aguilar. Copyright © 2018 by Elena Aguilar. Reproduced by permission.

Value	Missed Opportunity	Intention

From *The Onward Workbook: Daily Activities to Cultivate Your Emotional Resilience and Thrive* by Elena Aguilar. Copyright © 2018 by Elena Aguilar. Reproduced by permission.

A Letter to Vulnerability

We all carry psychological armor to protect us from risks inherent in being vulnerable. As Brené Brown writes in *Daring Greatly* (2015), vulnerability is the center of difficult emotion, but it's also "the birthplace of love, belonging, joy, courage, empathy, and creativity. It is the source of hope, empathy, accountability, and authenticity" (p. 34).

Write a letter to the vulnerability within you. What would you like it to know? What can you thank it for? What would you like to ask of it?

Here's how my letter to vulnerability starts: *Hello tender quiet part of me. I've made a warm fire and tea for us—let's talk. I want to know you better. I promise to make it safe for you to come out. I'm sorry that for many years I told you to stay away. I'm ready for you to come into my life.*

Artistic Depictions of Vulnerability

Go to your preferred online search engine and look for images of vulnerability. See what comes up.

Then search for "depictions of vulnerability in art." Look closely at a few of those images. Sit with them and spend some time getting to know them. Pay attention to how they make you feel and what thoughts go through your mind.

Reflect

What do you notice in the images that come up?

What have you learned about vulnerability through doing this exploration?

How did this exploration help you understand your own experience of vulnerability?

If you'd like, print out one (or more) of the images that particularly speak to you and stick them in here.

From *The Onward Workbook: Daily Activities to Cultivate Your Emotional Resilience and Thrive* by Elena Aguilar. Copyright © 2018 by Elena Aguilar. Reproduced by permission.

Destination Postcard: Self-Knowledge

What would it look and sound like if you knew yourself really well? Draw a picture of yourself with thought bubbles and labels that depict a you with acute self-knowledge. If you'd like, draw this you at work, surrounded by kids and colleagues. How might you be in that space?

Chapter Reflection

What were your biggest takeaways from this chapter?

Of the different activities in this chapter, which were most useful?

Which activities would you like to revisit periodically? How might you get that habit going?

What implications do the ideas in this chapter have for the work you do?

From *The Onward Workbook: Daily Activities to Cultivate Your Emotional Resilience and Thrive* by Elena Aguilar. Copyright © 2018 by Elena Aguilar. Reproduced by permission.

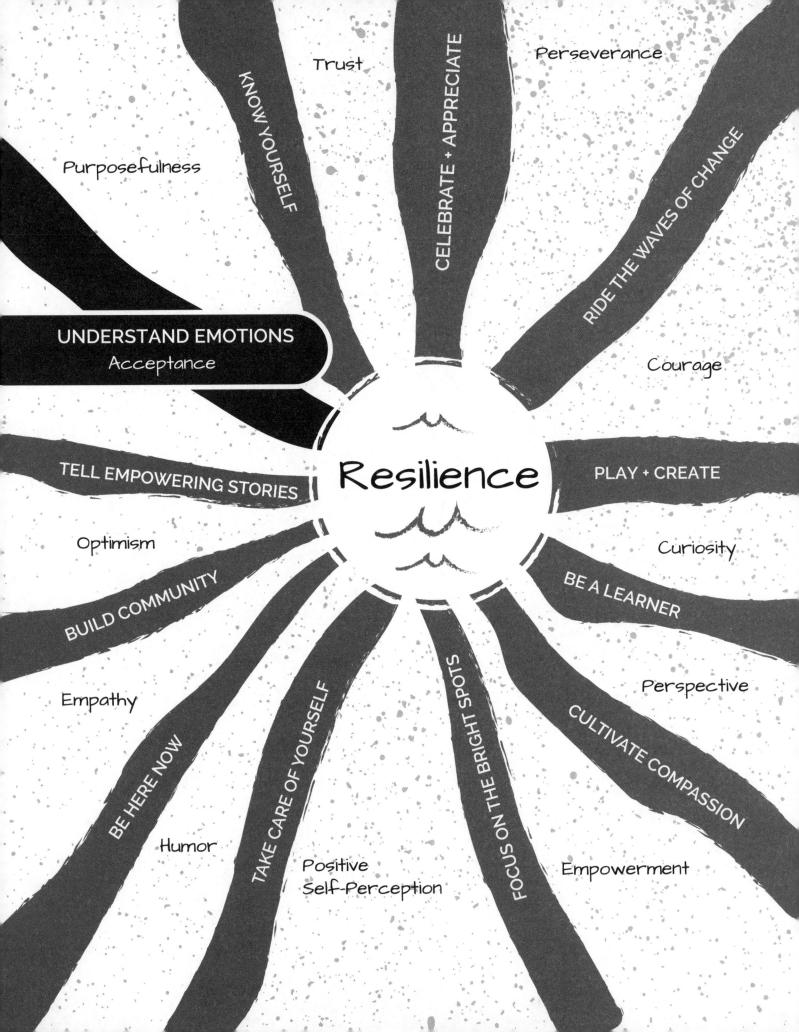

CHAPTER 2

Understand Emotions

Understanding emotions—accepting them and having strategies to respond to them—is essential to cultivate resilience. With an understanding of emotions, you can accept their existence, recognize where you can influence a situation, and let go of what is outside your control.

> *July: Summer is an ideal time to reflect on your emotions because hopefully you can sleep a little more, enjoy warm evenings, and find a few minutes for contemplation.*

A word of caution: Some of the activities in this chapter could open up a well of emotions for which you may want some support from a mental health professional. You can always skip an activity if you are concerned that it could raise memories or feelings that you feel uncertain about exploring.

Understand Emotions: Resilience Self-Assessment

The purpose of this self-assessment is to help you gauge the level of your resilience reservoir and to explore what might be draining or what could replenish it. The exercises that follow and the information in the corresponding chapter of *Onward* can boost your resilience by helping you recognize and respond to your own and others' emotions.

Imagine each circle here as a little *cenote* or reservoir within you, and fill it up according to how much each statement reflects a source of resilience. If you need something more concrete, imagine marks at ¼, ½, and ¾ full.

Before you start the exercises in this chapter, take this self-assessment and fill in the date. At the end of the month, take the assessment again. (You might even cover up your original markings with a strip of paper.) Is your resilience reservoir a little more full? If so, which practices do you want to keep up? If not, what else do you want to try?

Statement	Date:	Date:
I can recognize and name my and others' emotions.		
I am aware of the parts of an emotion cycle, and I recognize when I'm experiencing them.		
I have emotional literacy: I have the language to talk about emotions.		
I understand and can describe the four elements of emotional intelligence.		

I know the indicators of depression and anxiety and when to contact a medical professional.	◯	◯
I am aware of the role that physiology plays in how we experience emotions and moods.	◯	◯
I recognize the nonverbal expression of emotions in myself and in others.	◯	◯
I know what burnout is, and I recognize its signs.	◯	◯
I understand anger and why exploring and talking about it are valuable.	◯	◯
I understand how self-acceptance boosts my resilience, and I have strategies to accept myself.	◯	◯

KWL: Emotions

I am fond of the KWL (Know, Want to Know, and Learned) chart that's often used in elementary classrooms to introduce new material. Although my time as an elementary teacher was some 20 years ago, I find myself thinking through a KWL process as it relates to my own explorations. It brings things into focus, nudges me to raise good questions, and helps me feel accomplished.

You might fill in the first two columns now and then as you read Chapter 2 in *Onward* and as you do this workbook chapter, fill out the third column. Go ahead!

What do I KNOW about emotions (or think I know)?	What do I WANT to Know about emotions?	What have I LEARNED about emotions?

From *The Onward Workbook: Daily Activities to Cultivate Your Emotional Resilience and Thrive* by Elena Aguilar. Copyright © 2018 by Elena Aguilar. Reproduced by permission.

Beliefs About Feelings

Read these common beliefs about feelings. Indicate which ones you were taught and which ones you believe.

	I Was Taught This	I Believe This *A little; Sometimes; A lot*
Emotions don't need to be talked about.		
There is a right way to feel in every situation.		
Telling others that I am feeling bad is a sign of weakness.		
Men shouldn't cry.		
Negative feelings are bad and destructive.		
I can't control the way I feel.		
If I tell other people how I feel, they won't like me.		
If I ignore a feeling, it will go away.		
Letting others know how I feel is useless.		
Being emotional means being out of control.		
Women are hyperemotional.		
Emotions just happen for no reason.		
Painful emotions are the result of a bad attitude.		
It's not appropriate to talk about feelings at work.		
Other people have a better handle on their emotions than I do.		
If others don't approve of my feelings, I obviously shouldn't feel the way I do.		
Other people know better than I do how I'm feeling.		
Painful emotions should be ignored.		
Letting others know how I feel is risky.		
If I feel too good, something bad will happen.		

From *The Onward Workbook: Daily Activities to Cultivate Your Emotional Resilience and Thrive* by Elena Aguilar. Copyright © 2018 by Elena Aguilar. Reproduced by permission.

Reflect

What comes up for you in response to this activity?

How has your life been affected by the messages you received about emotions growing up?

Which beliefs about emotions that you hold would you like to shift?

From *The Onward Workbook: Daily Activities to Cultivate Your Emotional Resilience and Thrive* by Elena Aguilar. Copyright © 2018 by Elena Aguilar. Reproduced by permission.

Examining Coping Mechanisms

Which stressors do you face at work?

What are your usual coping strategies?

Where did you learn these coping strategies? What purpose did they serve then or are they serving now?

What might be some unintended consequences of coping in these ways?

How might your life be different if you modified or changed some of your coping strategies?

Watch the animated Pixar film *Inside Out* (2015). Then reflect on the following questions. The benefits from this activity are exponential if you discuss your reflections with someone else, so consider making plans to do this together.

Which ideas surprised you in this movie? Did you have any *aha!* moments?

Which ideas resonated with you?

What connections can you make to the suggestion that in order to feel true happiness we must also feel sadness?

How might this film help you think about and understand your own emotions?

How might this film help you think about and understand how your emotional landscape was formed by your childhood experiences?

What other thoughts or feelings does this movie raise in you?

Extension

Here are some ways to learn about the neuroscience shared in *Inside Out*. TEDEd Talks are a great resource for this learning and give us a break from sitting with so much text.

After watching one or more of these, pick a friend or colleague you think might share your interest in this topic and summarize the talk for him or her in under a minute. "I just watched this great TED Talk on . . . In it, the speaker . . ."

- **On memory:** Memories drive both the plot of *Inside Out* and most of the inner workings of Riley's brain. How does the brain store memories for later retrieval? Are there different types of memories? Learn about these questions in the TEDEd Talk called "What Happens When You Remove the Hippocampus?" by Sam Kean.

- **On sadness:** If Joy is the captain of this movie, Sadness is the navigator. *Inside Out* stresses the importance of sadness. It's not something we can just push away or avoid—it's critical for our emotional and social health. To understand the science behind this idea, watch the TEDEd Talk called "A Brief History of Melancholy," by Courtney Stephens.

- **On the brain:** Our brains are complicated and busy. Learn more about the various functions of our brain in a TEDEd Talk called "How Spontaneous Brain Activity Keeps You Alive," by Nathan S. Jacobs.

- **On sleep and memory:** Why do we need to sleep? In *Inside Out,* when Riley falls asleep, her memories head to long-term storage. Learn more in the TEDEd Talk called "The Benefits of a Good Night's Sleep," by Shai Marcu.

The Cultural Construction of Emotions

How we interpret, understand, and express emotions is culturally constructed and influenced by our assumptions about gender, race, class, and ethnicity. For example, in many places in the world, if a man cries, he is seen as weak—unless he's intoxicated, at a funeral, or at his daughter's wedding.

Being able to identify the cultural construction of emotions can be empowering as we recognize that we have choice in how we experience emotions. This understanding also helps us better understand others and our reactions to how they express their emotions.

Although it can be tempting to make generalizations about groups of people and how they express emotions, we need to be careful. There are so many intersections between culture, class, religion, generation, geographical region, and gender that it's dangerous to generalize. Each of those factors influences how people understand and express their emotions.

At the same time, when reflecting on ourselves, it can sometimes be useful to paint some broad strokes describing our emotional selves. For example, among members of my mother's Jewish side of the family, it's normal and acceptable to have loud, passionate, and intense conversations. To express your feelings in this way is normal. Yet when my mother communicated in this way with her New England Protestant in-laws, she was perceived as brash, rude, and disruptive.

Use the following prompts to gain insight into how you understand and express your own emotions.

When you think about how you understand and express emotions, what do you think has played the biggest role: Your culture, class, religion, generation, geographical region, or gender? Or what combination of these factors?

What messages do you think you've received about how someone of your gender should express anger? Sadness? Love?

How do you see others from the cultural/ethnic groups with which you identify express their anger, sadness, and love?

Do you see differences between the messages you've received about how someone of your gender and ethnicity should express strong emotions and how you have chosen to express them? What do you notice? Were those differences the result of a conscious choice?

Of the eight core emotions ("The Core Emotions" in this chapter), which do you feel is the most culturally constructed for you? Is your experience and expression of sadness or anger the emotion that feels most culturally constructed? Or perhaps fear?

Of the ways in which your expression of emotion has been influenced by culture, is there a way that you'd like to shift, expand, or change? (For example, perhaps you're a woman who has received the message that you shouldn't express anger—and this is something you intend to shift.)

The Core Emotions

Core Emotion	Fear	Anger	Sadness	Shame
Common Labels for This Emotion	Agitated Alarmed Anxious Apprehensive Concerned Desperate Dismayed Dread Fearful Frightened Horrified Hysterical Impatient Jumpy Nervous Panicked Scared Shocked Shy Tense Terrified Timid Uncertain Uneasy Worried	Aggravated Agitated Annoyed Antagonized Bitter Contemptuous (other than for self) Contentious Contrary Cranky Cruel Destructive Displeased Enraged Exasperated Explosive Frustrated Furious Hateful Hostile Impatient Indignant Insulated Irate Irritable Irritated Mad Mean Outraged Resentful Scornful Spiteful Urgent Vengeful	Alienated Anguished Bored Crushed Defeated Dejected Depressed Despairing Despondent Disappointed Discouraged Disheartened Dismayed Dispirited Displeased Distraught Down Dreary Forlorn Gloomy Grief-stricken Hopeless Hurt Insecure Isolated Lonely Melancholic Miserable Mopey Morose Neglected Oppressed Pessimistic Pitiful Rejected Somber Sorrowful Tragic Unhappy	Besmirched Chagrined Contemptuous (of self) Contrite Culpable Debased Degraded Disapproving Disdainful Disgraced Disgusted (at self) Dishonored Disreputable Embarrassed Guilty Hateful Humbled Humiliated Improper Infamous Invalidated Mortified Regretful Remorseful Repentant Reproachful Rueful Scandalized Scornful Sinful Stigmatized

Core Emotion	Jealousy	Disgust	Happiness	Love
Common Labels for This Emotion	Competitive Covetous Deprived Distrustful Envious Greedy Grudging Jealous Overprotective Petty Possessive Resentful Rivalrous	Appalled Dislike Grossed out Insulted Intolerant Nauseated Offended Put off Repelled Repulsed Revolted Revulsion Shocked Sickened Turned off	Agreeable Amused Blissful Bubbly Cheerful Content Delighted Eager Ease Elated Engaged Enjoyment Enthusiastic Euphoric Excited Exhilarated Flow Glad Gleeful Glowing Gratified Harmonious Hopeful Interested Jolly Joyful Jubilant Lighthearted Meaningful Merry Optimistic Peaceful Pleasure Pride Proud Relieved Relish Satisfied Thrilled Triumphant Up Zealous	Acceptance Admiration Adoring Affectionate Allegiance Attached Attraction Belonging Caring Compassionate Connected Dependent Desire Devoted Empathetic Faithful Friendship Interested Kind Liking Passionate Protective Respectful Sympathetic Tender Trust Vulnerable Warm

Naming Emotions

Naming emotions is much harder than it seems. The way you label an emotion influences how you express it. When you notice an emotion coming up, take time to consider it. If you feel angry, think about why you feel angry. Maybe you're actually feeling embarrassed or sad or jealous. Anger might be the secondary feeling, rather than the primary source of your upset.

- For the next few days, notice when you're having feelings. Use the "The Core Emotions" table to name your emotion. It can be helpful to carry these pages around with you. (You can also download them from the website, www.onwardthebook.com.)
- Keep track of the emotions you feel over the course of a few days; use sticky notes, a journal or this workbook, or an app on your phone to record the emotions that come up. You could also keep a list of the core emotions out and check the emotions off as they come up.

After a few days, reflect:

What did you notice about your emotions over the last few days?

Which core emotions did you experience most often?

Did anything surprise you?

How challenging did it feel to name the emotion?

Which emotions were you more likely to notice?

From The Onward Workbook: Daily Activities to Cultivate Your Emotional Resilience and Thrive by Elena Aguilar. Copyright © 2018 by Elena Aguilar. Reproduced by permission.

Exploring the Intensity of Emotions

Exploring the intensity of your emotions can help you better anticipate triggers, manage your response in the moment, and recognize changes over time.

Step 1: Record

Over the course of a few days at work, record a handful of core emotions, (use "The Core Emotions") including a brief note about the event that triggered the emotion. Assign the emotion a point value between 1 and 10—see the example here. Everyone's ranking of events will be different, so don't get too hung up on assigning a value.

Example:

	Emotion	Event	Ranking (1–10)
Day 1	*Sadness*	*I learned that a student I really care about is going into foster care and will change schools.*	4
	Anger	*The supplies I ordered three months ago still haven't come, and I can't start my science unit next week.*	7
	Happiness	*My partner teacher brought me a latte during prep.*	4

	Emotion	Event	Ranking (1–10)
Day 1			
Day 2			
Day 3			

Step 2: Reflect

What did you notice about your emotions during the days that you engaged in this exercise?

What understanding do you have of why you responded strongly to some events?

Recall a moment in which you experienced an intense emotion. How does your response in that moment compare with your reflection on the event now? Does it still seem to have merited an intense response?

What patterns do you notice in the intensity levels that you experience?

What patterns do you notice in the events or triggers of strong emotions?

Meditation

When you're in a fairly calm state, spend some time meditating on your anger. Sit quietly, close your eyes, and ask yourself: *What is its use?* Jot down your reflections here.

Reflection

When you experience anger, ask yourself if it's emerging from disappointment or a frustrated expectation. Ask yourself:

- What was my expectation?
- Can I release it and accept what is or how others are rather than how I think they should be?
- Can I acknowledge my part in the conflict?
- Can I see my part in contributing to the situation I am angry about?
- Will my anger benefit anyone, including me?
- What's the potential negative impact that anger might have: How might it harm my relationships and undermine my well-being?
- What does my anger have to teach me?

Reflect in writing about any or all of these questions.

From *The Onward Workbook: Daily Activities to Cultivate Your Emotional Resilience and Thrive* by Elena Aguilar. Copyright © 2018 by Elena Aguilar. Reproduced by permission.

Get to Know an Emotion Cycle

This exercise is worth doing many times. You can download this template from www.onwardthebook.com.

Identify a recent emotional experience that you want to reflect on. In a couple sentences, describe what happened:

Name the emotion and the degree of intensity you experienced:

Describe

1. Prompting event: What event triggered this cycle? This is the who, what, when, and where.

2. Interpretation: How did you interpret the event? This is the why.

3. Physical response: What happened in your body?

4. Urge to act: What did you want to do?

5. Action: What did you actually do? What did you say? Be specific.

6. Aftereffects: What was the consequence of what happened and how you responded?

From The Onward Workbook: Daily Activities to Cultivate Your Emotional Resilience and Thrive by Elena Aguilar. Copyright © 2018 by Elena Aguilar. Reproduced by permission.

Reflect

Where in your cycle do you think you could most easily make a change and steer your experience in a different direction?

Look at how you interpreted the event—stage 2. What other ways are there to see the situation? How might a different way to interpret the situation shift your emotional experience?

If you had an intense physical response (for example, you got a pounding headache, burst into tears, or started shaking), you most likely need to start with the physiological aspect. When your body is in high alert, you won't be able to think rationally. What could you do in the moment when you're experiencing an intense physical response?

Example of Getting to Know an Emotion Cycle

What happened: *I got really frustrated because my principal did a surprise observation, and it was only the first week of school.*
The emotion was frustration (or anger), and the level of intensity was a 6.

Describe

1. Prompting event: What event triggered this cycle? This is the who, what, when and where.
    My principal showed up in my classroom, unannounced, on the fifth day of school this year to do a formal evaluation.

(continued)

2. Interpretation: How did you interpret the event? This is the why.
   I interpreted this as she wanted to check up on me because my evaluation last spring wasn't great. She moved me to kindergarten, and I've never taught this before, and I feel like every move I make is being watched.

3. Physical response: What happened in your body?
   I felt my stomach tighten. I felt my breath get shorter.

4. Urge to act: What did you want to do?
   I wanted to either run from the room or tell my principal to get out.

5. Action: What did you actually do? What did you say? Be specific.
   I kept teaching. I ignored her. I focused on my kids. I wasn't as relaxed as usual, but I moved on in the lesson. My hands were shaking, though. I think I appeared really nervous.

6. Aftereffects: What was the consequence of what happened and how you responded?
   I felt sick all day. I felt exhausted and also angry. I feel like she's trying to catch me messing up so she can get rid of me.

Reflect

Where in your cycle do you think you could most easily make a change and steer your experience in a different direction?

To start with, I think I could intervene in my physical response. I got so nervous that I wasn't at my best.

Look at how you interpreted the event. Is there any other way of seeing the situation? If so, might taking that stance change the rest of your emotional experience?

Maybe she came in because she wants to help me. When we had our debrief conversation a couple days later, she actually had some useful ideas. She used to be a kindergarten teacher. I also know that she observed everyone in the first two weeks, so I guess I wasn't being singled out. But I didn't know this when she came in. Maybe I need to give her more of the benefit of the doubt.

What could you do in the moment when you're experiencing an intense physical response?

Taking really deep breaths always helps me. I think I'll put up a sign in my classroom that says, "Breathe!" That might help me remember when I get anxious.

From *The Onward Workbook: Daily Activities to Cultivate Your Emotional Resilience and Thrive* by Elena Aguilar. Copyright © 2018 by Elena Aguilar. Reproduced by permission.

A Day of Observing Your Emotions

Today, set a timer on your watch or phone to go off every half hour. When it goes off, pay attention to your underlying emotions at that moment. The purpose is to pay attention to your base state for a day. *(Am I generally happy? sad? angry?)* and reflect on the impact that base state has.

Keep a log or consider using an app called the Mood Meter (www.moodmeterapp .com). Then reflect:

What did you notice about your emotions today?

In thinking about your emotions, how typical was today?

How did it feel to keep focusing awareness on your emotions throughout the day?

Were certain emotions more susceptible to judgment than others? If so, do you have any thoughts on why?

From *The Onward Workbook: Daily Activities to Cultivate Your Emotional Resilience and Thrive* by Elena Aguilar. Copyright © 2018 by Elena Aguilar. Reproduced by permission.

Relaxing Your Body: The Body Scan

Unless we are experiencing pleasure or discomfort, we are often unaware of our body. The body scan technique allows you to experience your body as it is, without judgment. You may notice tension you were unaware of, a clenched jaw or tight shoulders, and be able to release that tension. This exercise invites you to draw your attention to different parts of your body, from the feet to the face; to bring mindful awareness to bodily sensations; and to relieve tension wherever you find it.

To get the most out of this practice, use it three to six days per week for four weeks. You can do it lying down or sitting. If you are new to the practice, it is best to use an audio recording like the one found at www.onwardthebook.com, or you can use the script here for yourself or to lead others through the practice.

The Body Scan

Close your eyes if it's comfortable and bring your attention into your body.

Whether you're seated or lying down, notice the feeling of your body pressing into the chair or floor.

Take three deep breaths. As you take a deep breath, you are bringing in more oxygen, enlivening your body. And as you exhale, connect with a sense of relaxing more deeply.

Notice your feet on the floor and the sensation of your feet touching the floor, or your body on the floor and the sensation of your back against the floor.

Notice the weight and pressure of your body, its heat.

Notice your legs against the chair. Is there pressure? Heaviness? Lightness? Notice your back against the chair. Or notice your body against the floor. Just notice.

Bring your attention into your stomach area. If your stomach is tense or tight, let it soften. Take a breath.

Notice your hands. Are they tense or tight? See if you can allow them to soften.

Notice your arms. Feel any sensation in your arms. Let your shoulders be soft.

Notice your neck and throat. Let them relax and be soft.

Soften your jaw. Let it be soft.

Notice your face and facial muscles, and let them be soft.

Then notice your whole body. Take one more breath.

Be aware of your whole body as best you can. Take a breath. When you're ready, open your eyes.

From *The Onward Workbook: Daily Activities to Cultivate Your Emotional Resilience and Thrive* by Elena Aguilar. Copyright © 2018 by Elena Aguilar. Reproduced by permission.

Where Emotions Live in Your Body

Where do you physically experience strong feelings?

Draw an outline of a body in the space here. Consider each of the eight basic emotions one by one, and indicate where in your body you sense it. Use colored pencils and different lines to capture the experience of that emotion. For example, perhaps anger feels like jagged arrows in your throat. Use this process as a way to visualize your emotions and how they show up in your body.

Muscle Relaxation

When you are in the grip of an intense emotional response, the quickest way to begin relaxing your body is simply to think about releasing tensed muscles while you slow your breathing. Just imagine your muscles releasing with every exhale.

Where do you tense up when you feel strong emotions? Your shoulders or neck? Jaw? Stomach? Right now, practice breathing into those places and imagine them softening.

As you practice this kind of breathing and relaxation, imagine that you're floating around yourself, watching yourself do this. How does it feel to breathe in this way and relax your body?

Next time you are in the grip of a strong emotion, you'll be more likely to remember to breathe and relax your tensed muscles if you've "practiced" in the way I'm suggesting and if you've visualized yourself doing this.

Write a note to yourself on what you want to remember about this idea and practice:

Nonverbal Communication: The Interviews

Identify a few people you trust within your personal and professional circles. Tell these people that you're working on honing your awareness of your nonverbals and your emotions, and that you want to know how they experience you. Ask them the questions here, and record some of their responses. Appreciate their honesty.

What do you remember about my body language when we first met? How did you interpret my body language?

How do you experience my nonverbal communication now, while we're talking?

When it comes to my nonverbals, is there anything I could do that would make you feel more comfortable?

What do you think someone who doesn't know me as well as you know me would say about my nonverbal communication? What do you think others perceive in my body language?

Reflect

How did it feel to engage in this exercise? What did you learn?

The Biography of My Emotions

Write the biography of your emotions in a series of short vignettes. Imagine each core emotion as a character, and narrate its story. Here's the beginning of an example:

At three years old, Anger learned to be quiet and put on a smiley face and hide in the corner. This is what Anger heard from her mother: "Nice girls don't shout!" And so Anger got small and hard . . .

Start with whichever emotion is calling you to understand it: Sadness, anger, envy, fear, joy. Which one would you like to know better?

Reflecting on Regrets

Recall a time when you expressed an emotion (in your personal life or at work) in a way that you regret. Remember this event as if you were watching a movie: See yourself from the outside. Imagine that you're operating the camera, and widen the perspective so that you can see the surrounding context. Which contextual factors contributed to the way you expressed your feelings? Get curious about what was going on. Practice compassion and self-forgiveness. Write about what you remember, notice, and understand now.

A visualization:

Invite your emotions over for tea. Visualize them walking in the door and taking a seat at a table. Or if you'd like, perhaps invite them to sit on a comfy couch. Offer them a woolen throw. Light a fire. If it's a warm day, perhaps you could sit outside on a colorful blanket. Set out something yummy to eat—finger food—and a steaming pot of herbal tea. Then invite each emotion to share its story. What does joy want to tell you? When anger is welcomed, and treated with respect, what does it need to say?

As your emotions speak to you, listen with curiosity and compassion. Accept whatever they need to say to you—they're guests at your tea party. They'll be well behaved if you respect them, accept them, and let them share their stories. Whenever you want, you can ask them to leave—it's your house. But see what happens if you are a generous host and listen well.

Reflect

What did this visualization bring up for you? What did you learn about your emotions?

From *The Onward Workbook: Daily Activities to Cultivate Your Emotional Resilience and Thrive* by Elena Aguilar. Copyright © 2018 by Elena Aguilar. Reproduced by permission.

Lessons About Strong Emotions

Much of what we believe about our strong emotions are lessons we were taught. We received those lessons when we were young. As a teacher, you are now in charge of designing the lessons. So what lesson would you like to teach yourself and others about these emotions? You're writing the curriculum guide now—so what content will you teach?

	Lessons I Was Taught	Lessons I Will Teach
Example: Fear	There is so much of it. We must be very afraid, and we must be afraid of fear too.	Fear is unavoidable—it's part of being a human. But it doesn't have to take over. It can be acknowledged, and I can learn from it, but I don't need to be afraid of it.
Fear		
Anger		
Sadness		
Shame		
Jealousy		

(continued)

From *The Onward Workbook: Daily Activities to Cultivate Your Emotional Resilience and Thrive* by Elena Aguilar. Copyright © 2018 by Elena Aguilar. Reproduced by permission.

Disgust		
Happiness		
Love		

Reflect

What did it feel like to do this exercise?

What did you learn about emotions from doing this exercise?

From The Onward Workbook: Daily Activities to Cultivate Your Emotional Resilience and Thrive by Elena Aguilar. Copyright © 2018 by Elena Aguilar. Reproduced by permission.

Thanking Your Emotions

Your emotions want to serve you, but sometimes they just don't know how. In spite of how messy they can be, you can acknowledge their efforts and thank them. Exhibit 2.1 is my appreciation for my emotions.

Complete the following statements.

Thank you, sadness. You've helped me understand . . .

Thank you, fear. You've helped me recognize . . .

Thank you, anger. You've helped me learn . . .

Thank you, disgust. You've helped me see . . .

Thank you, shame. You've helped me recognize . . .

Thank you, envy. You've helped me understand . . .

Thank you, happiness. You've helped me learn . . .

Thank you, love. You've helped me see . . .

From *The Onward Workbook: Daily Activities to Cultivate Your Emotional Resilience and Thrive* by Elena Aguilar. Copyright © 2018 by Elena Aguilar. Reproduced by permission.

Exhibit 2.1: Thanking My Emotions

Thank you, sadness. You've helped me understand that your pain is tied to my joy. Sadness arises because of loss, and you help me see that I need to feel joy and connection.

Thank you, fear. You've helped me recognize how I can stay safe in this world. You have given yourself to protecting me.

Thank you, anger. You've helped me learn about what I value. You've helped me draw limits and boundaries around how people can treat me. You've energized me at times and helped me speak and act.

Thank you, disgust. You've helped me see who I want to be in this world. You've helped me draw boundaries and say no. You've helped me see what I want to do with my life.

Thank you, shame. You've helped me recognize my fears and anger. You've helped guide me toward authenticity and integrity. You've helped me take ownership of my behaviors and words.

Thank you, envy. You've helped me understand what I need in this world. You've directed me to self-appreciation and compassion. You've pushed me to be my best self.

Thank you, happiness. You've helped me learn that I need you and that that's okay. You've shown me what life is all about. You've guided me to my values.

Thank you, love. You've helped me see that I need you, I deserve you, and I'm better with you. You are all there is. You are why I am here.

Reflect

What did it feel like to engage in this exercise?

What insights did you get into your emotions?

From *The Onward Workbook: Daily Activities to Cultivate Your Emotional Resilience and Thrive* by Elena Aguilar. Copyright © 2018 by Elena Aguilar. Reproduced by permission.

Thanks, but No Thanks

Now that you've acknowledged your emotions and appreciated them for their efforts to guide and protect you, it's time to give them some corrective feedback as well. Tell them what you need from them. You'll see my reflection on this activity following the space for you to write.

Complete the following statements:

Thank you, sadness. I appreciate your efforts, and from now on, I'd like to ask you . . .

Thank you, fear. I appreciate your efforts, and from now on, I'd like to ask you . . .

Thank you, anger. I appreciate your efforts, and from now on, I'd like to ask you . . .

Thank you, disgust. I appreciate your efforts, and from now on, I'd like to ask you . . .

Thank you, shame. I appreciate your efforts, and from now on, I'd like to ask you . . .

Thank you, jealousy. I appreciate your efforts, and from now on, I'd like to ask you . . .

Thank you, happiness. I appreciate your efforts, and from now on, I'd like to ask you . . .

Thank you, love. I appreciate your efforts, and from now on, I'd like to ask you . . .

Elena's Reflection: Thanks, but No Thanks

Thank you, sadness. I appreciate your efforts, and from now on, I'd like to ask you to be more direct about needing attention. You don't need to hide behind anger. I promise not to be so afraid of you. Let me know when you need some time.

Thank you, fear. I appreciate your efforts, and from now on, I'd like to ask you to check in with reality a little more often. Sometimes you sound the alarm when it's unnecessary. I know you're trying to protect me, but I promise to reasonably assess the situation if needed. So just turn it down a little. I'll be okay.

Thank you, anger. I appreciate your efforts, and from now on, I'd like to ask you to take a moment before breaking down my front door. Please check in with sadness first to see if you are mixed up in something. When you do need to come over, please make your appearance and know that I will see you right away. You are welcome to stop by, but be a good guest.

Thank you, disgust. I appreciate your efforts, and from now on, I'd like to ask you to give me some space for curiosity when you show up. I'd like to understand you better. Please give me a chance.

Thank you, shame. I appreciate your efforts, and from now on, I'd like to ask you to minimize your visits to only those that are truly necessary to keep me alive and to help me preserve healthy relationships with others.

From *The Onward Workbook: Daily Activities to Cultivate Your Emotional Resilience and Thrive* by Elena Aguilar. Copyright © 2018 by Elena Aguilar. Reproduced by permission.

Thank you, envy. I appreciate your efforts, and from now on, I'd like to ask you to consider that abundance is a law of the universe and that there's enough to go around. Know when you've linked arms with insecurity and fear—because sometimes you show up tangled with another emotion.

Thank you, happiness. I appreciate your efforts, and from now on, I'd like to ask you to be more insistent on demanding my attention. The other emotions are noisy and occupy a great deal of my energy. It's okay for you to speak up and call to me. I promise to listen.

Thank you, love. I appreciate your efforts, and from now on, I'd like to ask you to turn up your volume and radiate light. If you are all there is, then you have permission to be stronger than all the other emotions. Don't let me forget.

Exploring Moments of Emotional Intensity

List five moments of intense emotion during your years as an educator. These can be highs or lows or a combination—whichever feel as though they were the most emotional. Mine include when I had to call Child Protective Services because one of my students was being abused, when I attended the high school graduation of kids I'd taught in second grade, and when my school went through a challenging leadership transition.

Describe the event briefly and then see if you can label some of the emotions you experienced. Most likely, there were a number of emotions that surfaced.

The Moment	Description of the Event	The Emotions

From The Onward Workbook: Daily Activities to Cultivate Your Emotional Resilience and Thrive by Elena Aguilar. Copyright © 2018 by Elena Aguilar. Reproduced by permission.

Reflect

What do you notice about the events you selected? Are there any common themes?

What did you learn from this exercise?

How to Breathe

When you're in the grip of a strong uncomfortable emotion, breathing is one of the most effective ways to calm your mind and body. If you remember nothing else when you're caught up in anger, fear, or sadness, remember to breathe. But there's a very specific kind of breathing that's most effective. It has three parts:

1. Inhale to a count of six.
2. Hold your breath for two counts.
3. Exhale to a count of six.

Repeat this routine *five* times for greatest impact. It literally changes what's going on in your brain that is contributing to the intensity of the experience.

This routine will be most helpful if you've practiced it and strengthened the mental muscles that will help you remember how to do it. So right now, practice this breathing routine five times.

Jot down a few words: What did you notice about how this kind of breathing made you feel?

Over the course of the next couple of days, make it a goal to do this three-step breathing routine at least 10 times—in moments of emotional intensity and in moments of emotional ease. You'll be strengthening your memory of this practice so that you can use it when you really need it. Each time you practice breathing, shade in one of the heads here so that you have a record of your practice.

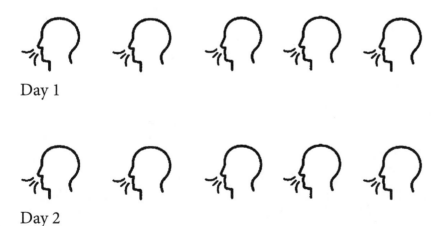

Day 1

Day 2

From *The Onward Workbook: Daily Activities to Cultivate Your Emotional Resilience and Thrive* by Elena Aguilar. Copyright © 2018 by Elena Aguilar. Reproduced by permission.

How can you remember, when you're in the grip of intense emotion, to breathe? Which cues could you place around you? Perhaps you could write the word *Breathe* in big, bold letters and post it on your classroom or office door. Or how about a temporary tattoo on your forearm? Or a screensaver with this word? Identify a way to prompt yourself to remember—and take action to set up that prompt. Right now.

RAIN: Dealing with Uncomfortable Emotions

RAIN is an acronym for a four-step process that you can use in any situation in which you experience a strong emotion that causes confusion and stress. This process gives you a place to turn, a thing to do to help manage the experience. The acronym was coined around 2005 by Michele McDonald and is based on mindfulness practices.

R	A	I	N
Recognize what's going on	**Allow** the experience to be there, just as it is	**Investigate** with kindness	**Nonidentify** with whatever is going on

Recognize: Recognizing means consciously acknowledging the thoughts, feelings, and behaviors that are affecting you. Name your emotions.

Allow: Allowing means letting the thoughts, emotions, feelings, or sensations you have recognized to simply be there. Often when we have an unpleasant experience, we pile on the self-judgment, numb ourselves to our feelings, or focus our attention elsewhere. Allowing creates space to make wise decisions.

Investigate: Investigating with kindness means calling on your curiosity and directing your attention to your present experience. Ask yourself: *What's going on in my body? What is calling for attention? What am I believing? What does this feeling want from me?* Unless you engage in this inquiry with kindness toward yourself, you won't be able to gather a complete picture of what is going on. You will need to incorporate some self-compassion practices here to get the most from this process (see Chapter 7). Try simply placing your hand on your heart or cheek as you investigate.

Nonidentify: You are not your limiting emotions, thoughts, sensations, or stories. Nonidentification is the step in which you loosen your sense of who you think you are and create more expansiveness around your sense of self. Emotions come and go like the weather; who you are remains steady underneath.

Practice

1. Recall a few times recently when you experienced a strong emotion. Take a moment to put yourself back in the experience, and use RAIN to explore the feelings that came up for you. Then reflect here.

2. Write out the acronym and what each step means, in your own words. Post this on a wall where you can see it regularly or on a small note card that you can tuck into your pocket. The hardest part of this exercise is remembering to use it—and the more you use it, the easier it is to remember.

3. When you use RAIN, take as much time as you can—even if it's just one minute—to go through the process.
    a. Notice which steps you find most useful: The recognition? The investigation?
    b. Is one of the steps harder?
    c. At which step do you feel the greatest relief?

4. As soon as possible after using RAIN, capture a few words of reflection on the experience. How did the steps help you manage the moment? What did you learn?

Noticing Physical Cues

Pay attention to physical feelings—not so much the story of why you're feeling what you're feeling, but the sensations themselves. If you're feeling irritated with your principal, what does irritation feel like in your body? Where do you sense it? How does it feel as a mood? By doing this, you'll heighten your recognition of your feelings and then have more choice about how to respond in that moment.

Today, pay attention to the physical sensations that arise in connection to emotions. At the end of the day, jot down a few observations and reflections on this experience.

There are a number of online surveys that can help you assess your level of stress. I find it useful to do these occasionally to have a baseline or to check in on my stress level.

Take the Perceived Stress Scale test: https://www.bemindfulonline.com/test-your-stress/. It's free and brief. After you take it, respond to the following prompts.

How do you feel about the results?

What, if anything, surprised you? What did you learn from taking it?

What are the implications of this assessment? Do you want to do anything different?

Quick Calm: Grounding

This exercise can help you quickly calm yourself and relax. Try it when you experience a surge of uncomfortable feelings such as fear or anger. By engaging your five senses, you'll bring yourself into the present moment.

1. Close your eyes or find a place to gaze where you can draw your attention inward.
2. Take five slow, deep breaths.
3. When you open your eyes, name five things you can see around you.
4. Name four things you can touch or feel.
5. Identify three things you can hear.
6. Name two things you can smell.
7. Name what you can taste right now.

Remember this exercise by counting—five, four, three, two, one—and by prompting yourself: Five deep breaths and five things I can see; four things I can touch; three things I can hear, two things I can smell, one thing I can taste.

In the space here, or on another piece of paper, draw a simple representation of this concept. If you'd like, post this somewhere that you can see during the day to remind you of this exercise.

From *The Onward Workbook: Daily Activities to Cultivate Your Emotional Resilience and Thrive* by Elena Aguilar. Copyright © 2018 by Elena Aguilar. Reproduced by permission.

Recognizing Cognitive Distortions

Distortions or inaccurate thoughts can reinforce negative thinking and uncomfortable emotions. These distorted thoughts might be one of the greatest threats to our resilience. Heightening our awareness of which kinds of thinking errors we fall into and what sends us into these ways of thinking can help us move out of them. Cultivating this practice of recognizing our distorted thinking and shifting it takes a great deal of time and attention and so we'll return to it in Chapter 3 of this book.

These are some kinds of cognitive distortions:

- **Black-and-white thinking:** Thinking about things as right or wrong, all-or-nothing, great or horrible. With either-or thinking, there is no middle ground or gray area. If a lesson you'd planned didn't go exactly as you'd hoped, you might declare it a total failure.
- **Overgeneralizing:** Interpreting events in terms of "always" or "never." "My principal never tells me anything I'm doing well!"
- **Catastrophizing:** Thinking everything is going to go wrong. You tell yourself, *This will be a disaster.*
- **Mental filtering:** Drawing conclusions based on one selected fact, situation, or event. You might think back to your first year teaching and remember having the flu in the winter, and you might say, "I was sick my whole first year of teaching."
- **Personalizing:** Taking responsibility or blame for something bad that you had no control over. Assuming that someone's behavior is "all about me." You tell yourself, *It must be my fault somehow.*
- **Mind reading:** Interpreting someone else's behaviors (facial expressions or nonverbal communication) with no input other than your own thoughts, and not checking your assumptions. You think, *That new teacher doesn't like me because she never smiles.*
- **Disqualifying the positive:** You ignore or explain away any positive fact or experience. You rationalize that something good doesn't count. If you have a day where kids are on task, you say, "Today was a fluke. Tomorrow they'll be out of control again."
- **Magnifying or minimizing:** Giving something more credit or importance than it deserves or doing the opposite and giving it less credit or less importance than it actually calls for. This is "making a mountain out of a molehill" (or the reverse).

Activity

For the next five days, track your patterns of thinking. Put a tally mark in each box when you notice yourself falling into one of these thinking patterns. At the end of the five days, use the reflection prompts.

Cognitive Distortion	Day 1	Day 2	Day 3	Day 4	Day 5
Black-and-White Thinking					
Overgeneralizing					
Catastrophizing					
Mental Filtering					
Personalizing					
Mind Reading					
Disqualifying the Positive					
Magnifying or Minimizing					

Reflect

Was there a thinking pattern that you fell into more often? Did you notice a dominant cognitive distortion?

Can you identify an incident that happened that spurred you into a way of thinking? Can you trace that way of thinking back to earlier experiences in your life?

What was the impact of one way of thinking? If you told yourself, *That new teacher doesn't like me,* what did that thought lead you to do or not to do?

What kinds of events send you into new ways of thinking? Can you identify any patterns in those events?

A Letter to Anger

Write a letter to anger. Imagine it as a character—either inside you or elsewhere. What do you need to say? Here's the beginning of my letter to anger:

Anger: Sometimes I fear you will consume me. You surprise me sometimes—you show up when I'm not expecting you and then your power seems greater than anything I've ever known.

Artistic Depictions of Anger

Go to your preferred online search engine and look for images of anger—or other terms that reflect anger, such as rage, frustration, or irritation (see "The Core Emotions" in Chapter 2 for these terms).

See what comes up, then search for "depictions of anger in art."

Look closely at a few of those images. Sit with them and spend some time getting to know them. Pay attention to how they make you feel and what thoughts go through your mind.

Reflect

What do you notice in the images that come up?

What have you learned about anger through doing this exploration?

How did this exploration help you understand your own experience of anger?

If you'd like, print out one (or more) of the images that particularly speak to you and stick them in here.

Destination Postcard: Understand Emotions

What would it look and sound like if you understood emotions? Draw a picture of yourself with thought bubbles and labels that depict a you who has high awareness of your emotions. If you'd like, draw this you at work, surrounded by kids and colleagues. How might you be in that space?

From *The Onward Workbook: Daily Activities to Cultivate Your Emotional Resilience and Thrive* by Elena Aguilar. Copyright © 2018 by Elena Aguilar. Reproduced by permission.

Chapter Reflection

What were your biggest takeaways from this chapter?

Of the different activities in this chapter, which were most useful?

Which activities would you like to revisit periodically? How might you get that habit going?

What implications do the ideas in this chapter have for the work you do?

CHAPTER 3

Tell Empowering Stories

How you interpret and make sense of events is a juncture point where emotional resilience increases or depletes. You make the choice about what story to tell. When you tell empowering stories, your optimism may expand, and optimism is a key trait of resilient people.

August: Your thoughts are the keys to unlocking reserves of resilience. Start the year with this key habit.

Tell Empowering Stories: Resilience Self-Assessment

The purpose of this self-assessment is to help you gauge the level of your resilience reservoir and to explore what might be draining or what could replenish it. The exercises that follow and the information in the corresponding chapter of *Onward* can boost your resilience by building your awareness of how you interpret experiences and situations and helping you choose more beneficial interpretations.

Imagine each circle as a little *cenote* or reservoir within you, and fill it up according to how much each statement reflects a source of resilience. If you need something more concrete, imagine marks at ¼, ½, and ¾ full.

Before you start the exercises in this chapter, take this self-assessment and fill in the date. At the end of the month, take the assessment again. (You might even cover up your original markings with a strip of paper.) Is your resilience reservoir a little more full? If so, which practices do you want to keep up? If not, what else do you want to try?

Statement	Date:	Date:
I am aware of many of the thoughts I have. I can recognize that a thought is a thought and not a fact or "the" truth.	◯	◯
I am aware of how my thoughts influence my feelings.	◯	◯
I can catch myself in a thought that doesn't make me feel good.	◯	◯
I recognize and interrupt thoughts that undermine my resilience.	◯	◯

I know where some of my unproductive thoughts come from.	◯	◯
I can shift and reframe my thoughts when I want.	◯	◯
I am intentional about crafting the narratives of my life. I interpret the events of my life in a way that fosters my resilience.	◯	◯
I know why it's important to tell my stories to others, and I do so.	◯	◯
I have strategies to build my optimism, and I know why it's an essential disposition for cultivating resilience.	◯	◯
I am aware of how stories in the school, in organizations, and in broader society affect how I tell my stories.	◯	◯

Three Good Things

The story of your life is formed by what you notice each day.

Every night this week, set aside 10 minutes before you go to sleep. Write down three things that went well today and why they went well. It is important that you have a physical record of what you wrote. The three things need not be earthshaking in importance ("First period was calm and focused"), but they can be important ("I was invited to present on a panel of science teachers"). Next to each positive event, answer the question "Why did this happen?"

| Monday | |
The Good Thing	Why Did This Happen?

From *The Onward Workbook: Daily Activities to Cultivate Your Emotional Resilience and Thrive* by Elena Aguilar. Copyright © 2018 by Elena Aguilar. Reproduced by permission.

Tuesday

The Good Thing	Why Did This Happen?

Wednesday

The Good Thing	Why Did This Happen?

(continued)

Thursday	
The Good Thing	**Why Did This Happen?**

Friday	
The Good Thing	**Why Did This Happen?**

From *The Onward Workbook: Daily Activities to Cultivate Your Emotional Resilience and Thrive* by Elena Aguilar. Copyright © 2018 by Elena Aguilar. Reproduced by permission.

At the end of the week, review the good things that happened each day, and write a summary story of the week.

Intention Setting

You can set an intention at any time, for any amount of time. Intentions can sound like any of these:

- I'm going to be calm and patient with my fifth period today.
- I'm going to listen to understand in our grade-level team meeting.
- I'll be open to feedback in my evaluation conference.
- I'll enjoy the field trip.
- I want to be open to new ideas.
- I want to connect with my colleagues.
- I'm going to have an easy day.

An intention should feel good to declare. It also needs to be somewhat within your influence and control—for example, rather than "I'm going to get a great evaluation," a true intention is "I'm going to learn from whatever is in my evaluation."

Your assignment this week is to set as many intentions as possible, but at least five. You could have one intention per day, or you could set an overall intention for each day and then a supporting intention for different sections of the day (perhaps for different periods or for events).

For each intention, identify what it might look and sound like if you're holding it; "sound like" can be internal self-talk. For example, if your intention is to be open to new ideas during the PD session, then you might notice that your mind is thinking, *Hmm. That could be interesting. I'd be willing to try that,* rather than what your mind says when it's not open: *That'll never work. She has never tried that with my kids. Who has time for that anyway?*

Equally important is that you reflect on your intention at the end of the day. You need to have a moment to consider how you held your intention and how it worked for you. That moment isn't an opportunity for you to be self-critical and berate yourself if you didn't hold your intention; it's an opportunity for learning.

Monday

Intention	
What might it look and sound like if I'm holding my intention?	
Reflection: When did I notice myself holding it? How did it work for me?	

Tuesday

Intention	
What might it look and sound like if I'm holding my intention?	
Reflection: When did I notice myself holding it? How did it work for me?	

(continued)

Wednesday

Intention	
What might it look and sound like if I'm holding my intention?	
Reflection: When did I notice myself holding it? How did it work for me?	

Thursday

Intention	
What might it look and sound like if I'm holding my intention?	
Reflection: When did I notice myself holding it? How did it work for me?	

From *The Onward Workbook: Daily Activities to Cultivate Your Emotional Resilience and Thrive* by Elena Aguilar. Copyright © 2018 by Elena Aguilar. Reproduced by permission.

Friday	
Intention	
What might it look and sound like if I'm holding my intention?	
Reflection: When did I notice myself holding it? How did it work for me?	

The third law of motion in physics is that for every action there's an equal and opposite reaction. What you put out comes back to you. Before the thing that goes out, the action, there is the thought to create the action. Behind the thought is an intention—a motivation. That intention is the energy that is going to be returned to you. So taking time to create intentions, to design them as you want, is a high-leverage strategy to influence how you experience your life.

If you want to really mine the potential of this habit, set intentions every day for a month or for a year. Or set intentions every day forever.

Start a New Habit

Transitions—from summer back to the school year, for example—are a great time to start a new habit. The break in routines can wipe away old habits and make space for new ones to start. Now, as you transition back to school, is an optimal time to start a new self-care habit. And if you engage in this chapter during any other time in the year—it'll be just fine!

What habit would you like to start?

What are the steps you need to take in order to create that habit?

What would it feel like if you were engaging in this habit regularly?

Imagine yourself weeks or months in the future, once this habit is established. What is different?

Who might be able to help you keep this habit?

From *The Onward Workbook: Daily Activities to Cultivate Your Emotional Resilience and Thrive* by Elena Aguilar. Copyright © 2018 by Elena Aguilar. Reproduced by permission.

Reflect on Thoughts

This activity helps you cultivate one of the most effective mental habits to boost your resilience.

This week, your task is to catch yourself having an emotional response to an event and then to reflect on your thoughts. The sooner you can engage in the reflection the better, so you might want to take this workbook with you to school this week. If you can't get to the reflection until the evening, that's okay. But it's really important to go through this reflection process at least five times this week (even better if you do it five times in one day!). That will make it more likely that your mind will remember the questioning routine and use it even when you aren't sitting with your workbook. Also, this is another activity for which the impact will be triple if you write your reflections down.

Event 1:	
What was the first thing that went through your mind when the event happened?	
What are you telling yourself about it now?	
What is so upsetting about it?	

From *The Onward Workbook: Daily Activities to Cultivate Your Emotional Resilience and Thrive* by Elena Aguilar. Copyright © 2018 by Elena Aguilar. Reproduced by permission.

What memories did the event stir up?	
What do you think this says about you? About your life?	
What do you think this makes others think about you?	
What does this tell you about another person or other people?	
What are you worried might happen now?	

Event 2:

What was the first thing that went through your mind when the event happened?	

From *The Onward Workbook: Daily Activities to Cultivate Your Emotional Resilience and Thrive* by Elena Aguilar. Copyright © 2018 by Elena Aguilar. Reproduced by permission.

What are you telling yourself about it now?	
What is so upsetting about it?	
What memories did the event stir up?	
What do you think this says about you? About your life?	
What do you think this makes others think about you?	
What does this tell you about another person or other people?	
What are you worried might happen now?	

(continued)

From *The Onward Workbook: Daily Activities to Cultivate Your Emotional Resilience and Thrive* by Elena Aguilar. Copyright © 2018 by Elena Aguilar. Reproduced by permission.

Event 3:

What was the first thing that went through your mind when the event happened?	
What are you telling yourself about it now?	
What is so upsetting about it?	
What memories did the event stir up?	
What do you think this says about you? About your life?	
What do you think this makes others think about you?	

What does this tell you about another person or other people?	
What are you worried might happen now?	

Event 4:

What was the first thing that went through your mind when the event happened?	
What are you telling yourself about it now?	
What is so upsetting about it?	
What memories did the event stir up?	

(continued)

From *The Onward Workbook: Daily Activities to Cultivate Your Emotional Resilience and Thrive* by Elena Aguilar. Copyright © 2018 by Elena Aguilar. Reproduced by permission.

What do you think this says about you? About your life?	
What do you think this makes others think about you?	
What does this tell you about another person or other people?	
What are you worried might happen now?	

Event 5:

What was the first thing that went through your mind when the event happened?	
What are you telling yourself about it now?	

What is so upsetting about it?	
What memories did the event stir up?	
What do you think this says about you? About your life?	
What do you think this makes others think about you?	
What does this tell you about another person or other people?	
What are you worried might happen now?	

At the end of the week, or after you've done this five times, read through all five reflections. Do you notice any themes or patterns in your thinking?

What insights into your thinking did you glean?

How did it feel to engage in these reflections?

What Einstein Says About Stories

The world as we have created it is a process of our thinking. It cannot be changed without changing our thinking.
ALBERT EINSTEIN

If you want to change your life, you've got to deal with your thoughts.

Which of your recurring thoughts are most problematic in your life? What comes to mind first?

Imagine that you can pull these thoughts out and put them in a display case somewhere. What do you notice about them?

From *The Onward Workbook: Daily Activities to Cultivate Your Emotional Resilience and Thrive* by Elena Aguilar. Copyright © 2018 by Elena Aguilar. Reproduced by permission.

Exploring the Impact of Cognitive Distortions

You may acknowledge that your thoughts are undermining your emotional well-being and ability to thrive, and you may be committed to shifting them. This will take time and daily attention, given that our thoughts are deeply engrained in our mind and way of being. That's why I'm offering you another exercise (similar to the one in Chapter 2) to support you in this effort.

As I mentioned in Chapter 2, the first step in changing our thoughts is recognizing what's unhelpful or wrong about them. What psychologists call *distorted thinking* comprises a set of patterns. These ways of thinking are hard to see because usually they're habitual; we engage in them with little awareness and have done so for many years. When we experience a strong, distressing emotion, most of us leap to one or more of these unhelpful patterns of interpretation. Some of us might use all of them at one time or another, or we might have our favorites.

A first step to shifting your thoughts is to catch them more frequently when they appear. This exercise will support you to notice and name your thoughts. It will also guide you to think about the impact of holding these thoughts—and the impact on you when others hold these thoughts.

What follows are the most common patterns of distorted thinking. You may want to refer to Chapter 3 in *Onward* for examples of these kinds of distorted thoughts.

Distorted Thought	Description	Put a star by those that you know you fall in to	Jot down the initials of others whom you suspect think this way
Black-and-White Thinking	• Using words such as "always," "every," or "never" • Thinking about things as right or wrong, all-or-nothing, great or horrible • Seeing no shades of gray, no complexity in people or situations, no middle ground		

From The Onward Workbook: Daily Activities to Cultivate Your Emotional Resilience and Thrive by Elena Aguilar. Copyright © 2018 by Elena Aguilar. Reproduced by permission.

Jumping to Conclusions	• Drawing conclusions about a situation without knowing all the facts, or sometimes without any facts • Even without evidence, making negative assumptions • Feeling supremely confident in knowing how someone else feels about you; you can infer others' motivations and feelings without hearing a word from them • Feeling confident about predicting outcomes, which are almost always negative, about things that haven't happened • Interpreting other people's behaviors (including their facial expressions or nonverbal communication) with no input other than your own thoughts, and not checking your assumptions		
Unrealistic Expectations	• Getting upset when someone else or life in general doesn't measure up to how you think things "should" be • Holding uncompromising rules about how things should be • Blaming yourself and others for things that aren't controllable • Being relentlessly hard on others and on yourself • Using the word, "should" a lot and saying that you're not a perfectionist; you "just have high standards"		
Disqualifying the Positive	• Focusing on and magnifying the negative aspects of a person, situation, or experience • Ignoring or explaining away any positive fact or experience		

(continued)

Overgeneralizing	• Arriving at speedy conclusions with only one piece of evidence • Making conclusions based on one selected fact, situation, or event		
Catastrophizing	• Thinking that everything will go wrong; seeing worst-case scenarios and warning others about them • Telling yourself that a situation is horrific and intolerable		
Emotional Reasoning	• Believing that your feelings reflect the way things actually are; treating your feelings as facts		
Personalization	• Thinking everything is about you, especially the bad things • Being sure that anything negative is directed at you or that you are responsible for it happening • Taking the blame for things that you could not control • If something goes wrong, telling yourself, *It must be my fault somehow* • Feeling as though people do things specifically to get at you		

Reflect

Is there one pattern of thinking that you go to more often? Do you have a favorite?

How do you think you're affected by engaging in this kind of thinking? What are the unintended consequences of doing so?

From *The Onward Workbook: Daily Activities to Cultivate Your Emotional Resilience and Thrive* by Elena Aguilar. Copyright © 2018 by Elena Aguilar. Reproduced by permission.

What kind of distorted thinking in others do you find most challenging to be around? What impact does their distorted thinking have on you?

What do you think might be possible for you if you shifted your distorted ways of thinking?

Compare your experience with this activity and with "Recognizing Cognitive Distortions" in Chapter 2. What did you learn from each one? What did you learn from doing both?

Catch That Distorted Thought

This week, your task is simply to catch yourself in as many distorted thoughts as possible—again, it'll take daily attention to shift cognitive distortions—but it's worth the diligence! You might want to have your workbook close by so you can make tally marks at any moment, or you could just use a sticky note or a note on your phone.

Week of: [Date]	
Distorted Thinking	**Tally Marks**
Black-and-White Thinking	
Jumping to Conclusions	
Unrealistic Expectations	
Disqualifying the Positive	
Overgeneralizing	
Catastrophizing	
Emotional Reasoning	
Personalization	

At the end of the week, reflect:

How did it feel to do this activity? Which parts were challenging?

What did you learn from doing this activity?

How did it feel to catch yourself in a distorted thought?

Visually Depicting a Life Story

Either here on this page or on another sheet of paper (maybe a chart-size piece), draw the path of your life, identifying significant moments. Depict the twists and turns, the ups and downs. Start with Birth and end with Present Day. Use symbols, images, and colors. Use captions if you want. Afterward, reflect on the prompts that follow the drawing space.

From *The Onward Workbook: Daily Activities to Cultivate Your Emotional Resilience and Thrive* by Elena Aguilar. Copyright © 2018 by Elena Aguilar. Reproduced by permission.

Reflect

What story did you tell about your life through this creation?

How did you decide what to include and what to leave out?

How did audience affect what you drew? (If you knew you'd share this with colleagues, how did that affect what you included?) Would this have looked different if you knew that no one would see it?

How might someone who knows you well see your path? What might this person have included?

How might this look if you were drawing it to show your children? Your parents? Your principal?

Affirmations

Affirmations may sound hokey or New Agey, but there's science behind the concept: Saying affirmations to yourself raises your levels of feel-good hormones and pushes your brain to form new clusters of "positive thought" neurons. This is basic rewiring for your mind. It's simple, easy, and powerful.

Tailor your affirmations so that the language resonates for you—because you're going to say them only to yourself. They need to be short and positive and to feel good when you say them. The most powerful affirmations will be those that you create, but these will get you started:

- I'll get through this.
- I am powerful.
- I'm valuable, and I belong.
- Everything is connected.
- I am enough. I do enough.
- Every day, I'm a better teacher.
- Difficult moments pass quickly.
- I'm a badass, and I can deal with anything.

One of my most powerful affirmations is *Trust the process.*
Write down a couple of affirmations to use today:

At which specific moments in the day do you hope to use these affirmations? Can you anticipate the moments when they'll be most useful?

At the end of the day, come back here and reflect on what it felt like to use affirmations. What impact did they have?

From *The Onward Workbook: Daily Activities to Cultivate Your Emotional Resilience and Thrive* by Elena Aguilar. Copyright © 2018 by Elena Aguilar. Reproduced by permission.

If your life were a book, what would the chapters be called?

What would you like the chapters of your life to be called going forward? Think about this year by year, if you'd like, or in five-year periods.

What's the story you want to tell at the end of this school year? Write a couple of sentences in the past tense describing this school year. For example, "This was the best year ever! I made so much growth as a teacher!"

There's a saying, "You are the author of your life." How does this feel to you? Does it ring true?

Take Apart That Thought

Thoughts are not facts. This activity helps you deconstruct a thought and see that it is not necessarily true. You might want to copy the prompts on this page and keep them somewhere visible or accessible, or you can download them from www.onwardthebook .com. This week, do this activity at least three times. By repeating it, your mind will begin incorporating these ways of thinking. To reap the most benefit from this activity, do it every day for a month.

Take Apart That Thought: Example

The thought: My students don't respect me.	
Is it true?	Yes. I think so.
If I think it's true: How do I know it's true?	Because they won't listen to me, they talk over me, they call me names behind my back, they roll their eyes at me, they talk back when I tell them to do something.
Is there any other way to see the thought?	I don't know. Maybe they treat me this way because they just don't like me. Or maybe because they are angry that I'm holding high expectations for them. Or maybe because they don't trust teachers. I know that last year they had a number of teachers who quit or were let go. Maybe this is just how 8th graders act. Maybe I'm getting too triggered by them too quickly. Maybe I could do something different so that I don't get caught up in their attitudes. Maybe I don't respect them either.
How does this belief make me feel? What are the story lines I attach to this thought?	It makes me feel angry that they don't respect me. I don't feel valued as a teacher. I feel like the administration condones their behavior and won't do anything about it. The belief makes me feel hopeless, frustrated, and like I don't want to go to school.
What would things be like if I didn't hold this belief?	I guess I might feel better going to school. Maybe I could figure out a way to get my kids to listen to me and respond in a way that's better for all of us.

| What's a different belief I could substitute for this thought when it arises? | I could tell myself that I just don't know how to manage them effectively. Or maybe that I don't know how to form a good relationship with them. I could tell myself that I just don't understand them. I could tell myself that I don't know them and they don't know me. I could tell myself that they want to be respected and want to connect with me. I could tell myself that the "problem" isn't that they don't respect me; it's that we haven't figured out how to treat each other in a way that is healthy and good. I guess I play a part in that too. I could tell myself that we can figure this out. |

Take-Apart 1

The thought:	
Is it true?	
If I think it's true: How do I know it's true?	
Is there any other way to see the thought?	
How does this belief make me feel? What are the story lines I attach to this thought?	
What would things be like if I didn't hold this belief?	
What's a different belief I could substitute for this thought when it arises?	

(continued)

Take-Apart 2

The thought:	
Is it true?	
If I think it's true: How do I know it's true?	
Is there any other way to see the thought?	
How does this belief make me feel? What are the story lines I attach to this thought?	
What would things be like if I didn't hold this belief?	
What's a different belief I could substitute for this thought when it arises?	

Take-Apart 3

The thought:	
Is it true?	
If I think it's true: How do I know it's true?	

From *The Onward Workbook: Daily Activities to Cultivate Your Emotional Resilience and Thrive* by Elena Aguilar. Copyright © 2018 by Elena Aguilar. Reproduced by permission.

Is there any other way to see the thought?	
How does this belief make me feel? What are the story lines I attach to this thought?	
What would things be like if I didn't hold this belief?	
What's a different belief I could substitute for this thought when it arises?	

Which was the most useful prompt to ask yourself?

What did you learn about yourself by doing this?

Try This Thought

Even if you don't feel like an optimist, you can try on optimistic thoughts and fake it for a bit.

When you find yourself falling into thinking patterns that won't boost your resilience, try one of these resilience-boosting sayings:

- Don't sweat the small stuff.
- The glass might be half empty, but it's also half full.
- When life gives you lemons, make lemonade.
- There's a silver lining in everything.

Choose one of these and write it on a piece of paper, perhaps with thick markers. Post it somewhere you can see this month.

Notice when you look at it or when you call it to mind.

Notice what it feels like to run this thought through your mind. Perhaps you feel irritated by the suggestion; perhaps you feel a glimmer of relief.

What thought will you try today?

From The Onward Workbook: Daily Activities to Cultivate Your Emotional Resilience and Thrive by Elena Aguilar. Copyright © 2018 by Elena Aguilar. Reproduced by permission.

Optimism: Choices

Choose to be optimistic. It feels better.
HIS HOLINESS THE DALAI LAMA

How do you feel about the suggestion that optimism is a choice?

What would it take for you to make this choice?

What holds you back from being optimistic?

In your childhood, who was optimistic? What did it look and sound like to be optimistic?

Think of the people with whom you spend your time. Who has chosen optimism? What impact does this choice have on their lives?

Challenge That Thought

This is another activity that you've got to do in writing. Think about this as making a case against a thought, and by writing it down you can more clearly see what you believe and think. Use it when you notice that you're having a strong uncomfortable emotion. Try to engage in this reflection as soon as you can after experiencing the emotion.

This is a useful practice to do in response to those things that keep you up at night. Writing down your thoughts gets them out of your head so that you can start to figure them out. Writing also helps you internalize the steps and prompts so that you can draw on them more readily in a moment of emotional upset.

Do this activity at least twice this week. You can download more worksheets from www.onwardthebook.com. Following is an example of this exercise.

Challenge That Thought: Example

Prompting Event: What triggered the distress? Include the who, what, where and when.	A student came in for help 15 minutes before school on a day that a major assignment was due. I yelled at the student (not my proudest moment) that she should have asked for help sooner. She stormed out of the room and skipped class that day.
Feeling: Name the feelings (see "The Core Emotions" in Chapter 2).	Anger—specifically, frustrated, irritated, resentful.
Clarify Your Interpretation: What were your thoughts, beliefs, and assumptions about the situation?	I've dedicated five hours of class time to this assignment on top of what students should be doing at home. By waiting till the last minute, it's clear she's not taking the assignment seriously and doesn't respect my time. I bet her assignment is a mess. It's too late for me to give her any help.
Unhelpful Thought Patterns: Which category of distorted thinking did you fall into?	Jumping to conclusions. If I pause, I can see that there's a lot I'm assuming about why her request for help is coming at this particular moment.

Challenging Evidence: • Is there any other way to look at this? • What advice would I give to someone I love in this situation? • What evidence might someone else point out to show me that my thoughts aren't completely true? • Am I focusing on weaknesses and not considering my strengths? • What have I learned from past experiences that could help me now? • Might I see this situation differently in a few months, or years, than I do today? • Am I blaming myself, or someone else, for something I, or he or she, can't control?	The student had missed a few days of school recently, so I really didn't know what state her assignment was in. She's doesn't typically seek help outside of class, so something motivated her to do so this time. Moreover, she's usually guarded in class about revealing her weaknesses or confusion; it's unusual for her to ask for help *at all.* Finally, her class isn't until after lunch, so maybe she was planning to work on the assignment then.
More Balanced Interpretation: Rewrite your thoughts about the triggering event in a more balanced way. Stick to the facts.	This student really had to swallow her pride to see me for help, knowing it was last minute. The fact that she bothered at all is probably evidence that she *did* care about the assignment. I wish I had responded with curiosity and maybe even a little compassion. Maybe I could have helped her after all; she would have turned in the assignment on time, and our relationship wouldn't have been damaged.

Challenge That Thought—Event 1

Prompting Event: What triggered the distress? Include the who, what, where and when.	
Feeling: Name the feelings (see "The Core Emotions" in Chapter 2).	

(continued)

From *The Onward Workbook: Daily Activities to Cultivate Your Emotional Resilience and Thrive* by Elena Aguilar. Copyright © 2018 by Elena Aguilar. Reproduced by permission.

Clarify Your Interpretation: What were your thoughts, beliefs, and assumptions about the situation?	
Unhelpful Thought Patterns: Which category of distorted thinking did you fall into?	
Challenging Evidence: • Is there any other way to look at this? • Is there any evidence to suggest that this way of thinking isn't entirely true? • Am I jumping to conclusions that aren't justified by the evidence? • Am I focusing on my weaknesses and not considering my strengths? • What advice would I give to someone I love in this situation? • What would someone I love say to me about this situation? • What evidence might someone else point out to show me that my thoughts aren't completely true? • What have I learned from past experiences that could help me now? • Is this situation really as important as it seems right now? Might I see this situation differently in a few months, or years, than I do today? • Am I blaming myself, or someone else, for something I, or he or she, can't control?	

From *The Onward Workbook: Daily Activities to Cultivate Your Emotional Resilience and Thrive* by Elena Aguilar. Copyright © 2018 by Elena Aguilar. Reproduced by permission.

More Balanced Interpretation: Rewrite your thoughts about the triggering event in a more balanced way. Stick to the facts.	

Challenge That Thought—Event 2	
Prompting Event: What triggered the distress? Include the who, what, where and when.	
Feeling: Name the feelings (see "The Core Emotions" in Chapter 2).	
Clarify Your Interpretation: What were your thoughts, beliefs, and assumptions about the situation?	
Unhelpful Thought Patterns: Which category of distorted thinking did you fall into?	
Challenging Evidence: • Is there any other way to look at this? • Is there any evidence to suggest that this way of thinking isn't entirely true? • Am I jumping to conclusions that aren't justified by the evidence? • Am I focusing on my weaknesses and not considering my strengths?	

(continued)

• What advice would I give to someone I love in this situation? • What would someone I love say to me about this situation? • What evidence might someone else point out to show me that my thoughts aren't completely true? • What have I learned from past experiences that could help me now? • Is this situation really as important as it seems right now? Might I see this situation differently in a few months, or years, than I do today? • Am I blaming myself, or someone else, for something I, or he or she, can't control?	
More Balanced Interpretation: Rewrite your thoughts about the triggering event in a more balanced way. Stick to the facts.	

Identify Patterns

- At the end of the week, look for patterns. See if you noticed yourself falling more regularly into one or two kinds of distorted thinking. Jot down a few reflections and observations here.

- Look for trends in the events that upset you. (Maybe you are triggered most by colleagues or changes in your routine, or you experience more emotional upset on days when you don't eat lunch.) What do you notice about the events that upset you?

Interrupting Distorted Thoughts

We all have distorted thoughts sometimes. This week, your goal is to catch yourself in them and provide your mind with an alternate thought.

Let's consider alternate ways to think when your mind travels down a distorted-thinking lane.

If you tend to think this way . . .	Then interrupt that thought and ask yourself . . .	And try telling yourself . . .
Black-and-White		Things aren't black and white. There's always a gray zone.
Jumping to Conclusions		I need to get more information before drawing a conclusion. I could be way off.
Unrealistic Expectations		I need to step back and rethink my expectations. These are unrealistic.
Disqualifying the Positive	• Is there any other way to look at this? • Is there any evidence to suggest that this way of thinking isn't entirely true?	What *is* working? What's going well? Where can I find bright spots or strengths?
Overgeneralizing		I don't have enough information yet to make this claim. I could be way off.
Catastrophizing		Things rarely go as badly as I fear; in fact, most things have turned out to be fine.
Emotional Reasoning		My feelings don't necessarily reflect facts. I need to uncover my interpretations.
Personalization		Everything is not about me.

Use a black marker and write the prompts in the second column on a piece of 8½-by-11 copy paper. Put that paper up somewhere in your office or classroom where you'll see it this week.

Identify one distorted thought that you fall into more often and on another piece of paper, write the alternate thought (the statement in column 3) that correlates to it. For example, I catastrophize a lot, so on my paper it says, "Things rarely go as badly as I fear; in fact, most things have turned out to be fine." Post that paper in a place where you'll see it also.

When you catch yourself in a distorted thought, read the questions that interrupt a distorted thought ("Is there any other way to look at this?") and the alternate thing to tell yourself.

Your goal this week is to catch yourself and read the statements on the papers at least five times.

Bonus points if you keep a record of this activity in the table here.

Date and Time	Distorted Thought You Caught Yourself In

Problematic Core Beliefs

Problematic core beliefs are those you hold to be true all of the time. They are global, not situational. One of the problems with such core beliefs is that because they filter your world for you, they also filter out the evidence against them. If you hold a core belief of *I don't fit in anywhere*, you're unlikely to find a place where you feel you fit in, because your attention is drawn only to evidence that upholds this core belief. Although we experience our core beliefs as personal, the problematic ones tend to fall into a few common themes.

Read the descriptions of common problematic core beliefs and then rate each (on a 1–10 scale) according to how strongly you suspect it's lodged in you.

Problematic Core Belief	Description	Sounds like . . .	Rating (1–10)
Worthlessness	• A general sense that one is inferior, inherently flawed or incompetent. • Most common. • Drives many problematic behaviors. • Often behind depression.	I'm worthless. I'm not good enough. I can't get anything right. I'm stupid. I'm useless. I'm a failure. I'm always wrong. There's something wrong with me. Other people are better than me.	
Unlovability	• Assumes that others don't understand them and won't accept or approve of them. • Often reflects an overemphasis on status, beauty, money, and achievement.	I'm always left out. I'm not wanted. I'm unwelcome. I'm alone. I don't fit in anywhere. I'm not interesting. I'm going to be rejected. It's important to be admired. I'm only worth something if people like me.	

Lack of Trust	• Typically rooted in fear of abandonment. • Assumes that anyone to whom an emotional attachment is formed will disappoint or be lost. • Can overlap with core belief about being unlovable.	People are untrustworthy. I can't trust or rely on another person. People I love will leave me. I will be abandoned if I love someone. I'm not important. People will let me down.	
Helplessness	• Results in people assuming they lack control and cannot handle anything effectively or independently. • Making changes is very difficult. • A sense of powerlessness can cause people to try to overcontrol their environment or completely give up control. • Can see themselves as victims.	I can't handle this. I can't do it. I'm powerless. I'm trapped. I'm needy. I can't change. Other people are trying to control my life. Bad things happen all the time. The world is a dangerous place. People will hurt me if I let them.	
Superiority	• Leads to a sense of entitlement, which can lead to rule breaking, resentment of others' success, and unreasonable demands. • May come from compensating for feeling defective or socially undesirable.	If people don't respect me, I can't stand it. I deserve a lot of praise and attention. If I don't excel, then I'm inferior and worthless. If I don't excel, I'll just end up ordinary. I'm a very special person and others should treat me that way. I don't have to be bound by the rules that apply to other people. People should satisfy my needs. People have no right to criticize me. Others don't deserve the good things they get. People don't understand me, or get me, because I am special/brilliant/etc.	

(continued)

Self-Sacrific-ingness	<ul><li>May produce the kind of caretaking behavior that puts the needs of others ahead of their own.</li><li>May feel guilty and compensate by prioritizing the needs of others, believing they are responsible for the happiness of others.</li><li>Excessive apologizing is an indicator.</li></ul>	My needs are not important. It's not okay to ask for help. I have to do everything myself. If I don't do it, no one will. If I care enough, I can fix him/her/this. I shouldn't spend time taking care of myself. When I see others who need help, I have to help them. I'm only worthwhile if I'm helping other people. I have to make people happy.	
Perfectionism	<ul><li>Can look like conscientiousness and a strong work ethic, but they are taken too far.</li><li>Sense of self-worth is overly tied to external praise and accomplishments.</li><li>A tendency to think in black-and-white terms, hold rigid standards, and quickly discount positives.</li><li>Perfectionists believe they must strive to act and be at their best all the time in order to prove they are capable, worthy, and loveable.</li></ul>	I have to do everything perfectly. If I make a mistake, it means I'm careless/a failure/etc. People who make mistakes should have consequences. People should follow the rules or be punished. I have extremely high standards for myself and others.	
Negativity	<ul><li>Pessimists.</li><li>The glass is always half empty—whether looking at the world, themselves or others.</li></ul>	Life inherently sucks. Life is meaningless. Nothing ever works out for me. The world is falling apart. Nothing ever gets better. I'm not a pessimist; I'm a realist.	

From *The Onward Workbook: Daily Activities to Cultivate Your Emotional Resilience and Thrive* by Elena Aguilar. Copyright © 2018 by Elena Aguilar. Reproduced by permission.

Reflect

Are you able to achieve your vision or purpose in life while holding these problematic core beliefs? How do they hold you back?

How might you feel at home, or at school, and with friends and colleagues if you were operating from different beliefs?

How might you benefit from being free of these beliefs? What could be possible?

How did it feel to rate your problematic core beliefs? Were you surprised by how you rated any belief?

Has holding these beliefs served you? What has holding them allowed you to do, or to avoid doing?

Select one problematic core belief that you'd like to get rid of. What might be possible if you didn't harbor it?

Rilke on Love

Most people have (with the help of conventions) turned their solutions toward what is easy and toward the easiest side of the easy; but it is clear that we must trust in what is difficult . . . Love is perhaps the most difficult task given to us, the most extreme, the final proof and text, for which all other work is only preparation.

RAINER MARIA RILKE, *LETTERS TO A YOUNG POET*

What feelings or thoughts stir in you when you read this quote?

Challenge That Core Belief

When you have a rough emotional experience, use the prompts here to identify and challenge the core belief that led to it. In order to disrupt a problematic core belief, you'll need to amass a pile of evidence that refutes it. Think about this as a project to which you need to dedicate time—because you will. Repeat this exercise whenever you catch yourself operating from a problematic core belief.

What was the event that triggered the emotion cycle?

How did you interpret what happened?

If your worst interpretation of this situation were true, what would that mean about you? What would it mean about people in general? What would that mean about how the world works?

What's the problematic core belief you're holding? (See "Problematic Core Beliefs" for descriptions.)

How does this core belief make you feel?

From *The Onward Workbook: Daily Activities to Cultivate Your Emotional Resilience and Thrive* by Elena Aguilar. Copyright © 2018 by Elena Aguilar. Reproduced by permission.

How might this belief be hurting you? How might it hurt others?

How does this belief truly fit—or not fit—with your values?

What evidence is there for and against this belief?

Is this belief your own, or does it come from someone else? If it comes from someone else, was this person worth modeling or listening to in this area?

What would you have to believe in order to feel the way you want to feel?

"The Optimism of Uncertainty"

An optimist isn't necessarily a blithe, slightly sappy whistler in the dark of our time. To be hopeful in bad times is not just foolishly romantic. It is based on the fact that human history is a history not only of cruelty, but also of compassion, sacrifice, courage, kindness. What we choose to emphasize in this complex history will determine our lives. If we see only the worst, it destroys our capacity to do something. If we remember those times and places—and there are so many— where people have behaved magnificently, this gives us energy to act, and at least the possibility of sending this spinning top of a world in a different direction.

HOWARD ZINN, "THE OPTIMISM OF UNCERTAINTY"

What does this passage raise for you? What connections can you make?

Which "times and places" do you want to remember where people have "behaved magnificently"?

River and Rut Stories

Robert Hargrove, a business and life coaching guru and the author of *Masterful Coaching* (2000), distinguishes between two kinds of stories we tell: "river" and "rut" stories. Rut stories are those in which, as the name suggests, we get stuck and feel powerless. They cut us off from other people and from our own potential. Rut stories reflect distorted thoughts and problematic core beliefs. River stories, by contrast, allow us to feel open, connected, and optimistic. They reflect a commitment to learning, growth, and perseverance.

Hargrove describes a number of classic rut stories that I hear often in schools and that I've told myself. These are

- **The Victim Story:** We give away all our power to others ("the district," "those parents," "that group of kids") or the situation ("budget cuts," "turnover," "new standards").

- **The Tranquilizing Story:** When we don't achieve something we want or when we get ourselves in trouble, we come up with reasons and excuses to feel better. We may tell ourselves, "I did my best, but we didn't have a copy machine for the first half of the year, I had a cold for almost the entire winter, and I got a tough group of kids." Superficial numbing covers up our shame, guilt, and sadness.

- **The "Why Bother?" Story:** We tell this story when we want to stay in our comfort zone or avoid responsibility. This sounds like "I don't have the time," "There's no money," "I don't have the authority." There is an underlying attitude of resignation.

Which rut stories have you told?

How have you benefited from telling those rut stories? What has telling that story allowed you to do or avoid doing?

When you notice yourself telling a rut story,

1. Interrupt yourself. Say to yourself, *Hold on, that's a rut story.*
2. Dig down. Explore the assumptions you're making.
3. Zoom out: Consider other ways to view what happened or other data that you might not be considering.
4. Make a new story. Craft a new interpretation that is more inspiring, empowering, or accurate.

What can you do so that you'll remember these steps to transform a rut story?

From *The Onward Workbook: Daily Activities to Cultivate Your Emotional Resilience and Thrive* by Elena Aguilar. Copyright © 2018 by Elena Aguilar. Reproduced by permission.

The Life-Defining Moments

Identify three to five events in your life that were life defining. These could have been challenging events, wonderfully rewarding events, or a combination.

1.

2.

3.

4.

5.

Which of these moments has had the greatest impact on your life?

Which of these events holds the most meaning for you?

Write the story of at least one of these life-changing events. Write it just for yourself, without the intention of sharing with anyone. Tell yourself the story from beginning to end: What happened? How did you respond? Who was a part of the story? Use additional paper if you need (you can always glue, tape, or staple it in here if you want).

Reflect on that story. What did you learn from writing it?

What new insights did you get into that event in your life?

What would you like to share about it with others?

If you're engaging in the activities in this book with others, you might share your reflections on the experience of writing the story, rather than the story itself.

"Want To" and "Get To"

In Appendix B of *Onward*, "How to Make Lasting Change," the sixth principle is Activate Autonomy.

Think *want to* or *get to* rather than *have to* or *should*. Tell yourself, *I want to take a walk*, rather than *I should take a walk*; or *I want to grade these essays and see how my students are doing*, rather than *I have to read 50 papers*. Create "want-to" goals rather than "have-to" goals, which are usually externally imposed or come from your own sense of obligation or desire to avoid shame. You can choose to eat more healthfully because of fear, shame, or anxiety about your appearance, or you can choose to eat healthfully because you *want to* feel good and enjoy life more.

Have-to motivation can enable you to make positive changes for a while, but willpower and determination have their limits. Have-to motivation can intensify temptation because it makes you feel deprived, which undermines your self-control. Think *I want to turn off the TV and go to sleep early because when I get up at 5:30, I will be rested.*

Today, pay attention to the stories you tell about what you do. Which are want-to stories? Which are have-to stories? Which of your have-to stories can you transform into want to or get to?

At the end of the day, record your observations and reflections here.

The Untold Story

There is no agony like bearing an untold story inside you.
ZORA NEALE HURSTON

What does this quote raise for you?

What story do you want or need to tell?

To whom do you want or need to tell it? Why to them?

Why do you want or need to tell it?

Write the first paragraph or two of that story here.

From *The Onward Workbook: Daily Activities to Cultivate Your Emotional Resilience and Thrive* by Elena Aguilar. Copyright © 2018 by Elena Aguilar. Reproduced by permission.

Memory, Mood, and Story-Crafting

The stories we tell emerge from our emotions. We need to understand why we feel what we feel and where those feelings come from so that we can craft stories that our whole being can believe in. This is why many of us could benefit from working with a therapist who can help us tease out the connections between our life experiences, moods, and perception and interpretation of events.

Here's a provocative passage on this topic:

> Mood is not homogeneous like cream soup. It is more like Swiss cheese, filled with holes. The triggers are highly specific, tripped by sudden trails of memory: a faint fragrance, a few bars of a tune, a vague silhouette that tapped into a sad memory buried deep, but not completely erased. These sensory inputs from the moment float through layers of time in the parts of the brain that control memory, and they pull out with them not only reminders of sense but also trails of the emotions that were first connected to the memory. These memories become connected to emotions, which are processed in other parts of the brain . . . The same sensory input can trigger a negative emotion or a positive one, depending on the memories associated with it.

Esther Sternberg, *The Balance Within* (New York, NY: W. H. Freeman, 2001), pp. 32–33

What does this passage raise for you? What thoughts, feelings, questions, and connections?

"The Danger of a Single Story"

Stories have been used to dispossess and to malign. But stories can also be used to empower and humanize. Stories can break the dignity of a people, but stories can also repair that dignity.

CHIMAMANDA NGOZI ADICHIE

In her 2009 TED Talk, "The Danger of a Single Story," Chimamanda Ngozi Adichie, a Nigerian author, eloquently warned us that "the single story creates stereotypes, and the problem with stereotypes is not that they are untrue, but that they are incomplete. They make one story become the only story."

Watch this TED Talk and then reflect on these questions:

What do Adichie's words bring up for you?

What connections can you make to Adichie's ideas?

How might these ideas be relevant within your work context?

What implications are there for how you teach and lead?

From *The Onward Workbook: Daily Activities to Cultivate Your Emotional Resilience and Thrive* by Elena Aguilar. Copyright © 2018 by Elena Aguilar. Reproduced by permission.

Using Empathy to Expand Stories

If you have a fixed story about someone, one way to expand it or break out of it is to use empathy. Today you're going to identify someone who gets on your nerves, or even whom you really don't like. This could be a student in your class, a colleague, or even a boss.

If you can do so discreetly (but not in a creepy way), use your phone to take a picture of the person's shoes—yes, you read that correctly. If you can't do this, then pay attention to the person's shoes and sketch an image of them here:

Throughout the course of the day, imagine being in this person's shoes. Use whatever knowledge you have about her to imagine her putting on her shoes in the morning, getting to school, going through her day, leaving school at the end of the day, going home, and so on. Putting yourself in someone else's shoes is a metaphor to access empathy. In this case, I want you to actively imagine going through the day in this person's shoes. Let's hope they are somewhat comfortable shoes at least.

At the end of the day, record your reflections here. What was that experience like? How did you feel? How did this experience expand the story that you have about this person?

Examining Organizational Stories

In *The Fifth Discipline* (1990), Peter Senge, a renowned systems thinker, observes that the very nature of schooling emerges from negative mental models. "The whole system is focused on fixing kids," he writes, noting that when we engage in problem solving by focusing on something we want to get rid of, we're not actually doing transformational work (p. 45). We end up in a perpetually reactive mode, not digging deep enough to surface the underlying dysfunctions and change them.

What does this idea raise for you? What does your school focus on?

What color is love for you? Find a crayon or marker to color in this heart with the color of love.

If love were a musical instrument, what would it be? What would it feel like to hear it?

If love were an animal, what animal would it be? Why? Draw that animal here.

How do you show love? How do you want to be shown love?

Tell a story about being loved.

Tell a story about a student you loved.

The Pessimism-Optimism Scale

Write a few sentences about a challenge you faced at school. The challenge could be small, such as that your prep period is cancelled, a new student joins your class in the middle of the year, or there are no funds to attend the conference you'd hoped to attend. Or it could be bigger: You are informed, a week before school starts, that you have to teach a different grade level, your beloved principal is fired, or the district implements a new reading curriculum that replaces one you've taught for years.

Write down what happened:

Now, try to recall how you thought and felt at the time. You might feel differently now, or not, but check off the box that reflects how you thought at the time about the challenge that was presented.

Your Interpretation of What Happened

☐ (1) This situation is horrible. [or] I can't believe this is happening. It's going to thwart all the good work I've been doing. It's entirely [the district's/administrators'/changing demographics', etc.] fault. [or] It's all my fault. This is devastating; the risks are potentially catastrophic.

☐ (2) This is the fault of the [district/principal/changing demographics, etc.]. This situation is bad. The potential for damage is huge.

☐ (3) This is happening, but it doesn't have to be a barrier to what I'm doing. I can see how I might have played a role in creating the present challenge. I need to gather a lot of information so that I can assess the situation and make accurate judgments about what's possible.

☐ (4) This challenge isn't that bad. It's not going to be a problem. I understand why I'm dealing with it. I don't need to spend any more time understanding it. I don't need any more information about what's going on. The risks aren't that big. Things aren't that bad.

Your Interpretation of Future Possibilities

☐ (1) I don't see how I can make any difference at all in what's happening. I can't see how this could work out positively at all. I can only see a whole bunch of worst-case outcomes.

☐ (2) There's no way that I can make any difference. It won't be worth my effort to try to stop, change, or respond to what's happened. I have pretty low expectations that anything good will come of this. I really can't see much aside from all the problems, challenges, and negative potential.

☐ (3) I strongly believe I can influence the future, although there might be some constraints around what we can do. I believe that good things can happen, but it's going to take a lot of work. I see all the problems and challenges, but I'm focusing on the possibilities.

☐ (4) I am completely confident that I can positively influence what happens. I'm sure that I'll see the best-case outcomes. Things will work out perfectly. Everything will be fine.

In the two lists of statements, the first statement (1) reflects the perspective of an unrealistic pessimist. The second (2) is that of a realistic pessimist. The third (3) reflects the views of a realistic optimist, and (4) is how an unrealistic optimist thinks.

In the incident you described, were you an unrealistic pessimist, a realistic pessimist, a realistic optimist, or an unrealistic optimist?

It's not uncommon for our thoughts to cross stances, but often we'll notice that we are more of a realistic pessimist than we are a realistic optimist, for example. Noticing the blurry areas can help us nudge ourselves along the continuum.

Are you surprised by where you fell on the pessimism-optimism scale? Why or why not? Can you think of other incidents where your response might have been similar or different?

Think Like an Optimist

If you want to adopt the thinking patterns of a realistic optimist, then you need to know how they think. Realistic optimists

- Think about, reflect on, and emphasize the good things in life
- Are grateful for their blessings
- Don't complain when something bad happens
- Feel that nothing can hold them back from achieving success and reaching their goals
- Believe in abundance and are confident that the world offers plenty of opportunities for everyone to succeed

When you read these statements, what comes up for you?

Which of these statements feel easier to hold? Which ones do you already believe?

Which of these statements feel harder to hold? Which ones are you suspicious of?

Which of these statements do you want to try holding today? This week?

Write the statement on a piece of paper or a note card and carry it with you.

From *The Onward Workbook: Daily Activities to Cultivate Your Emotional Resilience and Thrive* by Elena Aguilar. Copyright © 2018 by Elena Aguilar. Reproduced by permission.

A Letter to Love

Let this be a love letter to love. Let yourself say whatever you want to say to love. Here's the beginning of my letter to love: *I think I owe you an apology, first. I think you've tried to come into my life in many places and times and in many ways, and I think I didn't recognize you. I want to know you better . . .*

From *The Onward Workbook: Daily Activities to Cultivate Your Emotional Resilience and Thrive* by Elena Aguilar. Copyright © 2018 by Elena Aguilar. Reproduced by permission.

Artistic Depictions of Love

Go to your preferred online search engine and look for images of love—or another term that reflects love, such as affection, compassion, or friendship (see "The Core Emotions" in Chapter 2 for these terms).

See what comes up, and then search for "depictions of love in art."

Look closely at a few of those images. Sit with them and spend some time getting to know them. Pay attention to how they make you feel and what thoughts go through your mind.

Reflect

What do you notice in the images that come up?

What have you learned about love through doing this exploration?

How did this exploration help you understand your own experience of love?

If you'd like, print out one (or more) of the images that particularly speak to you and stick them in here.

Destination Postcard: Tell Empowering Stories

What would it look and sound like if you told empowering stories? Draw a picture of yourself with thought bubbles and labels that depict you telling these stories. If you'd like, draw this you at work, surrounded by kids and colleagues. How might you be in that space?

Chapter Reflection

What were your biggest takeaways from this chapter?

Of the different activities in this chapter, which were most useful?

Which activities would you like to revisit periodically? How might you get that habit going?

What implications do the ideas in this chapter have for the work you do?

Resilience

Perseverance

Trust

KNOW YOURSELF

CELEBRATE + APPRECIATE

RIDE THE WAVES OF CHANGE

Purposefulness

UNDERSTAND EMOTIONS

Courage

Acceptance

TELL EMPOWERING STORIES

PLAY + CREATE

Optimism

Curiosity

BE A LEARNER

BUILD COMMUNITY
Empathy

Perspective

CULTIVATE COMPASSION

BE HERE NOW

TAKE CARE OF YOURSELF

FOCUS ON THE BRIGHT SPOTS

Humor

Positive
Self-Perception

Empowerment

CHAPTER 4

Build Community

We are social beings, and we need each other to thrive. A strong, healthy community can bolster us through challenging moments and bring joy to our lives. When we build community, we can build empathy for each other; and building empathy for each other helps us build community.

September: During the month when we're surrounded by new people, building strong relationships must be our primary goal. The community we build is foundational for our resilience.

Build Community: Resilience Self-Assessment

The purpose of this self-assessment is to help you gauge the level of your resilience reservoir and to explore what might be draining or what could replenish it. The exercises that follow and the information in the corresponding chapter of *Onward* can boost your resilience by helping you build strong and healthy communities that nurture you.

Imagine each circle as a little *cenote* or reservoir within you, and fill it up according to how much each statement reflects a source of resilience. If you need something more concrete, imagine marks at ¼, ½, and ¾ full.

Before you start the exercises in this chapter, take this self-assessment and fill in the date. At the end of the month, take the assessment again. (You might even cover up your original markings with a strip of paper.) Is your resilience reservoir a little more full? If so, which practices do you want to keep up? If not, what else do you want to try?

Statement	Date:	Date:
I understand the connection between the community I have around me and my emotional well-being.		
I can describe the kind of community that is most supportive and nourishing to me.		
I know how to build community with colleagues, students, students' parents, and others.		
I have colleagues I trust.		

I understand how my ability to understand and work with people of different backgrounds influences the strength of the communities I'm in.	◯	◯
My social network feels satisfying and supportive.	◯	◯
I can use my communication skills to strengthen social relationships.	◯	◯
I have strategies to deal with unhealthy conflict when it arises in my community.	◯	◯
I'm aware of my own body language and that of others—as well as how I interpret the nonverbal communication of others.	◯	◯
I know how to build my cultural competence, and I understand the connection between cultural competence and resilience.	◯	◯

Community Mapping

Think about these questions as they relate to the broadest terrain of your social networks. This landscape may include family, friends, social and professional groups, and perhaps other circles of community.

Which communities are you already a part of?

In which communities do you feel most accepted and comfortable?

Which communities do you learn with?

Which communities do you desire to be a part of or desire deeper connection with?

What might be a few things you could do to get closer to one of those communities with which you desire more connection? What might be something you could do today or this week?

Planning for Professional Community Building

Rank the following professional communities in the order you feel most connected. For example, you might feel most connected to your grade-level colleagues, so they'd be number 1, followed by your classroom community. Some categories may not apply to you because of your role. In that case, see if you can identify the community groups around you and substitute them.

Community Group	Ranking
Students	
Staff as a whole	
Coach, mentor, other staff support providers	
Grade-level team	
Department (or content area) team	
Site administrators/supervisor/manager	
Student support staff (counselors, specialists, etc.)	
Other school staff (custodial, office, food services, etc.)	

(continued)

Students' families	
Support staff outside your school (district coaches, university supervisors, others)	
Other:	
Other:	

Reflect

What did you learn about yourself from this activity?

What implications for action did you glean from this exercise?

What is one community with whom you'd like to form a stronger connection?

How might you do that?

From The Onward Workbook: Daily Activities to Cultivate Your Emotional Resilience and Thrive by Elena Aguilar. Copyright © 2018 by Elena Aguilar. Reproduced by permission.

Develop Cultural Competence: A Plan

Cultural competence is the ability to understand, appreciate, and interact with people from cultures or belief systems different from one's own; it is the ability to navigate cross-cultural differences in order to do something—be that teach students, collaborate with colleagues, or socialize with friends. These differences can be generational, racial, gendered, and so on. In order to build strong communities that can support you to be resilient, you'll need to develop your own cultural competence.

In order to be culturally competent, you must be able to do the following:

- Be aware of your own cultural identity, beliefs about difference, and unconscious biases.
- Have knowledge about the general role that culture plays (in enforcing norms, communication, emotions, relationships) as well as knowledge about specific other cultures.
- Effectively navigate difference. Self-awareness and knowledge don't automatically translate into the ability to do something.

Given this definition, what do you feel are your areas for growth?

What thoughts do you have about how you could make that growth?

From *The Onward Workbook: Daily Activities to Cultivate Your Emotional Resilience and Thrive* by Elena Aguilar. Copyright © 2018 by Elena Aguilar. Reproduced by permission.

Who might be a partner on this learning journey? Are there colleagues who might also join you in developing cultural competence? Are there people who might provide resources?

What might be a first step to develop cultural competence? What could you do today, or this week?

Trust: Reflecting on Experience and Assumptions

Write about someone you really trust. What makes you trust this person? How did that trust develop?

Write about what it feels like to really trust someone.

Write about a time as a child when you learned about trust—perhaps trust with peers.

Write about a time as an adult when your trust was broken.

From *The Onward Workbook: Daily Activities to Cultivate Your Emotional Resilience and Thrive* by Elena Aguilar. Copyright © 2018 by Elena Aguilar. Reproduced by permission.

Write about a time as an adult when you broke someone's trust.

What do you believe about trust? Is it hard to build? Does it take a long time? Is it harder to build with people who don't share your race or ethnicity, your background, your gender?

Write about someone you've recently begun to trust—perhaps a colleague, administrator, or friend. Describe how this trust has developed—what did the person do? What did you do? What's allowing this trust to grow?

What makes you not trust someone else? What are some big things that someone might do that would diminish your trust in him or her?

Write about a time when you've worked to repair trust that was broken. What happened? What did you have to do to repair trust? What made you willing to invest energy in re-building the relationship?

Relational Trust: Among Staff

In their book *Trust in Schools* (2002), Anthony Bryk and Barbara Schneider identify four key attributes of relational trust. Read the descriptions and think about the professional adult communities to which you belong in your school or organization. Respond to the reflective prompts as you go.

Respect Across Difference

Trust is grounded in respect that results from social exchanges. Respectful exchanges are marked by genuine listening to what each person says and by taking these perspectives into account in subsequent actions. When there are disagreements, individuals can feel valued if others respect their opinions. Without interpersonal respect, people will avoid each other, or there may be outward unhealthy conflict.

Do you see people acknowledging each other's dignity and ideas? What does this look and sound like? Has this happened recently?

Do you feel that your colleagues listen to you? What evidence do you have that staff listen to each other?

Think of a recent disagreement between people. What happened? How was it dealt with? What were the outcomes of the experience?

Do people interact in a kind way? How do you demonstrate kindness with peers?

Personal Regard

We have trust in others when we feel they are willing to extend themselves beyond the formal requirements, responsibilities, and roles of a job definition. We trust others who we feel are in alliance with us.

When was there a time that a colleague went above and beyond his or her responsibilities?

When have you been willing to go beyond your job definition? What did you do?

Do you feel that your colleagues care about you professionally and personally? Do you care about them professionally and personally?

Competence

In a school community, we depend on each other to reach our desired outcomes. Attaining those goals rests in great part on others' *role competence.* If skill, knowledge, and willingness to fulfill a role appear to be absent, trust is diminished. In addition, instances of negligence or incompetence, if allowed to persist, undermine trust.

Do you think your colleagues are willing and able to effectively fulfill their job responsibilities? Do you have doubts about the competence of some colleagues or supervisors?

Count the number of staff members for whom you have questionable confidence in their competence. What percentage of the total staff is this?

Do you wonder if colleagues question your competence? How might you address this?

Personal Integrity

When it comes to integrity, we need to trust that others will keep their word. Integrity also requires that people are guided by a moral-ethical perspective. Although conflicts frequently arise among competing individual interests within a school, a commitment to children must remain the primary concern.

Do people do what they say they'll do? Do you do what you say you'll do?

Do people put the interests of students first, especially when tough decisions need to be made? Are the interests of *all* students taken into account, or only those of some groups?

How to Build Trust

Building trust starts with acute awareness of self and with how we show up and engage with others. Mark an X on each line to indicate how strongly you agree or disagree with the statement.

Statement	Agree ——————— Disagree
I know who I am. I feel confident in my self-knowledge.	_____
My actions align with my core values.	_____
When I'm interacting with others, I'm aware of how I'm talking, listening, and engaging.	_____
When I'm interacting with others, I usually feel okay about myself. I like how I'm showing up.	_____
I'm aware of how I communicate nonverbally.	_____
I can control my nonverbal communication.	_____
I feel okay with the words I use when interacting with others.	_____
I rarely say or do things that I later regret.	_____
When I disagree with someone, I feel confident and comfortable with my response.	_____
I greet people when I see them.	_____
I have a good sense of what's appropriate to share about my personal life in a professional setting (I don't under- or overshare).	_____
I'm okay with receiving unsolicited or solicited feedback from others.	_____

Sometimes I ask for feedback from others.	_____
Even when feedback is hard to hear, I will reflect on it.	_____
When I sense tension or conflict with another person, I will bring it up (even if it's uncomfortable).	_____
I'm genuinely curious about other people.	_____
I ask other people appropriate questions about themselves. I express interest in who they are personally and professionally.	_____
I feel comfortable and confident talking with people I don't know well.	_____
I usually keep my commitments. I do what I say I will.	_____
When I don't keep a commitment, I take responsibility and don't make excuses or blame others.	_____
I'm willing to go above and beyond my job responsibilities when necessary.	_____
I set boundaries around what I will and won't do. I'm clear with others about why I'm setting my boundaries.	_____
I ask for help when I need it.	_____
I take responsibility for mistakes and acknowledge areas for growth.	_____
I appropriately share my goals or areas for growth with others.	_____
I offer genuine apologies.	_____
I work on my areas for growth and take action on feedback I've received.	_____

(continued)

From The Onward Workbook: Daily Activities to Cultivate Your Emotional Resilience and Thrive by Elena Aguilar. Copyright © 2018 by Elena Aguilar. Reproduced by permission.

I can give others positive and critical feedback when necessary.	_____
I recognize and acknowledge other people's strengths and contributions.	_____
I offer appreciations and acknowledgments regularly.	_____
If I have critical feedback to offer, I make sure that the great majority of my interactions with that person have been positive or neutral.	_____
I generally think that people are doing the best they can given the circumstances and the skills they have.	_____
I feel I have a great deal to learn from everyone around me (kids, their parents, colleagues, supervisors, custodial staff, and so on).	_____
I take ownership of what I do well and don't negate or downplay my skills.	_____
I forgive others.	_____
I forgive myself.	_____
It's not too hard for me to relax with others and (when appropriate) have fun.	_____
I am in the field of education because I'm committed to serving children.	_____
I'm committed to serving every child who comes into our schools.	_____

Reflect

What did you learn from engaging in this reflection?

Based on this activity, what do you feel are your strengths in building trust with others?

Given what you've learned from this activity, how might you strengthen the trust you build with others?

From *The Onward Workbook: Daily Activities to Cultivate Your Emotional Resilience and Thrive* by Elena Aguilar. Copyright © 2018 by Elena Aguilar. Reproduced by permission.

Body Language: Reflecting on Myself

How do you look when you're feeling relaxed and content? Draw a picture.

How do you look when you're feeling anxious? Draw a picture.

How do you look when you're feeling angry? Draw a picture.

From The Onward Workbook: Daily Activities to Cultivate Your Emotional Resilience and Thrive by Elena Aguilar. Copyright © 2018 by Elena Aguilar. Reproduced by permission.

How do you look when you're feeling sad? Draw a picture.

Now look at your drawings. What do they tell you? Are you surprised by anything?

What kind of feedback have you received from others about your body language? Have people commented on the amount you smile, or on whether you "look upset" often or seem angry?

How do you think others perceive your body language? How do you think they interpret some of your nonverbal cues?

How do you feel about the way your nonverbal cues are interpreted? Are they accurate? Do you wish your cues were interpreted differently?

What messages about body language do you think are conveyed in the cultural group to which you belong?

If you didn't do the activity "Nonverbal Communication: The Interviews" in Chapter 2, consider doing it now. When you're feeling brave, ask someone you trust, someone who knows you personally and/or professionally, what he or she notices about your body language and how he or she interprets those observations. Write down what the person says here. If you're feeling really brave, ask a few people and capture their responses.

If you've asked for some feedback on your body language, how did that feel? What did you learn? What, if anything, might you do differently?

From *The Onward Workbook: Daily Activities to Cultivate Your Emotional Resilience and Thrive* by Elena Aguilar. Copyright © 2018 by Elena Aguilar. Reproduced by permission.

Body Language: Reflecting on Others

What do you notice most in the body language of others?

What kind of body language do you remember seeing in your family of origin? How did people express emotions through their bodies?

What kind of body language in others makes you feel comfortable and relaxed?

What kind of body language in others makes you feel uncomfortable?

Think of a nonverbal cue that makes you uncomfortable. How do you interpret it? (For example, *If someone doesn't make eye contact with me, I've interpreted that as disinterest in the conversation.*) See if you can identify a few nonverbal cues and how you interpret them.

Choose one of those interpretations of someone else's nonverbals and see if you can identify where that interpretation comes from. (For example, *When I was growing up, I was told to make eye contact when talking with someone.*) Where do your interpretations come from?

Think of someone whom you perceive as being different from you. Perhaps this person is of a different ethnicity, religion, sexual orientation, or gender. Can you identify some nonverbal ways that this person communicates that you don't understand?

What are some of the ways that your students communicate nonverbally? What do you notice about their body language?

What comes up for you when interpreting your students' nonverbal communication? Does it feel challenging? Easy?

From *The Onward Workbook: Daily Activities to Cultivate Your Emotional Resilience and Thrive* by Elena Aguilar. Copyright © 2018 by Elena Aguilar. Reproduced by permission.

Body Language: Fake It Till You Become It

Body language affects how others see us, but it can also affect how we see ourselves. Social psychologist Amy Cuddy explains how "power posing"—standing in a posture of confidence, even when we don't feel confident—can positively affect testosterone and cortisol levels in the brain, and might have an impact on our chances for success. Cuddy suggests that we can change other people's perceptions of us, as well as our own body chemistry, by changing body positions. Watch Amy Cuddy's 2012 TED Talk, "Your Body Language Shapes Who You Are."

Reflect

Cuddy says that "body language has an immediate effect on other people's judgment." Do you agree with this? What have been some examples of this in your life?

How does the idea of "fake it until you become it" apply in your context as a teacher or leader? How is this relevant to you?

Try power posing before teaching, before attending or running a meeting, or before anything that might make you feel a little nervous. Reflect on the experience and impact.

From *The Onward Workbook: Daily Activities to Cultivate Your Emotional Resilience and Thrive* by Elena Aguilar. Copyright © 2018 by Elena Aguilar. Reproduced by permission.

Body Language: Rewiring Your Brain

Researchers say that smiling is good for building community. As a person who sometimes has to consciously prompt myself to smile, I find this research annoying. But for the sake of community, resilience, and justice, I'm willing to smile more. And I have found that I feel better when I do.

This strategy is based on the facial feedback theory of emotion, which argues that your brain is always monitoring what's happening in your body and adjusting your mood based on what it notices.

Try this: Slump forward, curl in on yourself, furrow your brow, and frown. Sit like that for 30 seconds or so and then notice whether your mood changed at all. Many of us will feel a little gloomy after adopting that posture. That's because our brain has registered our muscle tension, heart rate, posture, breathing, and facial expressions as unhappy.

So let's try the reverse. Research suggests that just putting yourself in a happier position can boost your mood. Get a pencil or a chopstick and put it in your mouth as you see me doing in the photo.

This position recruits the muscles of a genuine smile. Try it. How do you feel?

The tricky thing is that if you think really hard, *This is supposed to change my mood,* it may not work. But see what happens if you just go with it, settle into your silly smile, and register the flavor of pencil paint . . . What do you notice?

Jot down your observations and reflections here.	Draw a picture of yourself with the pencil in your teeth.

Here are a few more body-brain rewiring routines to try:

- When you're feeling insecure, stand tall or sit up straight. Broaden your shoulders. Elongate your neck. Imagine creating a centimeter or more of space between each vertebra in your back.
- If you're feeling anxious around someone with whom you don't have any reason to be anxious, lean toward the person.
- If you're in physical or emotional pain, hug yourself.

What Does Community Mean to You?

What does community mean to you?

What do you need in a community in order to feel that it's a source of strength and support for you?

Describe a community in which you've felt accepted and supported.

From *The Onward Workbook: Daily Activities to Cultivate Your Emotional Resilience and Thrive* by Elena Aguilar. Copyright © 2018 by Elena Aguilar. Reproduced by permission.

Now, ask two colleagues and, if you are a teacher, at least two students and perhaps even a couple of parents, the three questions you just answered. In the space here, write down what they say.

How are the descriptions of community that you heard similar to your own? How are they different?

What implications were there about how you build community with colleagues, students, and parents?

Sixty Ways to Build Community at School

Community strengthens through the hundreds of little actions we take every day. Read this list and put a star next to those that you've already done or regularly do. Pick several to try this month, and schedule those on the calendar or someplace where you'll remember to do them. Add your own ideas as well! If you do one of these every day for a month, I guarantee that your community will be far wider, deeper, and stronger than ever before.

1. Ask some students (if they're old enough) to take you on a tour of their neighborhood. If you teach young children, ask one of their parents to take you on a tour.
2. Shop in the stores where your students shop.
3. On a Sunday morning, walk around the neighborhood where your students live.
4. Ask your students what their favorite restaurants are and try one.
5. Host a back-to-school potluck for your students and their families, even if you teach 130 students. Bring a member of your family or a friend to that potluck.
6. Learn the names of your students' parents/guardians (especially if you have fewer than 35, you should be able to remember their names). Find out if they prefer to be addressed by their first or last name.
7. Smile when you talk to your students and to their families.
8. Have lunch with students occasionally. Or if you teach 30 kids or fewer, have lunch with pairs of kids in the beginning of the school year so that after a few weeks, you've had lunch with all your students. They can bring their lunch. You bring cookies or strawberries.
9. Do home visits. (But first, do some learning about how to make home visits comfortable and meaningful for all.)
10. If you teach a reasonable number of students, meet in person with all of their parents/guardians during the beginning of the year. Ask one good question—perhaps, "What do you think is most important for me to know about your child?" and make the purpose of the meeting to listen to them.
11. Send postcards to all of your students before school starts to introduce yourself.
12. Accept invitations to students' special events (birthday parties, quinceañeras, First Communions, and so on) and, especially if you're in a new community, try to attend as many as possible.
13. Identify a colleague you'd like to know better, and initiate lunch, a walk, or some other activity with him or her.

From *The Onward Workbook: Daily Activities to Cultivate Your Emotional Resilience and Thrive* by Elena Aguilar. Copyright © 2018 by Elena Aguilar. Reproduced by permission.

14. Ask to observe a colleague whom you admire. When you observe, write down all the bright spots and highlights. Share those with the colleague.

15. Ask a colleague, "What's the most impactful book you've read related to our work?"

16. Initiate a book study with colleagues.

17. Ask a colleague, "Why did you become a teacher?"

18. Even if you're an introvert and you hate staff social events, force yourself to go. Go for an hour. It won't be that bad, and it'll be worth it.

19. Ask your principal to tell you about a student he or she cared deeply about.

20. Tell your supervisor a few things you appreciate about him or her.

21. Ask your principal (or supervisor) if he or she has any professional goals that he or she would be willing to share with you.

22. Ask your principal (or supervisor) what he or she loves about his or her job.

23. Bring a house plant to front office staff.

24. Ask front office staff if there's anything you could do to make their work easier.

25. Say good morning/afternoon when you walk through the front office.

26. Ask the custodial or lunchroom staff what they enjoy doing when they're not at work.

27. Ask the custodial or lunchroom staff if there's a student they have connected with or whom they really like.

28. Ask the custodial or lunchroom staff about their experience as a student.

29. Tell the custodial or lunchroom staff what you appreciate about them.

30. Tell a colleague that you're aware that you're not supposed to have favorite students, but ask, "Who is your favorite kid this year?"

31. Show a colleague a piece of student work that you're really excited about.

32. Eat lunch at least once a week with a colleague or two.

33. Eat lunch in the cafeteria with your students (even just once).

34. Attend an athletic event, play, or concert that your students participate in.

35. When you welcome your students to class, stand at the door and express enthusiasm at seeing them.

36. Greet each student by name as he or she enters your classroom. Shake hands or give a high five.

37. On Monday, chat with a few students as they arrive or during recess or lunch and ask, "Tell me about a moment this weekend when you felt happy."

38. Go on an appreciation hunt. Look for every little thing to appreciate in your students' or colleagues' actions. Name those things in an authentic way: "Kathryn, I really appreciate that you always greet me in the morning. It makes me feel welcomed."

39. Introduce people to each other who might appreciate and learn from each other.

40. Ask for introductions: "I'm looking for another eighth-grade science teacher whom I can observe teaching this unit. If you can recommend anyone, I'd be grateful for an introduction."

41. Tell colleagues what you're working on learning as a teacher and ask for their help: "This year I'm working on being more organized. If you have any resources that might be useful to me, I'd love to know about them."

42. Ask a colleague, a staff member, or a supervisor if there's something you can help him or her with one day after school.

43. If your school has counselors or student support specialists, find a time to meet with them individually. Learn about what they do and how they can support you. Ask them why they got into their field. Ask them how you can make the most of what they can offer.

44. Surprise someone with a breakfast treat—a bagel or fruit salad.

45. Bring a small snack to share with your grade level or department during a meeting.

46. Host your grade level or department for a potluck dinner.

47. Pick up trash around school during lunch or after school.

48. Stand outside school during dismissal and greet families—especially those whose students you don't teach.

49. Take photos of your students during the first month of school, print them, and post them in your classroom or on a bulletin board.

50. Invite students to bring in and post photos of their family and loved ones.

51. Propose a bulletin board in the staff room where all the teachers post photos of themselves at the same age as the students they now teach (and then help create it if you get a positive response).

52. Post a few photos of your family, pets, or personal life in your classroom near your desk. Be thoughtful about the images you select.

53. Create an anonymous appreciation box in your classroom and perhaps in the front office, and invite your students and colleagues to leave notes for each other there. Open the box together and read appreciations once a month.

54. Host a Grandparents and Extended Family potluck lunch and get to know your students' families.

55. Celebrate the birthdays of students and staff with simple acknowledgments and appreciation.

56. Ask teachers at your school which other schools they think you should visit for ideas and inspiration.

57. Visit another school in your district or network, ideally during the day so that you can observe a class or two, but after school is worthwhile too. Walk through the halls and look for inspiration; knock on a door or two and chat with teachers.

58. When you meet teachers from other schools, ask them if there's something they do in their classroom that they feel really good about and would be willing to share.

59. Meet central office staff, learn about how they support school sites, and make a friend. Reach out and ask for help, resources, coaching, and feedback.

60. Meet your superintendent. Stalk the halls of the central offices, linger outside of board meetings, and then boldly introduce yourself. Offer an appreciation for his or her work and invite him or her to drop by your classroom any time.

How to Address Conflict

To build your skills in addressing conflict and to boost your confidence, identify someone with whom you're having a small conflict and deal with it. Here are some steps:

1. Open the conversation by naming that you are sensing conflict.
2. State your intention or purpose for the conversation.
3. Take responsibility for any part you played in the conflict, and know that the majority of the time we've all played some role.
4. Name specific behaviors that you feel have contributed to the problem.
5. Suggest solutions.
6. Invite the other person's reflections and input.
7. Be vulnerable and seek connection.

Here's what this can sound like:

Lisa, I'm not sure what's going on, but I feel like there's conflict between us. It makes me nervous to raise this with you, but I hope we can improve our collaboration, because I know I can learn from you, and our students will benefit. I think I may have been contributing to this tension with some of the terse emails I sent you. I've been frustrated when you don't respond to my emails. I'm not sure how to understand your lack of response. I'm hoping that today we can clarify how we will communicate with each other. I'd love to hear how you are thinking about what's been going on and what suggestions you have for how we can better collaborate.

Remember, tone of voice and body language matter.

Identify someone with whom you have experienced some conflict. Write down what you'll say, using the listed suggestions. Practice saying these things aloud, focusing on your tone of voice and body language. Then go and have the conversation. After, jot down a reflection on what happened and how you felt.

Neighborhood Exploration

This activity is most enjoyably done with others—colleagues, students, or their families. Whether you're new to the community or have worked there for many years, you'll be sure to discover something because this activity is also about the partnership with students.

If you're not sure whether the neighborhood is safe, ask colleagues for their opinion. Even in the roughest neighborhoods, there are times when people are going to school or work, doing shopping, going to church, and so on. Those neighborhoods are usually only truly unsafe during certain hours and on certain blocks. And if your kids live in those neighborhoods, it's probably even more important for you to walk around and learn more about their experience. Go with a colleague and/or with older students, and use common sense.

If your school is not a neighborhood school and your students' homes are spread out, you can still do this activity—you'll probably just need to drive between points.

- Print out a map of the neighborhood where your school is (or where the majority of your students live).
- Ask your students which places they really like or think you should see. Ask them what you could see that would help you understand them better. Mark those places on the map.
- You might also identify the homes of some of your students just so that you can walk past and see their block.
- Also identify destination points: Stores, parks, restaurants, other schools, historical sites, churches, and so on. Map a route.
- When you visit those places, take photos of the locations, of yourself in those places, and of the people you meet and talk with.
- Afterward, print some of these and put them up on the walls, or post them online in a place where your students can see. Share this community exploration experience with your students. Tell them what you learned and appreciated.

Implications for Leaders

This is a powerful activity to do with an entire staff before school starts. Group people in teams, add a competitive element if you want (points for the greatest number of sites visited, for trying new foods, for talking to *x* number of people, and so on), and offer prizes. Be sure to debrief the experience with staff.

From The Onward Workbook: Daily Activities to Cultivate Your Emotional Resilience and Thrive by Elena Aguilar. Copyright © 2018 by Elena Aguilar. Reproduced by permission.

An Anthropologist in the Lunchroom

The staff lunchroom can be a fascinating place if you analyze it from the unbiased stance of a social scientist. Taking this stance might also help deepen your relationships with colleagues by extricating you a little from your judgment of others, so give it a try.

If you never eat in the staff lunchroom, this activity might feel a little awkward, but do it anyway. Show up on a day when you're feeling good—well-enough rested, okay-enough about work, emotionally balanced enough. You may never feel great, so don't wait for that day.

Anthropologists sit on the sidelines, but others don't see them that way. They're both in the group and outside the group, observing what happens.

Notice where people sit and how they cluster. Notice what and how people eat. Notice who talks, who talks the most, who listens, and who laughs. Notice what people talk about and how conversations get started. Generate questions in your mind about what you're noticing. The questions need to be nonjudgmental and truly curious. For example:

- I wonder if that's what she eats every day . . .
- I wonder if he made that food himself or if someone else made it . . .
- I wonder what kinds of things they spoke about when they first started teaching . . .
- I wonder what this room was like 10 years ago . . .
- I wonder whether these teachers talk to each other outside this room . . .

After you do your staff lunchroom fieldwork, jot down your reflections on the activity and the questions you came away with about your school, staff dynamics, and individuals.

Research Community Outside of School

List all professional communities that you could be a part of—for example, other schools in your district, networks of teachers who teach the same content, virtual communities of educators, professional associations, and so on.

Ask others—coaches, mentors, colleagues, supervisors—if they have suggestions for networks that you could explore. Say, "I'm trying to connect with other educators. I'm interested in . . . I'm working on developing . . . Do you have suggestions for people or organizations or networks to connect with?" Write down their ideas here.

Gather emails, websites, phone numbers, and so on. Write them down here—or somewhere you can access them.

Identify two people or organizations that you commit to connecting with. Give yourself a due date to reach out and make contact.

A Corsage of Community

Draw the outline of a big flower with many petals and draw your face in the middle. Inside each petal, write the name of someone from your professional and/or personal community who supports you. Add as many petals as you need or want.

Now, add a few more blank petals. Who else would you like in your support network? Perhaps you have a general sense of what's missing. For example, maybe you want an older, wiser veteran educator or a fiery, inspirational colleague. Maybe you want a therapist or a yoga teacher or a rock-climbing buddy. Who else do you want in your community? Go back and write some words in the blank petals to indicate the people in those roles.

From *The Onward Workbook: Daily Activities to Cultivate Your Emotional Resilience and Thrive* by Elena Aguilar. Copyright © 2018 by Elena Aguilar. Reproduced by permission.

Building Your Social Network

Psychologists say that there are a variety of relationships that we need in order to feel socially nurtured; a deep and wide social network is essential for resilience. Complete the following table to help you reflect on the kinds of social relationships in your life. There may be some relationship roles for which you don't have anyone, and that's to be expected.

Relationship Role	The Name of Someone Who Fills This Role	On a 1–5 scale, how strong do you feel this relationship is?
Someone to have fun with outside of work		
Someone older and wiser		
Someone I can mentor		
Someone I can turn to in need		
Someone who shares my professional role		
Someone with whom I can be physically and emotionally intimate		
Someone with whom I can learn new things		

From *The Onward Workbook: Daily Activities to Cultivate Your Emotional Resilience and Thrive* by Elena Aguilar. Copyright © 2018 by Elena Aguilar. Reproduced by permission.

Reflect

How did you feel as you engaged in this activity?

It's likely that for one or more of the types of relationships, you aren't satisfied with your relationship. Of these, which social relationship do you want to prioritize cultivating?

How could you cultivate the kind of social relationships you want? What could you do, today, to bring people into your life who could play the roles that you feel are missing?

Storytelling

Telling stories is good for our physical and communal health. When we tell stories and listen to others tell stories, our bodies produce more oxytocin. This is a good thing. Oxytocin is the "feel-good" hormone that makes us feel connected to others. It also helps us deal with tension and conflict when they inevitably arise. We can all use as much oxytocin as we can get.

Storytelling can happen organically, or it could be something incorporated into a grade-level meeting, PD time, or a one-on-one meeting.

Here are some storytelling prompts:

- Tell me a story about a time in your life when you felt really happy.
- Tell me about someone in your life who has taught you a lot.
- Tell me about a challenging moment in your life when you learned a lot.
- What's your favorite thing to do on the weekend? Describe a weekend when you got to do this.
- If you weren't an educator, what would you be doing? Which life experiences have led you to imagine this?
- In a parallel universe, what's your life like?
- If you could be any other living creature, what would you be? Why?
- What body of water is most like you? Why?
- If you could go anywhere in the world, tomorrow, where would you go and why?
- Tell me about one of the greatest adventures of your life—adventure can be anything you imagine.
- When you were 5 or 10 years old, what did you want to be? What were you like at 5 or 10 years old?
- What's something that other people do that you're terrified of doing, but that a tiny part of you would like to do one day?
- What's a risk you've taken in the last few years?
- When you were a child, whom did you admire? Whom did you want to be like?
- What fictional character would you like to be? Which fictional characters have had an influence on your thoughts or feelings?
- Tell me about someone in your life who is really important to you.
- Tell me a story about love.
- Tell me a story about heartbreak.
- Tell me a story about a good friend.
- Tell me a story about a friendship that was challenging.
- Tell me a story about what you were like when you were the same age as the students you teach.

From *The Onward Workbook: Daily Activities to Cultivate Your Emotional Resilience and Thrive* by Elena Aguilar. Copyright © 2018 by Elena Aguilar. Reproduced by permission.

Listening to Your Own Listening

When we listen, our minds take journeys. They make connections, they disagree, they ask questions. Sometimes this is okay, and sometimes it can be problematic because we stop hearing what the speaker is actually saying. This exercise will help you cultivate awareness of how you listen so that you can become a better listener.

First, read the descriptions of the mental journeys and, in the second column, put a check by those that you know you take occasionally or often when listening to someone else. Then go out and set an intention to listen mindfully to someone speak—perhaps a colleague, your boss, or a friend or partner. After you spend some time listening, as soon as possible come back to this tool and indicate in the third column (How did I listen?) where your mind went while you listened. Don't be hard on yourself if you didn't entirely fulfill your intention—just use this as a tool to notice what your mind does.

You can also use this tool with a partner to practice. One person can talk for a minute or so about anything he or she wants, while you track your listening.

Mental Journey	Which journeys do I know I take?	How did I listen?
Connection: I want to interject with a connection to what the speaker is saying.		
Fix it: I want to offer a solution or some advice, or suggest something that can be done. I want to fix it!		
Disagree: I want to interject with a disagreement—to discuss or debate something the speaker is saying.		
Question: I want to ask a clarifying question so that I can have more information or understanding. Or: I want to ask a probing question so that the speaker can explore his or her thinking more deeply.		
Uncomfortable feeling: I'm experiencing an uncomfortable emotion because of what the speaker is saying. (I'm feeling annoyed, impatient, angry, judgmental, bored.)		
Comfortable feeling: I'm experiencing a comfortable emotion because of what the speaker is saying. (I'm feeling caring, excited, enthusiastic, appreciative.)		

Spacing out: My mind is wandering to an unrelated topic—I'm spacing out or distracted by unrelated thoughts.		
Planning an exit strategy: I'm considering options for how to get out of the conversation.		
Other: (Describe)		

Reflect

After using this tool a few times (it's a great one to have copies of—you can download it from www.onwardthebook.com), respond to these questions:

What trends have you noticed in your listening?

What insights did you get into the journeys your mind takes?

What strategies do you have for keeping your mind from wandering too far?

Expansive Listening

As we cultivate awareness of how we listen, and as we become aware that we often listen with judgment or to fix a problem, we need alternate ways of listening. Our mind wants to be a good servant, so we need to direct it and tell it where to go and, in this case, how to listen.

Listen through these ways of listening one at a time. Imagine that they are radio stations and flip through the channels, listening for what's available on each station.

You can do this in the same way that you engaged in the "Listening to Your Own Listening" activity.

Listen . . .	Suggestions
For the big picture	Listen for the whole, the interconnectedness, the intersection of systems; see the person and situation embedded within the many moving pieces; see the forest and the trees.
With love	Listen with an open heart, with the knowledge that your heart will not break and that it can hold the pain and suffering of many; be present with and understand the humanity of the person who speaks.
For pain	Listen for pain, without trying to fix it; listen to hear the raw emotions under the story.
With humility	Listen with gratitude for the trust that's bestowed on you. Be humble in the face of emotion and experience.
With curiosity	Listen without an attachment to how you think things should be right now, without conjuring up the past or clinging to notions of the future. Be willing to be surprised. Let go of assumptions.
With compassion	Suspend judgment of yourself and others, appreciating and accepting that everyone makes choices based on her knowledge and skills and what makes sense given her history and worldview.
With confidence	Listen with confidence in yourself, in your abilities to listen expansively and respond from that expansion; be confident in the other person's abilities to solve his own problems.
For relationships	Listen to build healthy relationships with others who might be resources; listen for untapped sources of strength and nourishment.

From *The Onward Workbook: Daily Activities to Cultivate Your Emotional Resilience and Thrive* by Elena Aguilar. Copyright © 2018 by Elena Aguilar. Reproduced by permission.

For possibility	Listen with the conviction that there are other ways that things can be, with belief that the other person can discover those ways; listen for unseen potentials.
With hope	Listen while remaining unattached to outcomes, but with deep conviction that transformational possibilities exist that you may not perceive.

Reflect

What thoughts and feeling does this tool raise for you?

Of these various ways of listening, which one resonates most with you? Why?

Which way of listening do you want to commit to using today? Tomorrow?

Which way of listening feels the easiest?

Which way of listening feels the hardest?

How do you want to be listened to?

Listening: The Interviews

Interview three people you trust about how they experience you as a listener. I know, this is a scary proposition, and it may be hard. But do it anyway. You'll get feedback that's useful, and you may also strengthen your relationship with the people you interview.

Ask these questions:

- What do you notice about me when I'm listening?
- What feedback can you give me about my listening?

Jot down some of their responses.

Reflect

What did this activity raise for you? How did it feel?

What did you learn from this activity?

What implications are there for you based on this feedback?

From The Onward Workbook: Daily Activities to Cultivate Your Emotional Resilience and Thrive by Elena Aguilar. Copyright © 2018 by Elena Aguilar. Reproduced by permission.

Am I in a Toxic Culture?

Of course, not all communities—especially those in schools—function optimally at all times. It can be helpful to recognize when a community you're in has developed a toxic culture so that you can work with others to bring health back into the community. Explore your school or organization's culture using the exercise here. Use a 0–5 scale to rate your agreement with each statement: 0 = Not true and 5 = Absolutely true.

Indicator of Toxicity	Rating
Teachers conduct routine, boring classes.	
Staff obsess over enforcing rules about student behavior.	
There's a focus on unimportant outcomes.	
Concern is expressed only about small groups of students (often elite students such as advanced band students, gifted and talented students, or athletes).	
Teachers are siloed in classrooms, departments, or grade levels.	
Staff organize into antagonistic camps.	
Staff perpetuate negative attitudes toward students and work.	
Staff are disengaged and just go through the motions.	

(continued)

Students are disengaged and just go through the motions.	
Faculty meetings are hostile.	
Anyone who tries to improve the school culture is attacked.	
Old grudges between people are right below the surface and explode easily.	
Negative stories are told about kids, parents, the past, the current leader, and the district.	
Students are seen as a burden.	
In the staff room, negative stories are told about students.	
Gossip is rampant.	
The good old days are talked about.	
A "This too shall pass" attitude is expressed about new initiatives, programs, or leaders.	

The heroes are those who oppose change.	
Teachers arrive just as school starts and leave right when it ends.	
TOTAL	

Totals:

Over 80: Your school is highly toxic. You should probably figure out how to get out, unless you are a person with a great deal of decision-making power.

Over 60: Your school is toxic. You'll need to don some intense protective armor and make some allies if you want to stay and fight the good fight.

Over 40: Your school is on a toxic path. Find others who want to intervene (they are there), and do something about it.

Over 20: Your school has some toxicity sprouting. It may not be too hard to reverse course if you can find allies who want to pull out those weeds and build a healthy culture.

From *The Onward Workbook: Daily Activities to Cultivate Your Emotional Resilience and Thrive* by Elena Aguilar. Copyright © 2018 by Elena Aguilar. Reproduced by permission.

Reflect

How did this exercise make you feel? What emotions came up?

Which of the 20 indicators of toxicity hit home, surprised you, or upset you the most?

What do you feel compelled to do now? What kind of action could you take?

From The Onward Workbook: Daily Activities to Cultivate Your Emotional Resilience and Thrive by Elena Aguilar. Copyright © 2018 by Elena Aguilar. Reproduced by permission.

What to Say When People Don't Talk Nicely About Kids or Their Families

There were many times when, as a new teacher, I didn't know how to respond when veteran teachers made disrespectful comments about students. This happened again, further into my career, when I joined a new staff. I didn't want to alienate my new colleagues, and I didn't know what to say when they spoke disparagingly about students.

I heard comments like these:

- That kid is going to end up just like his older brother. You're wasting your time on him.
- What can you expect from him? You've met his mother, right?
- She doesn't care about her grades.
- That kid's an asshole.
- I've been assigned to teach reading intervention to our delinquents-in-training.
- Those parents don't care about their kids.

I was often so taken aback that I didn't know what to say, or I got angry and said something I later regretted, or I walked away. Then I'd replay the incident a hundred times in my mind and come up with all kinds of responses that I'd wish I had said.

Here are some things you can say when you hear comments that undermine the community you're committed to building with your students and their families:

- That comment makes me feel sad.
- I feel uncomfortable talking about kids that way.
- My experiences with that kid/that kid's family have been different. I've seen good things.
- What makes you feel like they don't care?
- I wonder why it seems like he doesn't care? I'm curious to understand that.
- All parents care about their kids.
- All parents care about their kids; maybe we just don't see or hear their care.
- All parents care about their kids; I'd like to understand how her mother expresses her love.
- I know that all parents care about their kids, even though it seems like her actions express a lack of caring. I wonder what's making it hard for me to understand her caring?

- Are you willing to understand his mother better? It sounds like you don't understand her.
- I'm curious about where your beliefs come from. Would you be willing to talk about that with me?
- What's led you to believe this? Did you feel different as a new teacher? What happened?
- It sounds like you're experiencing some strong emotions [anger, hopelessness, sadness, frustration, etc.]. I don't share those feelings.
- It sounds like you're experiencing some strong emotions [anger, hopelessness, sadness, frustration, etc.]. How do you think your feelings impact on the students we teach?
- I hear your sadness/frustration. I don't think it's right to express that to me in the way you did.
- I hear your sadness/frustration, and I care about you. I don't want to talk about students that way, but I'm willing to listen if you want to unpack those feelings.
- I never give up on kids.
- Please don't talk about kids like that with me.

Reflect

Of these statements, which do you feel you might be able to say? Select a couple that you might feel comfortable with and would like to remember.

Try saying one of those statements out loud, right now. Say it standing or sitting in a confident position. Say it over and over until your body and mind remember how to say this statement comfortably.

Which thoughts or feelings might get in the way of your being able to say one of these statements?

What could you do when one of those thoughts or feelings shows up and gets in the way of saying one of these statements? Depict that in the cartoon strip here.

How would it feel to be able to say something, perhaps to use one of these statements, when you hear disparaging comments about your students or their communities? Visualize yourself saying one of these. How do you look? How do you feel?

How to Ask Questions

Good questions come from good listening—so start there. Refining your listening is deep work. You'll find the roots of your struggles with listening in your sense of self, in your anxieties and insecurities, and in your unmet needs and desires. At the same time that you're digging into your triggers and your feelings about other human beings, you can also incorporate technical elements of listening that will help you make quick improvements.

Technical Listening Tips

- Take slow, deep breaths while you listen.
- When the speaker finishes or pauses, say, "Thank you. Tell me more."
- Don't talk too much if your intention is to listen—not more than a third of the total time.
- Speak slowly.
- Don't hurry your questions or responses.
- If you want, say "I need a moment to think," before you respond.
- During your moment to think, look out a window and let your mind wander. Don't worry about what the other person is thinking about your taking time to think.
- Soften the space between your eyebrows, relax your arms, let your jaw drop, and smile slightly.
- Think mostly about the place from which you are listening and make a choice to do so from a place of love.

Of these tips, which ones feel as though they'd be most useful to you?

What additional one to three tips might someone who knows you well offer to improve your listening?

Today, as you go about your day, ask generous questions. Speak slowly. Don't talk too much. At the end of the day, reflect:

What was challenging about this exercise?

What impact did your questions and listening have on the other person?

How did you feel engaging with others in this way?

From The Onward Workbook: Daily Activities to Cultivate Your Emotional Resilience and Thrive *by Elena Aguilar. Copyright © 2018 by Elena Aguilar. Reproduced by permission.*

A Letter to Fear

What would you like to say to fear in general? To the fear inside you? Write it a letter. Say whatever you want to say—don't be afraid! Here's the beginning of my letter: *Okay, fear. You sit down right there and let me talk. I won't hurt you. I just need to get some thoughts off my chest because you play too big of a role in my life. I understand that you want to help me, but you're going to have to back off . . .*

Artistic Depictions of Fear

Go to your preferred online search engine and look for images of fear (see "The Core Emotions" in Chapter 2 for these terms).

See what comes up, and then search for "depictions of fear in art."

Look closely at a few of those images. Sit with them and spend some time getting to know them. Pay attention to how they make you feel and what thoughts go through your mind.

Reflect

What do you notice in the images that come up?

What have you learned about fear through doing this exploration?

How did this exploration help you understand your own experience of fear?

If you'd like, print out one (or more) of the images that particularly speak to you and stick them in here.

From *The Onward Workbook: Daily Activities to Cultivate Your Emotional Resilience and Thrive* by Elena Aguilar. Copyright © 2018 by Elena Aguilar. Reproduced by permission.

Destination Postcard: Community

What would it look and sound like if you had the kind of community you want? How would that feel? How might you be different? Draw a picture of yourself with thought bubbles and labels to depict you in a healthy, resilient community.

Chapter Reflection

What were your biggest takeaways from this chapter?

Of the different activities in this chapter, which were most useful?

Which activities would you like to revisit periodically? How might you get that habit going?

What implications do the ideas in this chapter have for the work you do?

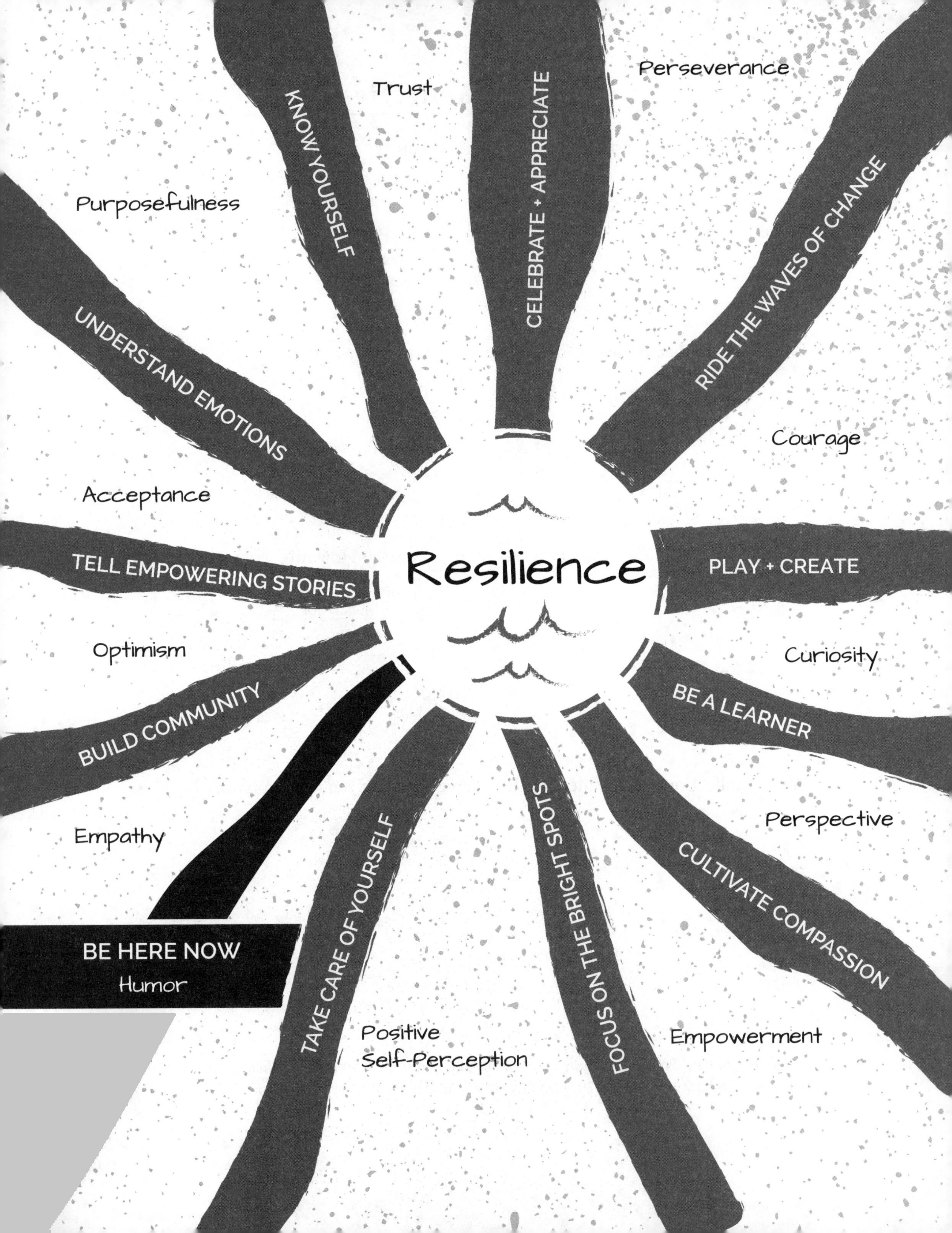
Resilience
KNOW YOURSELF
Trust
CELEBRATE + APPRECIATE
Perseverance
RIDE THE WAVES OF CHANGE
Courage
PLAY + CREATE
Curiosity
BE A LEARNER
Perspective
CULTIVATE COMPASSION
Empowerment
FOCUS ON THE BRIGHT SPOTS
Positive
Self-Perception
TAKE CARE OF YOURSELF
BE HERE NOW
Humor
Empathy
BUILD COMMUNITY
Optimism
TELL EMPOWERING STORIES
Acceptance
UNDERSTAND EMOTIONS
Purposefulness

CHAPTER 5

Be Here Now

Learning to be in the present moment, without judging it, boosts our resilience. It can allow us to feel accepting and clearheaded about our options for response. When we're fully present, we're more likely to find appropriate levity to moments of challenge and to relieve stress by finding humor in a situation.

October: As we move into the fall, our energy wanes, and we're triggered more easily. Learning to be in the present moment enables us to cultivate awareness of our emotions and make choices that foster our resilience.

Be Here Now: Resilience Self-Assessment

The purpose of this self-assessment is to help you gauge the level of your resilience reservoir and to explore what might be draining or what could replenish it. The exercises that follow and the information in the corresponding chapter of *Onward* can boost your resilience by helping you keep your mind on the present moment so you can manage worry and make clearheaded decisions.

Imagine each circle as a little *cenote* or reservoir within you, and fill it up according to how much each statement reflects a source of resilience. If you need something more concrete, imagine marks at ¼, ½, and ¾ full.

Before you start the exercises in this chapter, take this self-assessment and fill in the date. At the end of the month, take the assessment again. (You might even cover up your original markings with a strip of paper.) Is your resilience reservoir a little more full? If so, which practices do you want to keep up? If not, what else do you want to try?

Statement	Date:	Date:
I understand what mindfulness is and how it can help me build my resilience.	◯	◯
I know a few ways to practice mindfulness, and I use them with some consistency.	◯	◯
When I'm experiencing a strong emotion or faced with another person's strong emotion, I use mindfulness practices to help me respond with intention.	◯	◯
I use mindfulness practices to determine how I want to interpret things that happen.	◯	◯

From *The Onward Workbook: Daily Activities to Cultivate Your Emotional Resilience and Thrive* by Elena Aguilar. Copyright © 2018 by Elena Aguilar. Reproduced by permission.

I'm aware of the neuroscience that validates mindfulness.	◯	◯
When I find myself worrying a lot about something, I have ways to deal with these thoughts.	◯	◯
I use mindfulness practices to strengthen my cultural competence.	◯	◯
I use mindfulness practices to tap into feelings of joy and contentment.	◯	◯
I use humor mindfully and with intention to cultivate resilience and strengthen relationships.	◯	◯
I know how mindfulness can help me make decisions about how to deal with the 65,000 thoughts I have every day.	◯	◯

The Raisin Meditation

When we taste with attention, even the simplest foods provide a universe of sensory experience.

JON KABAT-ZINN, MINDFULNESS TEACHER

One of the most widely used methods for cultivating mindfulness is to focus your attention on each of your senses as you eat a raisin. This exercise is often used as an introduction to the practice of mindfulness. Try it alone or with colleagues or even with students. You can also find this as an audio recording on the website, www.onwardthebook.com. Here are the steps:

1. **Holding:** First, take a raisin and hold it in the palm of your hand or between your finger and thumb.
2. **Seeing:** Take time to really focus on the raisin; look at it with full attention—imagine that you're from another planet and you've never seen anything like this. Let your eyes explore every part of it, examining the folds and ridges, the lighter and darker crevices, and any asymmetries or unique features.
3. **Touching:** Turn the raisin and explore its texture. Do this with your eyes to enhance your sense of touch.
4. **Smelling:** Hold the raisin beneath your nose and inhale. Notice its smells and fragrances. Notice anything happening in your mouth or stomach.
5. **Placing:** With your eyes closed, slowly raise the raisin up to your lips. Notice how your hand and arm know exactly how and where to position it. Gently place the raisin in your mouth. Without chewing, spend a few moments focusing on the sensations of having it in your mouth, exploring it with your tongue.
6. **Tasting:** When you are ready, prepare to chew the raisin, noticing how and where it needs to be for chewing. Then, very consciously, take a bite and notice what happens, experiencing any waves of taste as you continue chewing. Without swallowing yet, notice the sensations of taste and texture in your mouth and how these may change over time, moment by moment. Also pay attention to any changes in the raisin itself.
7. **Swallowing:** When you're ready to swallow the raisin, see if you can first detect the intention to swallow as it comes up so that you experience this consciously before you swallow the raisin.
8. **Following:** See if you can feel the raisin moving down into your stomach, and sense how your body feels after completing this exercise.

This exercise helps cultivate mindfulness as you pay attention to your senses. It also can help you increase enjoyment of food and become more attuned to hunger and fullness signals and therefore avoid overeating or "emotional eating."

Jot down a reflection on this activity. What would you like to remember about it? If you want to draw your raisin, go ahead!

The Joy Collage

This activity can help you gain insight into joy, which for many of us is an elusive emotion.

Collect some magazines and a piece of heavy paper or cardboard, grab a bottle of glue, and find a place where you can spread out. Now, go through the magazines tearing out images that represent joy for you. If you want, you can use scissors to cut them out, or you can tear the paper with your fingers, which can create a nice effect. Then paste your collection of images onto the heavy paper or cardboard.

The key to getting the most from this activity is not to spend too much time thinking about the images—go with your quick reactions. Let this be playful and fun and let yourself be drawn to whatever image speaks to you of the experience of joy.

If you'd like, you can photograph your creation, print that photo, and paste it in here as a record of your exploration.

Right Here, Right Now

This is a simple meditative phrase to repeat at any time you feel anxious or unsettled, or when you find yourself worrying about the future or ruminating over the past. Simply say to yourself, *Right here, right now, everything is okay.*

I'm willing to bet that 98% of the time, for most of us everything *is* okay. This phrase can reground you in the present moment. As you say it to yourself, sense your body—run your awareness over your skin, shoulders, jaw, scalp. This kind of body scan helps you get back into the present as well. When you say the phrase to yourself, focus on the word *okay*. For me, okay is a powerful word; it means that the present moment is not my fantasy moment, but it's also not painful emotionally or physically. I love the word okay. It's fine for life to be okay a lot.

Of all of the practices I have tried and used, this is one of the easiest, quickest, and most effective for me when I find myself fluttering out of the present. Try it while you're settling your students into a Do Now, when you're walking your class to lunch, when you're sitting in a meeting that you don't want to attend, when you're running late to school, when you're working your way through a stack of papers to grade. Most likely, during those moments that can feel stressful, everything is still okay.

The challenge is to remember to use this phrase. So how might you do that? Do you want to write these words on your forearm today? Or write them on your whiteboard? Or create a screen saver with this phrase? Set yourself up to remember.

Write down your plan for remembering to try this strategy this week:

Blowing Bubbles

It is tempting to believe that mindfulness can only be practiced in moments of silence and stillness, which in turn can make it seem like a *serious* practice. But many people who regularly practice mindfulness attest to the fact that it is a wellspring of joy and contentment. To help us remember this, it can be helpful to practice mindfulness during moments of play and relaxation.

Explore the ideas here for experiencing mindfulness during play. Pick one and try it today, perhaps with your own children or students or colleagues.

- Bubbles! Focus on taking slow, deep breaths as you inhale, and on exhaling steadily to fill the bubble. Pay close attention as the bubbles form, detach, float away, or pop.
- Pinwheels! Use the same tactics as for blowing bubbles by bringing mindful attention to a spinning pinwheel.
- Balloons! Blow up a balloon and use gentle motions to keep it from touching the ground. Imagine the balloon to be very fragile. Notice the sensation of it touching your fingertips. Pay attention to its movement in the air and the movement of your body in response.
- Trampolines! If you have access to a trampoline, spend a few minutes jumping on it without shoes. Notice the sensations throughout your body as you push up. Feel the breeze as you move through the air—against your skin, through your hair. Notice the sounds of the springs supporting you and sending you soaring.
- Play dough! Grab a ball of play dough or clay and start kneading it. Squeeze it through your fingers or roll it between your palms. Pay attention to its smell, its colors, its temperature, its texture.

How else could you practice mindfulness during play?

From The Onward Workbook: Daily Activities to Cultivate Your Emotional Resilience and Thrive by Elena Aguilar. Copyright © 2018 by Elena Aguilar. Reproduced by permission.

Being anchored in the present moment helps you practice appreciation and see the bright spots. It also goes the other way: Practicing gratitude can help you stay anchored in the present. We often think that happiness comes from big wins or achievements, but the sum total of all the little things is often greater than the big things.

This week, focus on the little things by sending at least one thank-you email or text each morning—two short minutes to take stock of the present and appreciate those who are making it better.

Write the names of the people you'll thank this week:

MONDAY:

TUESDAY:

WEDNESDAY:

THURSDAY:

FRIDAY:

SATURDAY/SUNDAY:

Mindfulness on Yard Duty

Engaging your senses fully is a form of mindfulness. Our habitual approach to taking in sensory information is to make judgments about what we see: We like this; we don't like that. This leaf is pretty; that one is ugly. Mindfulness is about experiencing the leaf without judgment.

So here's how to do stealthy yard duty mindfulness practices (of course, you can substitute another activity or place—perhaps a staff meeting, a walk between appointments, a passing period, or any other moment of the day). Start with sight because 80% of what we learn comes from this dominant sense. Stand quietly, with your eyes open. Don't focus on only one thing; just notice what's in your visual field. What colors do you see? What shapes do you see? What patterns? Textures? Notice the light; pay attention to movement. All without judgment.

Now notice sounds. Do you hear sounds that are familiar? And perhaps others that have always been there in the background but to which you've grown so accustomed that you no longer notice? If you're listening to people speaking, pay attention to the cadence, pitch, pace, and intonation of their words. All without judgment.

Shift your awareness to smell. If you're lucky, you work in a place where you want to inhale pleasant scents. Or maybe you're in a stuffy classroom or a city lot that smells toxic. Whatever it is you smell, you're always smelling, but you're probably rarely conscious of it. So just bring awareness to odors for a few moments and try to do this without judgment. You might be surprised.

Activating your awareness of sight, sound, and smell, without judgment, will bring you into the present moment and help anchor you in the here and now. It can feel calming and energizing. And you can do it quickly, while still being an adult presence on the yard (or wherever else you are).

Try this today, and then this evening, come back and jot down a few words about what you experienced.

Mindful Eating

There are moments throughout the day when you can engage in mindfulness as a way to calm and center yourself. Mindful eating is a practice of bringing your full attention to eating. When we eat mindfully, we smell our food before eating it, slowly chew each bite, and savor the flavors and textures. I know that many of you probably eat lunch while doing several other things at once (if you eat lunch at all), so my suggestion here might seem radical.

Today, eat your lunch mindfully. Slowly. Savor each bit. Chew 25 times, or even just 5. In the evening, come back here and jot down a reflection on this experience. Don't judge yourself about whatever you experience—it's all fine. It just is what it is.

The Myth of Multitasking

Let's acknowledge what blocks us from mindfulness: Multitasking and perpetual busyness. Contrary to popular belief, humans are cognitively unable to multitask. It contributes to stress, undermines our ability to connect with others, and erodes professional skills. The human brain can focus on only one thing at a time. It takes in information *sequentially*. When we attempt to focus on multiple tasks at the same time, we have to switch back and forth between tasks, and, therefore, we pay less attention to both. We can't concentrate on two distinct, input-rich activities that require attention. Sure, you can talk on the phone and drink water at the same time, but you can't engage in a pair-share and write a text message at the same time without missing something, making a mistake, or losing time.

Neuroscientists explain that when you are interrupted and have to switch your attention back and forth, it takes, on average, 50% longer to accomplish the task. Each time you switch tasks, your brain runs through a complex process of disengaging the neurons involved in one task and activating the neurons needed for the other. Switching back and forth wastes time, tires your brain out, and lowers the quality of whatever you're doing—be that listening or writing an email or grading papers.

So why do we do it? First, multitasking can feel good. It actually stimulates dopamine production, and dopamine makes us feel happy. According to scientist Daniel Levitin in his book *The Organized Mind* (2015), "Multitasking creates a dopamine-addiction feedback loop, effectively rewarding the brain for losing focus and for constantly searching for external stimulation" (p. 96). What makes it even worse is that our prefrontal cortex has a novelty bias, which means our attention is easily hijacked by something new. If you identify as a multitasker, beware! You might be addicted to the experience.

Multitasking also gives us the *illusion* of productivity, but that may be because we don't notice when we start making mistakes or when our focus deteriorates. The information we take in while multitasking is also harder to remember later. Another problematic consequence of this habit: Multitasking prompts the release of adrenaline and other stress hormones, which contribute to short-term memory loss and long-term health problems.

I know how much you need to get done, and I know how busy you are, but stop dividing your attention. Instead, take frequent breaks between intervals of sustained, focused attention, and you will feel much better and get more done. Staying focused on one thing at a time is mindfulness in action.

Today, set an intention to do one thing at a time. When you feel tempted to try to multi-task, remind yourself of your intention. Bring your awareness to the one thing you're doing, while holding soft awareness of the feelings that come up as you try to stay focused. At the end of the day, jot down a few reflections on this experience.

Mindful Walking

Walking meditation is another form of mindfulness that you can practice at work, or at any time. Most of our walking is utilitarian; we walk to get from here to there, to get the kids to the cafeteria or the library, or to get to our car or the bus. Even when we go for a walk in the park, our attention is often captured by other things—a podcast, a conversation with a friend, or thoughts about the past or future. Mindful walking is deceptively simple.

Here's how to do it: Allow your attention to rest on the coordinated rhythms of walking. Walk at a pace that is slightly slower than normal. Feel the changing sensations in your feet as you walk. Feel the contact with the ground, and notice the sensations in your legs, hips, shoulders, and arms as you move. Walk for 2 minutes or 20.

Try this today. Then come back and jot down a few words about what you noticed.

Tagore on Joy

I slept and dreamt that life was joy. I awoke and saw that life was service. I acted and behold, service was joy.

RABINDRANATH TAGORE

What does this quote raise for you? What connections can you make with it? How does it make you feel?

Ice Cube Meditation

Hold an ice cube in your hand for as long as it takes to melt. Let the water drop onto your lap or the table. Observe your sensations, feelings, urges, thoughts, and desires. Afterward, record those observations here.

What were the sensations you experienced? Freezing? Burning? Cold? What else?

Discomfort: On a 1–10 scale, how uncomfortable was it to hold the ice cube?

How did the discomfort shift over time?

What thoughts did you have?

What emotions did you have?

From The Onward Workbook: Daily Activities to Cultivate Your Emotional Resilience and Thrive by Elena Aguilar. Copyright © 2018 by Elena Aguilar. Reproduced by permission.

A Tree in a Storm

You'll need a sheet of paper and watercolor paints (or colored pencils) for this activity. If you have watercolor paper, use that for this activity.

Divide your paper into three sections. In the first, using a black or brown crayon, draw yourself as a tree. What kind of tree are you? What season are you in? Do you have fruit? Include deep roots, foliage, and any creatures that might live on or around you.

In the second section, using the crayon, draw yourself as the tree again, but this time, draw and paint a storm passing by. You can use other colors for the storm if you want. You can make it as big or mild as you want. You may need to change an element of the tree; you may want to draw some leaves blowing off, or branches bending.

In the third section, draw yourself as a tree after the storm. What do you look like?

We can think of strong, uncomfortable emotions as storms that pass by. When we can imagine ourselves as a tree with deep roots, it can help us manage the experience and remember that it's temporary.

Project Silliness

This month, the disposition we're exploring is humor. Humor can help us shift our perspective on something, expand our mindset, and illuminate more choices and options when we feel stuck. Humor can also lighten a difficult situation and help us accept our humanness and foibles. It's gentle and playful and helps us not take life too seriously.

Silliness can open paths to humor. Your goal for the next week is to explore silliness—to consider what it is, to ask others about their definitions of silliness, and to try a few things that might be silly. Because you're *exploring* silliness, take a growth mindset—know that this is a disposition that you can cultivate and that it might feel awkward and uncomfortable. And do it anyway.

What could you do this week that's silly? Wear something silly? Greet your students with a song and dance? Propose that your PLC meeting conducts five minutes of the agenda using only charades? Brainstorm some ideas here.

Now, go out and try to do at least one silly thing, if not more.

At the end of the week: What did you do this week that was silly? What did it feel like?

Identify a Choice Point

Trying to cultivate new habits? Here's a tip from Thaler and Sunstein's book *Nudge* (2009): By identifying a "choice point," you can prime yourself to form good habits. If you want a peaceful wake-up routine, but as soon as you open your eyes, you reach for your phone and read email, then the choice point is to leave your phone in another room. New habits are built around dozens of miniscule choice points that we can set up in our daily life to send us in the direction we want to go. By identifying those choice points, you can create the conditions that will help you be successful.

A choice point establishes an environment that encourages and supports the changes you want to make. If you want to exercise first thing in the morning, leave your shoes and exercise clothes within arm's reach of your bed. If you know that the Internet sucks you in every time you work on lesson plans, turn your Wi-Fi off. By identifying choice points, you can also create action triggers such as checklists, routines, and other specific, visible, and intentionally created triggers that lead to new behaviors. Identifying choice points helps us make change and new habits inevitable.

Based on what you read in *Onward* about the habit Be Here Now, and perhaps what you've tried in this workbook so far, what's a change you'd like to make? What are the choice points that will help you build a new habit?

From *The Onward Workbook: Daily Activities to Cultivate Your Emotional Resilience and Thrive* by Elena Aguilar. Copyright © 2018 by Elena Aguilar. Reproduced by permission.

Treasure Chest of the Ordinary

This month's habit, Be Here Now, anchors us in the ordinary and everyday experiences that we often overlook. These moments can bring us tremendous joy if we pay more attention to them. If we count those little moments, we definitely have more mundane and pleasant moments than we have big milestones—weddings, births, and so on. Researchers tell us that what seems ordinary in the moment can take on unexpected significance later when, in looking back, we appreciate a simple moment of contentment. We rarely document the ordinary times because we underestimate the pleasure of revisiting them and overestimate our ability to remember them. In this activity, you'll document the ordinary and store it away. Here are the steps:

1. Create, assemble, or identify the "chest" in which you want to store your treasures. This could be a notebook, a scrapbook, or a digital folder.
2. Write about the following (and skip any you don't want to write about):
   - The last social event you attended
   - A recent conversation with a colleague
   - How you met a new friend or acquaintance
   - A good day at work
   - The name of a song you recently heard
   - What you ate for dinner last night
   - A book, article, poem, or TV show you recently read or watched
3. Include artifacts like these:
   - A recent photo of a mundane moment
   - A recent status update you posted on social media
   - A screenshot of a text message

When compiling your artifacts, focus on school or work life if you want, or cast a wider net. Let yourself be guided by the ordinary and mundane. You don't need to look for highlights and special moments.

4. Store your Treasure Chest of the Ordinary in a place where you won't see it. Set a reminder on your calendar or phone to revisit it three months from now.
5. After three months, look through your treasure chest. Does anything seem particularly interesting or meaningful, looking back on it now? Does anything surprise you? What does it feel like to look back at those moments?

This is a great activity to do quarterly. (So if you're a planner, pull out your calendar and schedule this for a few months from now.) And if you have friends or colleagues who are also doing this workbook, this is a fun activity to share.

From *The Onward Workbook: Daily Activities to Cultivate Your Emotional Resilience and Thrive* by Elena Aguilar. Copyright © 2018 by Elena Aguilar. Reproduced by permission.

Mindful Breathing

The most basic form of mindful breathing is simply to focus your attention on the inhale and exhale of your breath. You can do this while sitting, lying down, or even standing. You may find it easier to maintain focus if you close your eyes. It's helpful to set a timer to sustain your attention.

The essence of the practice is this: Simply observe each breath without trying to change it. Focus on the rise and fall of your chest, or the sensation of air on your nostrils. Your mind way wander. You might get distracted by thoughts or bodily sensations. That's okay. Just notice whatever happens and gently bring your attention back to your breath.

The instructions here are also included as a guided meditation on the website, www .onwardthebook.com.

Mindful Breathing
1. Find a relaxed, comfortable position. You could sit on a chair, on the floor, or on a cushion. Keep your back upright, but not too tight, and rest your hands wherever comfortable.
2. Notice and relax your body. Relax any areas of tightness or tension. Let the chair or cushion hold your body. Just breathe.
3. Tune in to your breath. Feel the natural flow of breath moving in and out of your body. You don't need to do anything to your breath—just let it move naturally. Notice where you feel your breath in your body—in your belly, chest, throat, or nostrils. Follow the sensations of each breath, noticing how when one breath ends, the next begins.
4. You might notice that you start thinking about other things. If this happens, it is not a problem. Just notice that your mind has wandered. Softly, in your head, you can say *thinking* or *wandering*. Then redirect your attention back to breathing. If you'd like, you can count the breaths—inhale, 1, exhale, 2—restarting at 10, 12, or 20.
5. Continue to focus on your breath for 5 to 10 minutes. If you get lost in thought, just return to your breath.

It's best to do this exercise regularly, at a designated time. The more you practice mindful breathing, the greater the impact during mundane daily events as well as during difficult moments. Think of the daily practice as training for a race—for those moments when you need your mind and body to efficiently move into high performance to deal with a stressful moment.

From *The Onward Workbook: Daily Activities to Cultivate Your Emotional Resilience and Thrive* by Elena Aguilar. Copyright © 2018 by Elena Aguilar. Reproduced by permission.

If you are engaging in the exercises in this book with colleagues or a team, consider starting some meetings with five to seven minutes of breathing meditation. Try it once and just see how your meeting changes after everyone has spent some time focusing on his or her breath.

The "Not-Right-Now" Shelf

We all have thoughts that try to hijack us from our work. They sneak up while we're planning or delivering a lesson, when we're in the middle of a meeting, or when we're in conversation with a concerned parent after school. These thoughts can distract us, fuel our irritation or anger, or make us feel insecure and anxious.

A simple way of dealing with these thoughts is to tell them, *Not right now* and place them on a mental shelf. This lets those thoughts know that you're not ignoring or repressing them, but that you'll return to them when the time is right. You don't need to get caught up in every thought that goes through your mind.

In order to train your mind to use your Not-Right-Now shelf, you'll need to construct it and practice using it. Right here, in the space provided, sketch out a shelf. Label it Not-Right-Now. Then think back over the last few days and see if you can identify any distracting thoughts. Name them and write them on the shelf. I like to think of those thoughts as books that I'll someday get to—so I draw the shape of a book and label it with the thought.

Having a visual of this mental concept will make it easier to remember to use as things come up. For the next couple of days, when you notice a thought or feeling surfacing at an inopportune time, write down the thought in a few words. Later write it on the shelf you drew. Doing this for a few days gets your brain into the habit so that you can later use this strategy without needing to write down your distracting thought. You'll be able to just visualize it.

In Figure 5.1, you'll see an example of my Not-Right-Now shelf. I've noticed that when I go back to my mental shelf at a later point to look at the thoughts I'd stacked up, many of them no longer feel relevant or necessary to explore. Then I imagine stacking them in a paper sack and saving them for a garage sale. If someone else is interested in them, he or she is welcome to them. Otherwise, I'll just drop them in the recycling bin one day.

Figure 5.1: Elena's Not-Right-Now Shelf

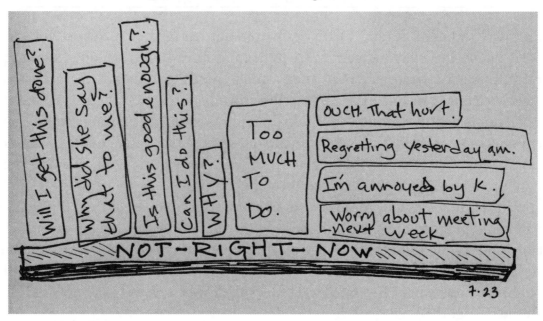

Draw your Not-Right-Now shelf in this space:

Sixty Seconds

I know it's hard to find time to do all of these resilience-boosting things. But you can find 60 seconds, right? Ideally, give yourself 60 seconds every hour that you're at school—we're only talking about a total of six or seven minutes! But if that feels undoable, dedicate 60 seconds once a day for this activity. Set an alarm so that you don't forget to do this practice. Close your door, turn off your lights, and engage in 60 seconds of recovery time—because that's what this is, and it can make a profound difference in the subsequent 59 minutes.

The Practice
1. Close your eyes.
2. Bring awareness to the palms of your hands or the soles of your feet, or both.
3. For 60 seconds, imagine all the tension leaving your body, draining out of you through your hands and feet.

That's it.

Can you try doing this every hour, for one day?

After you try this a few times, jot down a few words about how you experienced this practice. What did you notice? How did you feel afterwards?

Meet Your Telomeres

After you learn about telomeres, I'm hoping you'll be even more inclined to sit down and focus on your breath. Telomeres live at the end of each strand of DNA and protect our chromosomes—they are often compared to the plastic caps at the end of shoelaces. When telomeres shorten or fray, our cells age faster, making us more susceptible to disease and dementia. Long and strong telomeres keep us feeling young and healthy.

So how do you take care of your telomeres? By producing telomerase, an enzyme that slows, stops, or perhaps even reverses the telomere shortening that happens with age. And guess what helps your body produce more telomerase? Meditation! Research conducted by Elizabeth Blackburn, a Nobel Prize–winning molecular biologist, and her colleague Elissa Epel showed that meditation resulted in a substantial increase in telomerase in participants' blood. (They report these findings in their book *The Telomere Effect*, 2017). When compared to the control group, the meditators also observed their experiences in a nonreactive manner, felt increased purpose in life, and experienced a sense of control and decreased negative emotions. Although these feelings may be a psychological result of meditation, what blew the researchers' scientific minds was seeing the increased amount of telomerase in the participants' blood; this stuff is really important. And there aren't many ways to get it.

The human body can produce telomerase, but it can also shorten telomeres through long-term stress and repetitive negative thinking. "Telomeres are listening to your thoughts," explains Blackburn. Which is why, she says, considering the approximately 65,000 thoughts our mind processes a day, we need to be aware of our thinking: Negative thinking unravels and shortens those telomeres. And that's not good for our physical health. Blackburn (imagine her: a gray-haired scientist in a white lab coat) has become a leading advocate for meditation, as well as for sleeping, exercising, and eating well. We've known for quite a while that healthy eating, movement, and sleep are essential, but this research on telomeres now tells us why. And it tells us that meditation is key to caring for our cells.

What do you imagine your telomeres want to say to you?

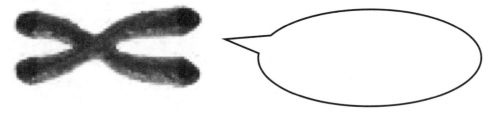

The Zen of Coloring

There are lots of studies on the effectiveness of art therapy in reducing stress, and coloring seems to offer some similar benefits. Doodling is a way for people to organize their thoughts and to focus. But coloring offers that relief and mindfulness without the paralysis that a blank page can cause. It's soothing. You don't have to make too many decisions. There's repetitive motion and limited space. Coloring patterns is like walking labyrinths. And in the end, you'll have something pretty.

Here are a few recommendations:

- *Adult Coloring Book: Stress Relieving Patterns* (2015), by Blue Star Coloring
- *One Zentangle a Day: A Week Course in Creative Drawing for Relaxation, Inspiration, and Fun* (2012), by Beckah Krahula
- Millie Marotta's books of animals (see www.milliemarotta.co.uk)

You can quickly and easily find a page to color online. Print it out right now and color it to get a taste of this experience!

Do Something Already

If you get stuck in your thoughts, they are most likely either ruminations over the past (regrets and such) or anxieties about the future. Although thinking is useful and important before taking action, some of us have a tendency to get caught up in our heads, going over and over what we want to, might do, or could do, and all the possible ramifications.

Is there something of a small to medium size that you have been wanting to do for a while? I'm not talking about resigning from your position or becoming an acrobat. I'm wondering about things like calling a therapist to make an appointment, asking a colleague to tea, signing up for a class, reaching out to an old friend, or telling your principal that you need more feedback on your teaching. What's something you want to do that you've been contemplating for a while that you could take action on today?

Now, go and do it. Get that ball rolling.

From *The Onward Workbook: Daily Activities to Cultivate Your Emotional Resilience and Thrive* by Elena Aguilar. Copyright © 2018 by Elena Aguilar. Reproduced by permission.

Walk a Labyrinth

Human beings have been constructing labyrinths for millennia. These ancient patterns have meditative powers and have held deep significance across a range of cultures. Unlike a maze, a labyrinth cannot be solved. There are no dead ends. There is a way in, and a way out.

A labyrinth can be "walked" with the eyes or with the feet. You need only a small amount of concentration to stay on the path, and the repetition is calming.

Use the resources noted here to locate a labyrinth in your community, and go walk it. Perhaps this could be a field trip that you take with colleagues. Alternatively, you could use a pencil to trace your way through the labyrinth included here (though walking one is best).

Resources
- www.labyrinthsociety.org
- www.labyrinthlocator.com

From *The Onward Workbook: Daily Activities to Cultivate Your Emotional Resilience and Thrive* by Elena Aguilar. Copyright © 2018 by Elena Aguilar. Reproduced by permission.

Soaking In the Satisfaction

Here's one of the steps to successfully building new habits: As you're building the new habit, after you implement it, pause to bask in the afterglow. Acknowledge yourself for doing it and for surmounting whatever obstacles showed up. Register the rewards in that moment and notice your positive emotions. Recognize that you're making progress toward your vision.

What's a new habit you're working on? Today, as you enact that habit, make sure you pause to soak in the satisfaction. It could be that you're trying to greet your students at the door with a smile. Take 10 seconds as you transition away from the door to soak in the satisfaction of having integrated that habit. Or perhaps you want to listen more during meetings. Pause for a moment of appreciation each time you harness your instinct to interject.

How can you remember to do this today? What cue might you give yourself to prompt yourself to do this?

Project Humor

Part 1: Reflection

Get to know your sense of humor. What is humorous to you? What do you find funny? Go ahead and brainstorm, letting every thought pour out of you.

Whose humor do you appreciate? These could be people in your life or actors or comedians.

Which of your own behaviors and beliefs can you laugh at? Note: You can't laugh at *yourself,* but you can laugh at the things you *do* or *think.* Can you think of a recent thing you did or thought that you could laugh at?

Part 2: Interviews

Ask a few friends or colleagues about their sense of humor. What do they find funny? Whom do they find funny? Which of their own behaviors and beliefs do they laugh at? You might decide to ask people whom you find funny or just people whom you feel close to or want to know better. Jot down some of what you hear. Capture recommendations for humorous books, TV shows, speakers, and so on.

Part 3: Exploration

What else could you do to explore humor? Take this opportunity to watch some TV shows that you've heard are funny or that others recommend. Listen to humorous speakers. Read a book—or listen to an audiobook—that you've heard is funny. Afterward, reflect on what you learned in this exploration. How has your own sense of humor expanded? What have you learned about your sense of humor?

Drawing Your Breath

Many mindfulness practices begin with bringing awareness to the breath. This is often done with the mind, but can also be powerful when done with the eyes and hand. There is a lot of value in this simple exercise, in terms of both relaxation and strengthening the attention and focus required by meditation. It's also a fun way to flex the creativity muscles we all have, as there's no right way to draw your breath. Here's what to do:

1. Get two sheets of paper and your preferred drawing medium (a colored pencil, a nice pen, oil pastels, or chalk). Lay the pencil on your paper and get settled into your seat.
2. Take a moment to observe your breathing without feeling the need to change it.
3. Visualize your breath and represent it as a line on your first sheet of paper.
4. Experiment with different kinds of lines as you observe your breath. Try changing your breath—making it faster, slower, smoother—and notice how this changes the lines on your page. Then change the lines and see if you can change your breathing to match.
5. After five minutes or so of experimentation, get the second sheet of paper. Now focus on the slow, deep breaths of relaxation. Again, draw lines to represent each breath. You might do this by inhaling and then drawing on the exhale, or by drawing the entire breath. Continue for a few minutes as you relax into the motion of breathing and drawing. Continue this for several minutes.

What did you notice about the natural quality of your breathing? Is it shallow or deep, slow or fast, even or irregular?

How did the lines and your breath shift by simply noticing or by consciously taking slow, deep breaths?

From *The Onward Workbook: Daily Activities to Cultivate Your Emotional Resilience and Thrive* by Elena Aguilar. Copyright © 2018 by Elena Aguilar. Reproduced by permission.

If you want, glue or staple this artifact here, or put it in the pocket or chest that you made for your resilience work.

Kale Is Not Required

If meditating seems like something that only kale-eating hippies do, then consider that meditation is now a practice taken up by the following people:

- Oprah meditates, of course. After bringing meditation practices to her company she said, "You can't imagine what's happened . . . People who used to have migraines don't, people are sleeping better, people have better relationships, people interact with other people better. It's been fantastic."
- Ellen DeGeneres also meditates and says: "[Meditation] feels good. Kinda like when you have to shut your computer down, just sometimes when it goes crazy, you just shut it down and when you turn it on, it's okay again. That's what meditation is for me."
- Dan Harris, ABC news anchor, became, as the title of his book declares, *10% Happier* (2014) through meditation.
- The Golden State Warriors (NBA champions!) are devoted mindfulness practitioners. Their core values are, in this order: Joy, mindfulness, compassion, and competition.
- Congressman Tim Ryan, who describes himself as "a half-Irish, half-Italian quarterback from Northeast Ohio," testifies to his conviction that meditation is the answer to many challenges in his book, *Mindful Nation: How a Simple Practice Can Help Us Reduce Stress, Improve Performance, and Recapture the American Spirit* (2012).
- Major General Walter E. Piatt, a 35-year-plus veteran of the Army now working in the Pentagon, advocates for mindfulness. In partnership with neuroscientists, he's brought meditation programs to trainees and veterans to increase focus and manage stress.

What associations do you have with meditators? Where do those associations come from?

Who do you know who meditates? Start asking around. You might be surprised. Ask them why they meditate and jot down what they say.

A Letter to Joy

Write a letter to joy. Imagine it as a character—either inside you or elsewhere. What do you need to say? Here's the beginning of my letter to joy:

Joy: What would I do without your presence in my life? You show up in the most unexpected places—a beautiful sunrise, my son's smile, an email of appreciation—and I am so grateful. I know I often look for you in "big moments," and then you appear while I'm taking out the trash . . .

Artistic Depictions of Joy

Go to your preferred online search engine and look for images of joy—or another term that reflects joy, such as bliss, cheer, or peace (see "The Core Emotions" in Chapter 2 for these terms).

See what comes up, and then search for "depictions of joy in art."

Look closely at a few of those images. Sit with them and spend some time getting to know them. Pay attention to how they make you feel and what thoughts go through your mind.

Reflect

What do you notice in the images that come up?

What have you learned about joy through doing this exploration?

How did this exploration help you understand your own experience of joy?

If you'd like, print out one (or more) of the images that particularly speak to you and stick them in here.

What would it look and sound like if you were fully present? Draw a picture of yourself with thought bubbles and labels to describe a you that is fully in the present moment. If you'd like, draw this you at work, surrounded by kids and colleagues. How might you be in that space?

Chapter Reflection

What were your biggest takeaways from this chapter?

Of the different activities in this chapter, which were most useful?

Which activities would you like to revisit periodically? How might you get that habit going?

What implications do the ideas in this chapter have for the work you do?

From The Onward Workbook: Daily Activities to Cultivate Your Emotional Resilience and Thrive by Elena Aguilar. Copyright © 2018 by Elena Aguilar. Reproduced by permission.

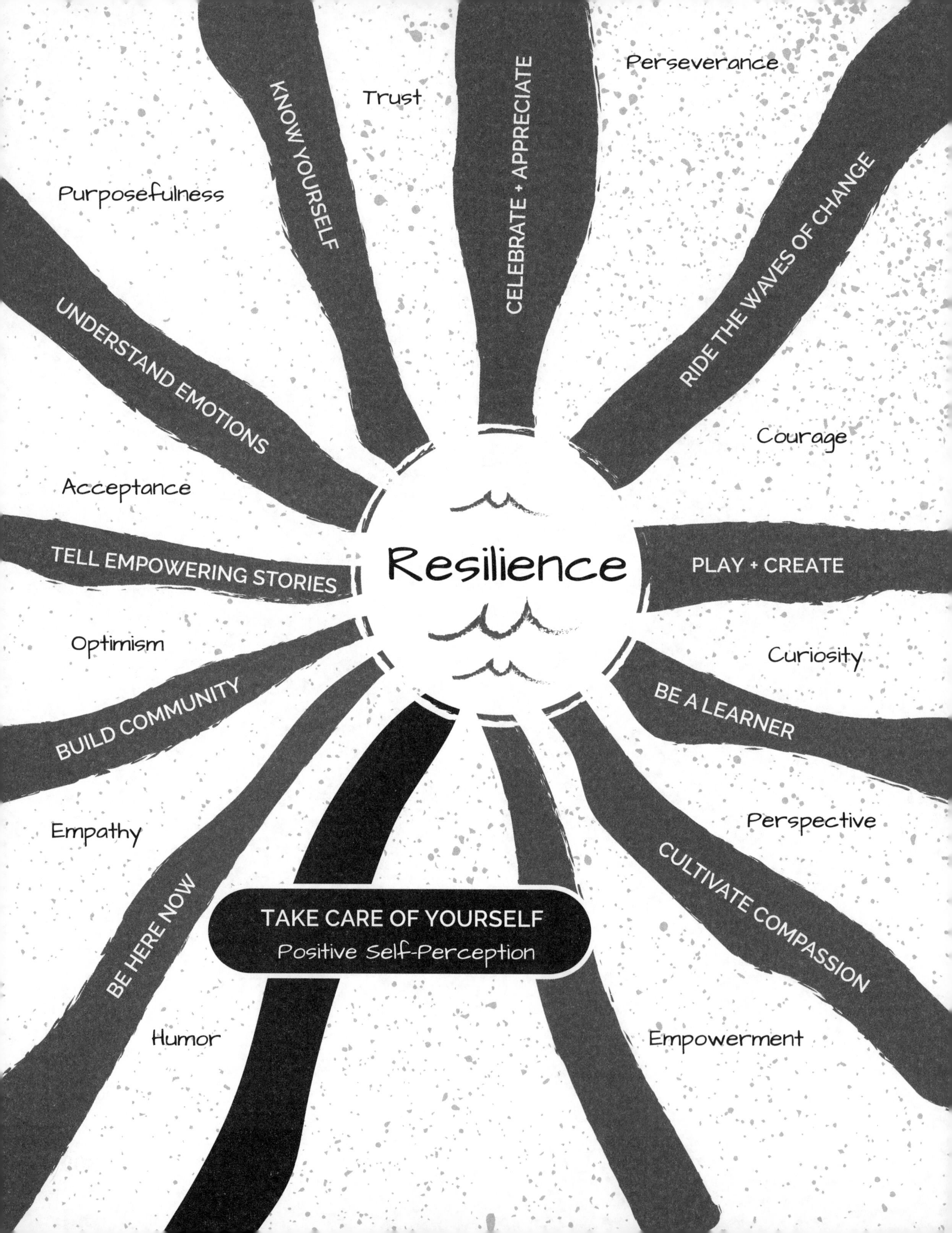

CHAPTER 6

Take Care of Yourself

Physical self-care and well-being are foundational for many other habits. When your body is cared for, you're better able to deal with emotions. Resilient people have a healthy self-perception, are committed to taking care of themselves, and accept themselves more or less as they are.

November: Self-care is the root of resilience when you're dragging yourself toward winter break and your emotions are raw.

Take Care of Yourself: Resilience Self-Assessment

The purpose of this self-assessment is to help you gauge the level of your resilience reservoir and to explore what might be draining or what could replenish it. The exercises that follow and the information in the corresponding chapter of *Onward* can boost your resilience by helping you give your body what it needs to be healthy—and see value in prioritizing that!

Imagine each circle as a little *cenote* or reservoir within you, and fill it up according to how much each statement reflects a source of resilience. If you need something more concrete, imagine marks at ¼, ½, and ¾ full.

Before you start the exercises in this chapter, take this self-assessment and fill in the date. At the end of the month, take the assessment again. (You might even cover up your original markings with a strip of paper.) Is your resilience reservoir a little more full? If so, which practices do you want to keep up? If not, what else do you want to try?

Statement	Date:	Date:
I believe that I deserve physical well-being and have a right to care for my body.		
I can put my own needs for physical well-being ahead of the needs of others when I want to.		
I know how to care for my body.		
I make choices every day that foster my physical well-being.		

From *The Onward Workbook: Daily Activities to Cultivate Your Emotional Resilience and Thrive* by Elena Aguilar. Copyright © 2018 by Elena Aguilar. Reproduced by permission.

I understand how my physical well-being affects my emotional well-being.	◯	◯
I understand what martyrdom looks and sounds like and how it undermines well-being. I avoid casting myself as a martyr.	◯	◯
I can say no to other people so that I can take care of myself.	◯	◯
I understand that perfectionism can undermine my self-care.	◯	◯
I understand that having a positive self-perception helps me care for myself and cultivate resilience.	◯	◯
I have an awareness of how our social, political, and economic history impacts my ability to care for myself.	◯	◯

Listening to Your Body

Sit for three to five minutes with your eyes closed and say this to yourself: *Body, I'm here with an open mind wanting to hear what you have to say. I'm listening. What would you like me to know?*

If you notice your mind drifting, just bring it back to this question and say it again to yourself. Try asking different parts of your body this question: *Shoulders, what do you want me to know? Stomach, what do you want me to know?* And so on.

Afterward, draw an outline of your body and speech bubbles near the parts that spoke to you. What did those parts say? Write the words in the speech bubbles.

What's My Gap?

Here's why I think we don't take care of ourselves:

- We're missing information that might convince us to take care of our bodies. Let's call this a **knowledge gap**. Sometimes we hear new information (or even something we've heard before) and it jolts us into behavior change.
- We don't have the ability to do it. We want to eat better, but where do we start? What exactly do we do? We all have **skill gaps** of different sizes. Self-care is learned, and sometimes instruction catapults us down a healthier path.
- We don't really think we need to take care of ourselves. This is a **will gap**.
- Deep down in our psyches, we don't think we deserve to take care of ourselves. We feel that our value is tied to our output and that if we don't work hard, people won't respect us, like us, love us, or want us. Our expectations for ourselves are astronomical, and we are never doing enough, so how could we possibly stop now? We don't say no to anyone; we take on too much work and overcommit. This is an **emotional intelligence gap**, because valuing self is at the center of emotional intelligence.

When you read these descriptions, what comes up for you?

Which gaps do you think you have? Which gap is the biggest?

How might you start to close one of those gaps?

Dream

Here's yet another reason why sleep is so important: Dreams play a key role in our emotional well-being. Sure, you can learn from your dreams, and perhaps you have brilliant ideas when you're dreaming. Dreaming can improve creative problem solving, say the experts. But the latest research from neuroscientists on the purpose of dreams closely links our emotional health and what happens when we sleep.

What they've found is that dreaming that occurs during REM sleep appears to take the painful sting out of difficult, even traumatic, emotional episodes experienced during the day, offering emotional resolution when you awake the next morning. Here's the fascinating science: REM sleep is the only time when our brain is completely devoid of the anxiety-triggering molecule noradrenaline. At the same time, when we dream, key emotional and memory-related structures of the brain are reactivated. This means that our memory can process the emotions in a brain free of a key stress chemical—in a calm environment. According to neuroscientist Matthew Walker (author of *Why We Sleep,* 2017), dreaming is like overnight therapy. Dreams help us take the sting out of painful emotional experiences during the hours we are asleep so that we can learn from them and move on with our lives.

Do you remember your dreams? Some tips for remembering them: Tell yourself before you go to sleep that you want to remember your dreams; let yourself emerge from unconsciousness in the morning slowly—keeping your eyes closed as you wake up and staying in that semiconscious state for as long as possible; and as soon as you are fully awake, jot down anything you remember about your dreams. Do this for a few days and you'll be more likely to recall your dreams.

When you wake up tomorrow morning, capture whatever you remember about your dreams here. Do they give you any insight into the emotional issues you're dealing with? What can you learn from them?

Self-Care Origin Stories

When you were a child, how did you see the adults around you taking care of themselves? How did your parents or guardians care for themselves?

Where do you think your beliefs and values about self-care come from? Which experiences have informed those values?

Are there any beliefs about self-care that you inherited from your family or that you've absorbed over the years that you want to give up? Which ones?

When You Are in Self-Care Crisis

Do you feel as though you're falling apart and can't figure out how to return to the classroom (or office) tomorrow? Here's an intervention plan that has pulled many educators back from the edge. You'll need to do some of these things every day for a week in order to feel better; then, once you're out of crisis mode, you can make a self-care improvement plan.

Seven Interventions

1. Sleep. Even if you won't be fully ready for tomorrow or your emails go unanswered, go to sleep. Aim to sleep for 30 minutes longer tonight than your average of the past three nights.
2. Ask for help. Say, "I'm having a really hard time right now. I'm not sure what to do, but I know I need to make some changes to the way I'm caring for myself. Could you help me figure this out?" And then make a couple of specific requests, such as:
   - "Could you take care of the kids so I can go to bed early?"
   - "Could you make me lunch tomorrow?"
   - "Please call my doctor and get me an appointment as soon as possible."
   If you can't think of what to ask for, say: "What do you think you could do to help me right now? I'm so exhausted I don't know what to ask for."
3. Complete the activity "Tracking Exhaustion" for a week.
4. Offer yourself the advice you'd give your best friend if you saw him or her in the state you are in. What would you tell your best friend to do? Heed that advice.
5. Take a one-minute break every hour and do this: Sit down, close your eyes, and visualize the tension and stress in your body pouring out of your hands. Take slow, deep breaths. Visualize your feet as portals to rejuvenating energy, and imagine energy surging up through your body from your feet.
6. Take a daily 20-minute walk outside, ideally in the sun.
7. Take one "next step" each day to initiate bigger change. Make a doctor appointment, buy vitamins, sign up for an exercise class, make a plan with a friend to go hiking, stock your refrigerator with nutrient-dense foods, download podcasts about healthy living, and so on. (See "Sixty-Five Ways to Care for Yourself" for more ideas.)

Tracking Exhaustion

Using a 1–10 scale, track your fatigue this week (1 = Very low fatigue/high energy; 10 = Very high fatigue/low energy). If possible, jot down your rating in the moment (in the morning, around noon, and in the evening), as opposed to at the end of the day in retrospect.

	Morning	Noon	Evening
Monday			
Tuesday			
Wednesday			
Thursday			
Friday			

If you find this useful, you might also consider tracking your exhaustion across a month. It can help you see patterns.

When you feel really tired, it can be hard to accurately assess how tired you are. Allocating a numeric value to your exhaustion can help you gain perspective and insight into your physical and emotional experiences.

After a week: What did you learn by tracking your exhaustion?

What implications are there for action?

Keep a Food Diary

I know you might want to skip this activity. I know this is going to bring up a lot. But do it anyway. Please! I really want you to become more resilient, to feel happier and more fulfilled every day, but if you aren't nourishing your body in the way it needs, you're not going to feel great. Keeping a food diary can be a first step toward making changes. You can do it here in the space provided, or somewhere else. You don't need to share it with anyone—so be completely honest. What you do with the data you gather is up to you.

	Breakfast	Lunch	Dinner	Beverages
Monday				
Tuesday				
Wednesday				
Thursday				
Friday				

From *The Onward Workbook: Daily Activities to Cultivate Your Emotional Resilience and Thrive* by Elena Aguilar. Copyright © 2018 by Elena Aguilar. Reproduced by permission.

What, if anything, do you want to change about your eating habits next week? What are three small shifts you can make?

Reflecting on Martyrdom

What came up for you when you read the section on martyrdom in Chapter 6 of *Onward*? What thoughts, connections, and questions arose?

When, if ever, have you felt a tendency toward martyrdom? What do you think were the underlying feelings you were experiencing?

What are the traits and qualities that you most admire in other educators? Which characteristics of your colleagues would you like to emulate?

If Your Body Could Talk

We make our bodies work so hard. Day after day, we ask them to do too much, and we rarely thank them. What would you like to say to different parts of your body? What would your body like to say to you? I've offered you some parts that you might want to talk to; feel free to add others. In order to hear what your body wants to say to you, you may need to sit quietly and listen. Your body might be shy about talking, especially if you've ignored it a lot.

Here's what my feet would like to say to me: *Elena, we love it when you wear wide, flat shoes. We love letting our toes spread out and wiggle.* And here's what I want to say to my feet: *Thank you for putting up with uncomfortable shoes. You do a great job of keeping my whole body moving. I'm going to lessen how often you're constrained in squishy shoes.*

Body Part *A little sketch of the part is welcome.*	What It Wants to Say to Me	What I Want to Say to It
Feet		
Neck		
Lungs		
Knees		

Digestive System		

Inside World and Outside World

This resilience-boosting idea comes to you with inspiration from Marie Kondo, the Japanese organizing expert and author of *The Life Changing Magic of Tidying Up* (2011). Kondo suggests that you pick up every object in your home and ask yourself if it gives you pleasure. If the answer is no, you thank it for having been in your life, and you send it off to its next life (donation or the dumpster).

Transferring this lesson to school is tricky: Don't try picking up the curriculum guide for the new math program and contemplating whether it gives you joy; but at home, Kondo's approach does work magic.

What I appreciate about Kondo's book is that she reminds us of how our emotional and mental well-being is connected to our physical space. When your classroom or office is a messy, cluttered, uninspiring place, your mind will have a much harder time getting settled, organized, and clear; therefore, your emotions might be unsettled.

Cleanup: Day 1—Toss It
- Today, after school, while you listen to good music or an interesting podcast, toss, recycle, and throw out as much as possible *in 15 minutes*. It's not the day to organize or clean; this is just tossing-time. Getting rid of clutter will make you feel better. You may need to repeat this Toss It step over several days.

Cleanup: Day 2—Organize
- On another day, spend *30 minutes* organizing papers, materials, supplies, student work, and so on. This step might also need to be repeated.

Cleanup: Day 3—Beautify
- Make your space more beautiful in some way—decorate, bring in a potted plant, post a photo of you and your dog, and so on. Again, limit your time to *15–30 minutes*.

Cleaning regularly in small chunks is key to organization. It's also realistic for people with busy lives. Here's why I suggest you limit your time: If you spend a whole afternoon cleaning or organizing, it's possible that you'll feel accomplished and that you'll love the feeling of an organized classroom, but it's also possible that you'll feel as though you've lost a huge chunk of time or that you'll need another huge chunk of time if things get disorderly again. You might leave late, heading home to plan for the next day or do whatever other work you need to do, having skipped your afternoon walk and healthy dinner, and you might feel that cleaning your room should not have been your priority that day.

From *The Onward Workbook: Daily Activities to Cultivate Your Emotional Resilience and Thrive* by Elena Aguilar. Copyright © 2018 by Elena Aguilar. Reproduced by permission.

Binge cleaning can be rewarding, and sometimes you need to do it, but making organization a smaller-scale, routine habit is more sustainable.

Make a Plan

Cleanup Stage	Date I'll Do It	What I'll Do	What I Accomplished
Toss It			
Organize			
Beautify			

Try Something New

Part 1: Planning

In my mid-40s, on a quest for exercise that I might love, I tried boxing. I was surprised that I liked it as much as I do, given that I have negative associations with boxing because of its violence. But I love that I can release so much energy through boxing—and I don't fight with people.

This month, I want you to try a new physical activity. In part 1 of this exercise, you'll plan. Then go and implement it. In part 2, reflect on the experience. What's a physical activity you've been curious about trying? What kind of physical activity feels as though it would be a stretch for you to try? Rock climbing, yoga, running a 10K, salsa dancing?

What would it take for you to do this activity? How can you make it happen?

How would you feel if you learned how to do this activity—or even if you just tried it once?

What could you do to take the first step toward trying this activity? Sign up for a class? Find a video online? Ask a friend to join you?

Take this first step now.

From *The Onward Workbook: Daily Activities to Cultivate Your Emotional Resilience and Thrive* by Elena Aguilar. Copyright © 2018 by Elena Aguilar. Reproduced by permission.

Part 2: Reflection

What did it feel like to try a new physical activity? Can you name the feelings that came up?

What did you learn about yourself?

What else would you like to try?

Bonus points if you include a photo in this workbook of yourself trying something new!

Charting Your Self-Care Story

Chart the history of your health efforts showing high and low points across the last 10 or 20 years of your life. (You can go back further if you want.) Label those points. Most likely, you'll see ups and downs.

What trends do you see? What are the implications for your self-care going forward?

Reduce Your Sugar Intake

Your task for this week is to pay attention to how much sugar you eat. Read ingredient labels. Pay attention to how sugar makes you feel. And see if you can reduce your intake just a little bit.

First, Some Information

Even if you don't think of yourself as someone who consumes a lot of sugar, you're most likely ingesting more than you think. Sugar, which also goes by the names glucose, fructose, honey, and corn syrup, is in 74% of packaged foods, including ketchup, pasta sauce, flavored yogurt, and salad dressing.

When sugar hits our tongue, our brain releases a surge of feel-good hormones, including dopamine, which makes us feel happy. As the brain's reward system is repeatedly activated by sugar, we become tolerant of it and caught in a cycle of cravings—we become addicted to it. We crave those dopamine hits and will suffer withdrawal symptoms if we give up sugar. (This process is physiologically similar to opioid addiction.)

Imagine a five-pound sack of sugar. Now imagine 30 of those sacks on your kitchen table—that's the amount of sugar that the average American eats in one year—an impressive 150 pounds of sugar. The toxic effects of sugar on the body and brain are becoming more widely known. Consider the following:

- Eating sugar causes blood sugar levels to spike and then plummet. The inevitable crash after drinking a soda or eating cookies can make you feel irritable, tired, foggy headed, or depressed.
- Too much sugar in your blood throws off your neurotransmitters. Neurotransmitters such as dopamine, serotonin, and norepinephrine are critical to regulating mood and energy. Serotonin, for example, makes us feel good and regulates sleep. It is what antidepressants work to boost. Sugary and high-carbohydrate foods stimulate serotonin production, which is why starches are known as comfort foods. But if you eat too many carbs, your serotonin pathways are constantly overworked, which eventually depletes the supply.
- Sugar consumption depresses the immune system. Sugar creates a 40–50% drop in the ability of white blood cells to kill bacteria and germs in our bodies for up to five hours.

Did you know: Political forces and big money have shaped in unseen ways what we eat. In the 1960s, the sugar industry paid scientists to downplay the link between heart disease and sugar, and to make fats the culprit. Fats, such as butter and healthy oils, were blamed for all health problems, and people were told to eliminate them from their diets. The sugar industry turned around and offered low-fat, high-sugar foods and made a lot of money. But, as you may know, many fats—such as the omega fatty acids found in olive oil, coconut oil, fish, avocado, and nuts—not only are healthy but also provide your body and brain with essential nutrition.

Tracking Sugar Consumption

Over the course of the next week, use this table to track your sugar consumption. While you do this, practice self-compassion—this isn't an opportunity for self-shaming or self-criticism—it's an opportunity to notice what you consume and how it makes you feel.

Day	Food I Ate That Contained Sugar	Observations on My Energy and Mood	What I Could Reduce, Substitute, or Cut Out
1			
2			
3			

(continued)

From *The Onward Workbook: Daily Activities to Cultivate Your Emotional Resilience and Thrive* by Elena Aguilar. Copyright © 2018 by Elena Aguilar. Reproduced by permission.

4		
5		
6		
7		

Planning for Better Sleep

Adults should sleep eight to nine hours per night. Unless you're living with a baby, chances are that getting more sleep is firmly within your influence and control.

Here are some tricks to better sleep:

- Go to bed 30 minutes earlier. Over the course of a few weeks, work yourself up to eight to nine hours per night.
- Don't drink anything with caffeine in the six hours before you want to sleep. Alcohol also disrupts sleep cycles; you might fall asleep easily, but it can wake you up later in the night.
- Relax before getting into bed. Try a warm bath, shower, or 10 minutes of meditation.
- Turn off screens an hour before going to sleep. The light from your devices obstructs your body's production of melatonin, which helps govern your internal body clock and regulates your sleep cycle. Or if you don't want to give up the screen, see whether you can put it in "night" mode, which switches from blue light to a warmer, darker palette that cues our brains to decrease activity.
- Keep devices out of your bedroom. If you can't do that, at least put them on the Do Not Disturb mode so a midnight text won't wake you up.
- Keep your bedroom dark. Remove devices with lights. Or wear a sleep mask.
- Keep your bedroom cool.
- Reserve your bed only for sleep and sex. And maybe reading for pleasure. Leave your laptop and curriculum guide out of it.

If you're not getting the sleep you want and you've tried all of the suggestions here, explore remedies for insomnia and talk to your doctor to rule out more serious physical issues.

Take Action

Identify action steps: Which of the things on this list could you try? Put a star next to those items.

From *The Onward Workbook: Daily Activities to Cultivate Your Emotional Resilience and Thrive* by Elena Aguilar. Copyright © 2018 by Elena Aguilar. Reproduced by permission.

Say goodbye: Getting more sleep will likely mean giving something up: TV time, social media browsing, wine in the evening, or working until the wee hours of the morning. What will you have to give up in order to sleep more?

Imagine the potential: What will you gain from more sleep? How could more sleep improve your life? Strengthen your resilience? Make you more effective at your work?

Plan: Make a list of the steps you'll take to get better sleep, in the order in which you'll do them. This might involve things like, *Find an app to dim my screens, buy dark shades for my windows, no more coffee after 3:00 p.m.,* and so on.

Be specific: What will your evening need to look like to ensure that you can go to sleep 30 minutes earlier tonight? Do you need to eat dinner earlier, get the kids to bed earlier, or turn off the TV by 9:00 p.m.? Create a plan for getting more sleep—and plan backwards from the total number of minutes you want to spend in bed.

Enlist support: Whose help do you need in order to get more sleep? Are there things that someone else needs to do or could do to help you execute your sleep plan? Identify these people and script what you'll say to them. For example, maybe you need to ask your kids to help with kitchen cleanup, or you need to tell your staff that you don't respond to email after 6:00 p.m. so that you can get through evening routines as scheduled.

Now, Go to Sleep Already!

After a good night's sleep, jot down some notes here. How did you feel in the morning? What did you notice about your mood and energy during the day?

What would it take for you to continue this healthy sleeping routine?

How to Get More Exercise

What are all the excuses you make for not exercising? Be honest. Write them down:

Here are three ways to make it more likely that you'll exercise:

- **Make it easy.** What would make it easier for you to exercise? Put your shoes next to your bed. Rent a locker so you can shower at the gym and go straight to school afterward. Find an exercise class close to school or home. Buy a used stationary bike on Craigslist. Do activities for which you don't need a lot of accessories or ideal weather or anything else that can become an excuse for not exercising.
- **Create external accountability.** Make a plan with a friend who will get irritated if you flake. Hire a trainer for a few sessions to get you going. Pay for a series of classes—you may be more motivated if you've paid for something and don't want to waste your money by skipping out.
- **Anticipate challenges and setbacks.** How will you exercise when obstacles get in the way: When the weather prevents you from running? Or you go on vacation? Or your favorite Pilates teacher leaves the studio where she teaches? Or you get sick and then even when you're better you've lost the routine and don't want to put those boxing gloves back on?

Create a plan to get more exercise. What do you need to do?

Movie Time!

These movies connect with this chapter's theme of self-care, specifically the value of good nutrition. Give yourself a break from reading and enjoy one.

Chef's Table. This is a Netflix series that is as much about people and their lives as it is about food. It's a beautiful meditation on what we eat, how we think about food, and the role that meals and eating play in our lives and society. This series is a delightful, uplifting treat that makes you think about what you eat, as well as about your purpose and passions in life. Season 3, episode 6, about chef Virgilio Martinez in Peru, is one of the most stunning documentaries I've seen. It evoked such strong feelings in me of joy, awe, and appreciation that I even shed tears.

Cooked. Michael Pollan is a writer whose book *Cooked* was turned into a fascinating Netflix documentary that explores different methods of cooking and their evolutionary and cultural impacts on humankind. This four-part series was filmed around the world. It's part history and part anthropology, and will most likely make you want to cook a wholesome, delicious meal for dinner. There are many elements of this documentary that would also be great to share with students in many grades and courses.

Supersize Me. If you eat a lot of fast food and want a jolt to reduce your intake, watch *Supersize Me.* In this 2004 documentary, Morgan Spurlock eats only McDonald's food three times a day for 30 days. The diet wreaks havoc on his physical health in terms of weight gain, high cholesterol, and high blood pressure, and it seriously affects his mental health. By the middle of the month of this fast-food diet, Spurlock suffered from massive headaches and depression, and he experienced long-term physical damage.

Self-Esteem Reflection

Mark an X along the line to indicate how strongly you disagree or agree with the statement.

	Strongly Disagree Strongly Agree
I think that overall, people find me boring to talk to.	
If I left any of my communities, people wouldn't care.	
I feel as though I let down the people I care about.	
I will never amount to anything significant.	
I have what it takes to socialize with others.	
I often feel like a failure.	
It's important to me to be liked by everyone I meet.	
I deserve to be loved and respected.	
When people point out my mistakes, I feel as though they're degrading me.	
I'm not confident that I've done a good job unless someone else points it out to me.	
I'm afraid of being rejected by my friends.	
I like myself.	
I modify my personality, appearance, or opinions in order to be accepted by others.	
Before making any decision, I ask others if I'm doing the right thing.	
When someone rejects my ideas, I feel insulted.	

From *The Onward Workbook: Daily Activities to Cultivate Your Emotional Resilience and Thrive* by Elena Aguilar. Copyright © 2018 by Elena Aguilar. Reproduced by permission.

The purpose of this activity is to provoke reflection and insight into your ability to deal with rejection and your general level of self-esteem. Which feelings came up for you as you did this activity?

What did you notice about the patterns in your responses?

What do your responses make you wonder about? What would you like to further investigate as it relates to your self-esteem and self-perception?

How Do I Perceive Myself?

Fill in the column below with **5 to 10** strengths and **5 to 10** weaknesses or areas for growth as they relate to your work and role (as a teacher, coach, administrator, and so on).

My Strengths	My Areas for Growth or Weaknesses

From *The Onward Workbook: Daily Activities to Cultivate Your Emotional Resilience and Thrive* by Elena Aguilar. Copyright © 2018 by Elena Aguilar. Reproduced by permission.

What do you notice about your strengths and weaknesses? What is the relationship between them?

How did it feel to create this list? What came up for you in the process or when looking at it?

What are the stories you tell yourself about your strengths and weaknesses? For example, an area of weakness for me is to establish clear boundaries around my time. The story I tell is that I do this because I haven't yet learned how and when to say no—not because I don't value myself.

What implications for action are revealed by this list? What are you inclined to do about your strengths or weaknesses?

The Best Homemade Chai

The following recipe for chai (spiced tea) is delicious and also a miracle elixir when you feel as though you're about to get sick. Cinnamon, ginger, and turmeric have anti-inflammatory properties, and coconut oil has good cholesterol. Read up on these herbs and spices if you want more information about how good they are for you. This recipe was shared by the writer Elizabeth Gilbert on her Facebook page some years ago. I've modified it a bit, and you should feel free to do so also until it tastes just as you like!

Bring 3 cups of water to boil.
Add:

- 2 to 3 cinnamon sticks
- 1 to 2 inches of diced raw ginger
- 1 teaspoon of whole black pepper corns
- 8 to 10 pods of cardamom, crushed

Bring to a boil and simmer, covered, for about 10 minutes.
Add 1–2 black tea bags if you want caffeine. This tea is just as delicious without black tea.
Simmer for 5 minutes.
Put the following into a big mug:

- A tablespoon of honey
- A teaspoon of turmeric powder
- A tablespoon of coconut oil

Take a few tablespoons of the chai, put them in the mug, and whisk until the honey, turmeric powder, and coconut oil are all blended.
Fill your mug about three-quarters full of hot strained chai.
Heat up or froth some milk or milk-like substance (almond milk or coconut milk are great).
Top off the mug with the hot milk and stir.
Sprinkle with cinnamon.

How Do Others Experience Me?

This exercise needs you to be very brave. You're going to ask others about their perception of your strengths and areas for growth—professionally and/or personally (that's up to you). You can be specific by asking, "What do you think are my top strengths and areas for growth?" or you can ask for more general perceptions.

Identify a few people in your professional and/or personal life with whom you feel somewhat safe and comfortable. However, in order to get useful feedback, you will need to cross over into the realm of not-so-safe and not-very-comfortable. Ask your best friend at work for feedback, and also the teacher on your team to whom you don't feel as close.

Tips
- Be truly open to feedback and encourage others to give it to you. Let them know that you're okay with hearing whatever they want to say.
- It can be hard to get honest feedback, so you might need to read between the lines— what didn't they say?
- If feedback really stings, there might be some real truth to it. However, you can also dismiss whatever you want. It's up to you what you do with the feedback you gather.
- Stay aware of your feelings as they surface, and consider opportunities to unpack and explore those feelings if they feel especially uncomfortable. What are your feelings trying to tell you?

Jot down a summary of what you hear:

Exploring Self-Confidence

How effective do you believe you are in handling and performing specific tasks? Self-efficacy plays an important part in determining your general level of self-confidence. Confidence is a general belief in oneself. By contrast, self-efficacy is the belief in one's capabilities to achieve something specific.

When you feel efficacious, you think, feel, and behave in a way that contributes to and reinforces your success and improves your well-being. You view obstacles as challenges to overcome, and you aren't afraid to face new things. You recover quickly from setbacks, because you view failure more as a result of external circumstances than internal weaknesses. In general, believing in your abilities affects your motivation, choices, determination, and resilience.

Reflect on the following prompts and indicate how you feel about the statement. Be honest with yourself. You don't need to share this with anyone. The purpose of this reflection is to gain insight into yourself.

Statement	Not at all	Rarely	Some-times	Often	Very often
I feel positive and energized about life.					
If something looks hard, I avoid doing it.					
I keep trying, even after others have given up.					
I do what I think is "expected" of me, rather than what I believe is "right."					
I handle new situations with relative comfort and ease.					

(continued)

I achieve the goals I set for myself.					
If I work hard to solve a problem, I can find the answer.					
People give me positive feedback on my work and achievements.					
I relate to people who work very hard and still don't achieve their goals.					
I have to experience success early when I'm trying something new or I won't continue.					
When I overcome an obstacle, I think about what I've learned.					
I believe that if I work hard, I'll achieve my goals.					
I have contact with people who have similar skills and experience and whom I consider successful.					
When I face difficulty, I feel hopeless and negative.					

After reflecting on these statements, do you feel that your self-confidence is strong and solid? Developing well? Or perhaps low? What does your gut tell you about your level of self-confidence after reflecting on these statements?

Do any of the statements feel contextual? That is, are there contexts in which you feel more confident than in others? Why do you think that is?

Along the same lines, can you draw a connection between your level of self-care and your confidence? For example, I know I feel much more confident after a good night's sleep and after talking with my best friend.

Fake It Until You Make It

The suggestion that you fake something until you make it is scientifically backed. If we tell ourselves we can do something or be a certain way (within a range of possibility, of course), we are more likely to believe it and be able to do it. For example, I can tell myself that I am going to get a lot out of our PD session this afternoon, that I'm going to find it interesting and useful, that I'm going to enjoy the opportunity to connect with my colleagues. I can tell myself that even though I'll be tired, I'll be glad I went. As I walk into the staff room for this meeting, if I keep telling myself this, my mind will be primed to have this experience.

This practice is a little tricky, because appearing disingenuous can have negative consequences. If you decide you want to "fake it" until you actually like an annoying student, that student may perceive your inauthenticity and trust you less. So when you explore this practice, find the edge of the fakeness that feels as though it could possibly be real—and only try faking something that you suspect could one day actually be true, such as that you could indeed appreciate the PD session or could like an annoying student.

What behavior or disposition could you fake a little bit today? Could you fake enthusiasm about going to school? Or fake self-confidence? You might look at the "Habits and Dispositions of Emotionally Resilient Educators" following the Introduction in *Onward* for ideas.

Identify a few moments today when you might fake a disposition or behavior. Perhaps when you walk into school and greet a particular staff member who is often cranky? Or when you see your department chair in the weekly meeting?

Jot down a plan for faking it today here:

Healthy Eating Reminders

Here are some reminders for healthful eating:

- Eat every two to three hours to stabilize your blood sugar. Going too long between meals sends blood sugar plummeting, engaging the stress response and causing mood swings.
- Eat breakfast, including a high-quality protein. Two boiled eggs is a fantastic teacher breakfast!
- Reduce or cut out processed foods such as boxed, canned, and packaged foods. If you don't know what an ingredient is, you probably shouldn't eat it.
- Reduce or limit sugar, soda, and hydrogenated and partially hydrogenated fats and oils.
- If you eat high-carb foods, eat them with fiber, fat, or protein, which slows the release of glucose into the bloodstream.
- Drink water. When researching the effects of dehydration, scientists at the University of Connecticut found that in addition to causing headaches and feelings of fatigue, dehydration prompted mood changes. Women, in particular, felt anxious and unable to concentrate when they were dehydrated. Drink water before you get thirsty, ideally around two quarts a day.
- Eat mostly whole foods—organic fruits and vegetables, some grains, wild fish, grass-fed meats, and raw nuts and seeds.

Which of these do you already incorporate into your life sometimes? Which do you incorporate regularly?

Which of your eating habits do you want to change?

Choose one habit to start changing. Make a small change. What is it?

Make a list of things you like to eat that are somewhat healthy for you. I keep the following list of Things to Eat because sometimes I just forget what's good for me—especially when I'm tired.

Elena's List of Things to Eat
- Blueberries—in smoothies.
- Japanese sweet potatoes with butter and cinnamon. This is comfort food.
- Almonds. I toss sacks of them in every bag, drawer, and cubby.
- Quinoa. This is a super-high protein, not actually a grain, but it kind of looks, tastes, and works like a grain.
- Avocados—which have super-good oils.
- Sardines, kippers, and other little fish. These have oils that we really need without the bad stuff that's found too often in tuna and salmon.
- Coconut oil. It's yummy and also contains a good oil—your brain needs these good oils for optimal functioning.
- Kale and all leafy greens, but you already know these are good for you, right?
- Beets. They do good things for your blood.
- Bone broth. Super-rich nutrients for your gut.

Make your list here (or somewhere that you can easily access it):

Loving Your Adrenals

In the middle of your lower back, resting on top of your kidneys, are your adrenal glands. Probably unbeknownst to you, the adrenals play a key role in the physiology of your emotional resilience. They produce important hormones, including adrenaline, dopamine, and cortisol, which regulate sleep cycles and energy. You need these hormones to feel good and manage stress. Your adrenals also play a critical role in controlling blood sugar, burning protein and fat, and regulating blood pressure.

When we encounter stress, our adrenal glands release hormones that increase our strength, focus, and awareness and help us do things such as managing a lively group of kindergarteners. Cortisol, the stress hormone, also has an anti-inflammatory effect that helps regulate your immune system. Inflammation is typically a sign that your body is fighting an infection, and cortisol prevents this reaction from getting out of control. Maintaining a balanced cortisol level—not too low and not too high—is an important part of your health. If stress repeatedly elevates your cortisol levels, your immune system may be weakened.

When the adrenals get worn out, they don't release the necessary hormones, and you may feel apathetic, depressed, irritable, anxious, and tired. To counter the adrenal glands' exhaustion, we crave stimulants. Caffeine and sugar can provide a quick boost, but over time, as most of us know, these stimulants have less and less of an effect.

So how do you care for your adrenals? If you suspect that they might be depleted, see a doctor. The best way to test for adrenal fatigue is with a saliva test. You might be amazed to find that if your adrenals aren't working well, you don't feel physically or emotionally well—and that pretty quickly, with medical care, your condition can change. For basic care of your adrenals, sleep, eat well, meditate, take a walk, and relax.

Just for fun, write a love note to your adrenal glands here. You've probably never appreciated them as they deserve to be appreciated.

Google "adrenal glands" so that you can see what they look like (they're one of the only organs in our bodies that isn't symmetrical—each one is a different shape). Then draw a little sketch of them here.

Who Needs to Yell at You?

Sometimes I think we need someone to yell at us and insist that we take care of ourselves. If you need someone to yell at you, give that person permission to do so. I've asked my son to yell at me to do my stretching if he sees me skip a day. (Our house is small enough that he knows when I don't do my morning stretches.) I gave him the words that I know I'll hear: "Mama, when you don't stretch, your back hurts. Get on your mat and stretch!" Who needs to yell at you? Whose permission do you need?

What would you like this person to say to you? Write it here, as if you were transcribing what he or she is saying. If you're inspired, you could also draw a picture of the person, with his or her words inside a speech bubble. You can see my example.

From The Onward Workbook: Daily Activities to Cultivate Your Emotional Resilience and Thrive by Elena Aguilar. Copyright © 2018 by Elena Aguilar. Reproduced by permission.

Maybe you don't need someone to yell at you. Maybe you just need someone to kindly remind you of your commitment and reason for self-care. Who could you ask to play a supporting role in your commitment to self-care? What would you like to ask this person to do? Be specific in that request.

Now, call or text this person. Make your request.

From *The Onward Workbook: Daily Activities to Cultivate Your Emotional Resilience and Thrive* by Elena Aguilar. Copyright © 2018 by Elena Aguilar. Reproduced by permission.

Reflecting on Perfectionism

What came up for you when you read the section in *Onward* about perfectionism?

Who do you know, yourself included, who may have a tendency toward perfectionism? What makes you think this?

What would you like to say to that person (who could be you) about your concern with his or her tendency toward perfectionism?

Part 1: Planning for Self-Care

At any point in this month of focusing on self-care, make a plan for a week of tending to your physical self. Be ambitious in your goals and plan, but also be realistic. There's no need to set yourself up for failure. However, I encourage you to see what happens if you devote as much time and energy as possible to your physical well-being for one week.

Step 1: Identify Goals

Create three self-care goals for the week. Examples: Sleep eight hours a night, eat a nutritious breakfast every morning, walk 20 minutes per day, eat a salad every day, drink only one cup of coffee per day. Be specific.

Goal 1:

Goal 2:

Goal 3:

Step 2: Make a Plan

What do you need to do in order to reach these goals? For example, if you want to eat a nutritious breakfast, you might need to do some shopping. If you plan to walk each day, you may need to throw your walking shoes in your car so that you can go straight from work. For each goal, identify the action steps that will lead you to accomplish it.

Goal 1
Action steps:

Goal 2
Action steps:

From *The Onward Workbook: Daily Activities to Cultivate Your Emotional Resilience and Thrive* by Elena Aguilar. Copyright © 2018 by Elena Aguilar. Reproduced by permission.

Goal 3
Action steps:

Now, go to your calendar and schedule these activities. Print out a copy of your calendar for the week and tape it in this chapter. Then heed your calendar. Do what it tells you to do, no matter what. Just for one week. At the end of the week, complete the reflection in part 2.

Part 2: Reflecting on a Week of Self-Care

Which of your goals did you accomplish?

What did it feel like to accomplish these goals?

What was challenging about accomplishing your goals?

What made it possible to accomplish your goals?

Which of your goals or activities seemed to have the greatest positive impact on your well-being?

What did you notice about your emotions and mood this week?

Which of these goals or activities do you want to continue next week? What do you need to do to make that happen?

Sixty-Five Ways to Care for Yourself

Need some new ideas for ways to care for yourself? Here are 65! Review them and check the ones that you sometimes do, and circle the numbers of others that you'd like to do. Flag this page and return to it when you want or need to.

1. Lie on the floor on your back and close your eyes.
2. Take 10 deep, slow breaths. Breath in for a count of five, hold for two, and exhale for a count of seven.
3. Find a recipe for kale chips and make a batch.
4. Give your feet an Epsom salts bath.
5. Start a 21-day liver detox cleanse.
6. Wake up at dawn to see the sunrise.
7. Go to a community acupuncture clinic and get a treatment.
8. Browse the listening library of Sounds True (www.soundstrue.com) and find something to listen to.
9. Run really fast for five minutes.
10. Walk slowly for 20 minutes.
11. Watch a funny movie or comedy special.
12. Listen to a piece of music that you loved when you were in high school.
13. Get a meditation coloring book and color.
14. Clean out a closet or messy drawer.
15. Make chai tea from scratch (see "The Best Homemade Chai" in this chapter).
16. Call an old friend with whom you haven't spoken for a while.
17. Take a bath.
18. Take a hot shower.
19. Walk around your neighborhood to notice colors and smell the flowers.
20. Find a photo of yourself at a time when you felt really content. Print it (if necessary) and put it somewhere you'll see every day.
21. Eat a piece of fruit slowly and mindfully.
22. Drink lots of water. Add a squirt of lemon or lime.
23. Discover new music you love. Play it loud.
24. Lie on the floor and stretch.
25. Sit in the sun for 10 minutes.
26. Hug a tree. Or just sit next to one.
27. Draw a tree. Or paint one.
28. Collect leaves from a tree and make them into a sculpture.

29. Watch the movie *Rivers and Tides.*
30. Stand or sit without shoes, with your feet and body in contact with the earth.
31. Have sex.
32. Learn about amino acids and consider taking some.
33. Eat oatmeal, with blueberries and almonds.
34. Smear oatmeal (or yogurt, banana, avocado, or papaya) on your face.
35. Go to an art museum. Sit in front of a piece of art for a while and just let it soak into you.
36. Find an exercise class to take. Try a new one.
37. Go to a library or local bookstore and browse a section that you usually wouldn't go into. Look at photography and art books. Check out graphic novels.
38. Get a tennis ball, put it under your neck and shoulders, and roll around on it.
39. Pet your pet (or find a pet to pet). Luxuriate in the textures of its coat and sweetness.
40. Get a manicure or pedicure.
41. Get a dry brush and brush your skin with it.
42. Make a big pot of soup that will last many days.
43. Float in a body of calm water.
44. Take a nap.
45. Go to sleep early.
46. Wake up and lie in your bed for five minutes doing nothing but feeling your body stretch and move.
47. Go to the grocery store on Sunday, buy healthy food, and make yourself lunches for the week. Or buy ready-made salads for lunch for the week. Or buy bags of pre-washed lettuce and some kind of healthy protein that you can eat for lunch.
48. Turn off notifications on your phone.
49. Spend a whole day without looking at your phone.
50. Reduce your intake of news.
51. Reduce your time spent on social media.
52. Make a date with a friend you haven't seen in a while.
53. Try a yoga, Pilates, or Qi Gong class (actually go to one—don't just follow a video).
54. If you play an instrument, play it. If you've always wanted to learn to play an instrument, get one. Find YouTube videos on how to play. Find a teacher. Play.
55. Consider going to a nutritionist, a chiropractor, a naturopath, or some kind of non-traditional healer and do some research. Find one. Make an appointment. Go.
56. Take all electronics out of your bedroom. Keep them out.
57. Get rid of things you don't need. Donate clothes. Declutter.
58. Wash your car. Or get it washed.

From *The Onward Workbook: Daily Activities to Cultivate Your Emotional Resilience and Thrive* by Elena Aguilar. Copyright © 2018 by Elena Aguilar. Reproduced by permission.

59. Make a date with a friend to do something in your area that you've never done that's outside and involves physical movement: Go kayaking, rock climbing, salsa dancing, rollerblading, ice skating, hang gliding, surfing, or jogging.
60. Walk in a neighborhood that you've never walked in.
61. Try a restaurant you've never tried.
62. Find an audiobook that relates to self-care (fiction, nonfiction) and listen to it.
63. Walk a labyrinth (see www.labyrinthsociety.org or www.labyrinthlocator.com).
64. Floss your teeth.
65. Try a floatation tank.

Can you add 15–20 of your own ideas? What are your favorite ways to take care of yourself?

A Letter to Perfectionism

Write a letter to your perfectionism, or any tendencies toward perfectionism. At the root of perfectionism is a fear of vulnerability and a fear of shame, as well as anxiety about not being accepted as you are. What do you want to say to this part of yourself?

Here's the start of my letter: *Hello, perfectionism. I'm curious about you. I'm not sure how much you live within me—sometimes I sense your presence more strongly, and other times I'm pretty sure that I'm free of you. The times when I've felt you more are when . . .*

From *The Onward Workbook: Daily Activities to Cultivate Your Emotional Resilience and Thrive* by Elena Aguilar. Copyright © 2018 by Elena Aguilar. Reproduced by permission.

Artistic Depictions of Perfectionism

Go to your preferred online search engine and look for images of perfectionism—or another term that reflects the stew of emotions that are involved in perfectionism, such as insecurity, anxiety, invulnerability (see "The Core Emotions" in Chapter 2 for these terms).

Then search for "depictions of perfectionism in art." Look closely at a few of those images. Sit with them and spend some time getting to know them. Pay attention to how they make you feel and what thoughts go through your mind.

Reflect

What do you notice in the images that come up?

What have you learned about perfectionism through doing this exploration?

How did this exploration help you understand your own experience of perfectionism?

If you'd like, print out one (or more) of the images that particularly speak to you and stick them in here.

Destination Postcard: Self-Care

What would it look and sound like if you invested deeply of your time and energy in self-care? Draw a picture of yourself with thought bubbles and labels that depict you caring for yourself in different settings.

Chapter Reflection

What were your biggest takeaways from this chapter?

Of the different activities in this chapter, which were most useful?

Which activities would you like to revisit periodically? How might you get that habit going?

What implications do the ideas in this chapter have for the work you do?

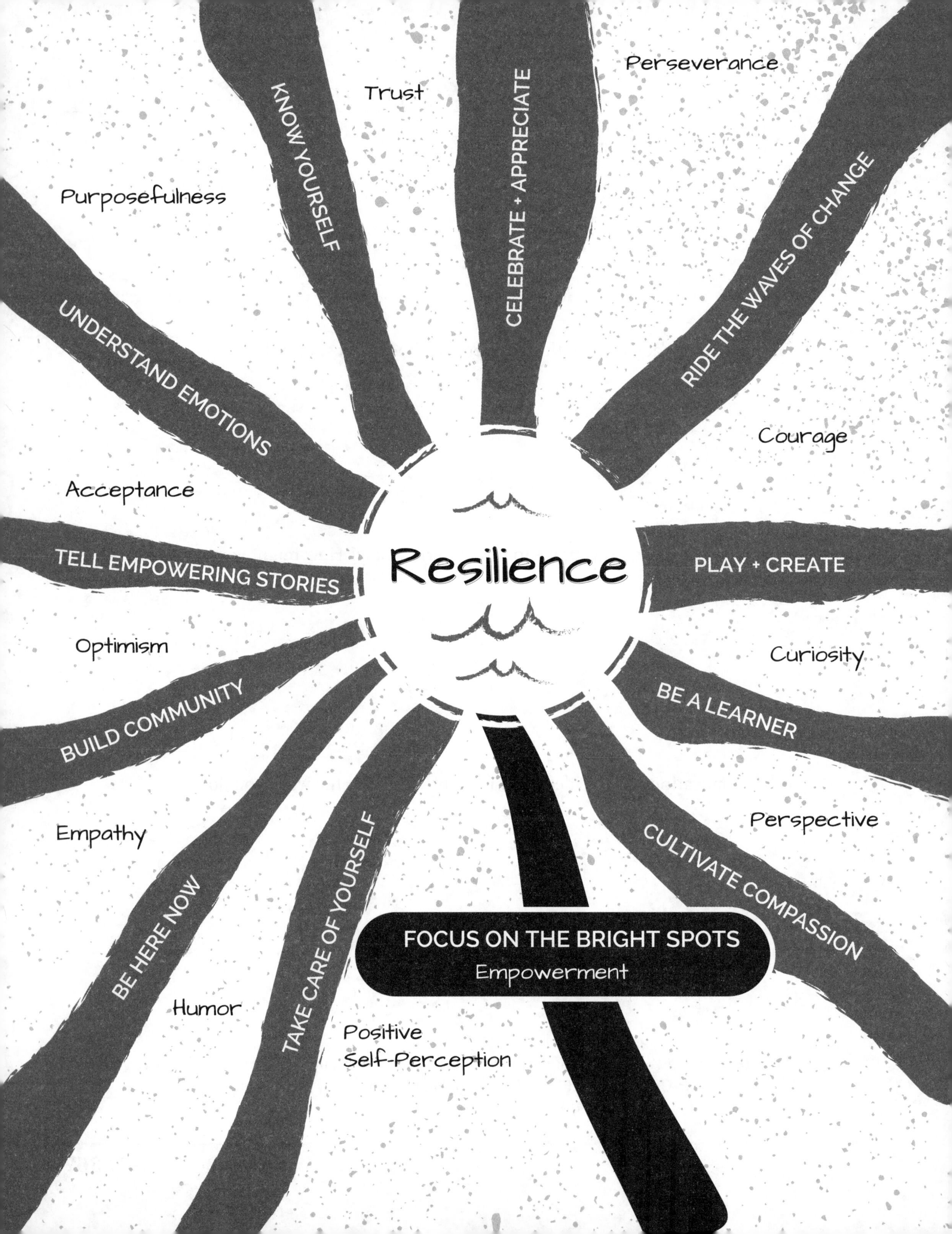
Resilience
KNOW YOURSELF
Trust
CELEBRATE + APPRECIATE
Perseverance
RIDE THE WAVES OF CHANGE
Purposefulness
UNDERSTAND EMOTIONS
Courage
Acceptance
TELL EMPOWERING STORIES
PLAY + CREATE
Optimism
Curiosity
BUILD COMMUNITY
BE A LEARNER
Empathy
Perspective
BE HERE NOW
TAKE CARE OF YOURSELF
CULTIVATE COMPASSION
FOCUS ON THE BRIGHT SPOTS
Empowerment
Humor
Positive
Self-Perception

CHAPTER 7

Focus on the Bright Spots

We can hone our attention to focus on our strengths, assets, and skills. This helps us generally feel better and enables us to respond to challenges more effectively. Focusing on strengths also boosts our levels of self-efficacy, and we feel more empowered to influence our surroundings.

December: When the days are short and you haven't recovered from the exhaustion of late fall, look for the light.

Focus on the Bright Spots:
Resilience Self-Assessment

The purpose of this self-assessment is to help you gauge the level of your resilience reservoir and to explore what might be draining or what could replenish it. The exercises that follow and the information in the corresponding chapter of *Onward* can boost your resilience by directing your attention to strengths, assets, and things that are going well.

Imagine each circle as a little *cenote* or reservoir within you, and fill it up according to how much each statement acts as a source of resilience. If you need something more concrete, imagine marks at ¼, ½, and ¾ full.

Before you start the exercises in this chapter, take this self-assessment and fill in the date. At the end of the month, take the assessment again. (You might even cover up your original markings with a strip of paper.) Is your resilience reservoir a little more full? If so, which practices do you want to keep up? If not, what else do you want to try?

Statement	Date:	Date:
I understand why a strengths-based approach helps us make behavioral changes.		
I understand why sometimes it feels hard to see the positive. I aim to do so anyway.		
I have strategies to direct my mind toward assets, what's working, and bright spots.		
When confronted by challenges, I can direct my thinking toward opportunities and possibilities rather than getting caught in a spiral of negative thinking.		

I have effective strategies to deal with strong emotions when they come up.	◯	◯
I have various ways of reflecting on what is happening, and I value the act of reflection.	◯	◯
I understand the role that sadness plays in the scope of an emotional life.	◯	◯
I feel I can make change in the areas in which I'm struggling.	◯	◯
If I'm struggling in an area, I know it's just because I haven't yet learned the skills to be successful there.	◯	◯
I feel I have a balanced view of things: I can see challenges *and* possibilities.	◯	◯

Find the Bright Spots

At the core of this month's habit is the ability to detect the early glimmers of something that's going well, and then to study it and expand or replicate it. Apply this practice to your skills and capacities as an educator. Identify your strengths, but also the things in which you show promise or potential and for which you have an inclination, and at which you could excel.

Part 1: Anticipate Bright Spots

What do you think you're good at as an educator? Which are the glimmering skills that you are excited to develop? Jot down as many ideas as you can.

Part 2: Go on a Quest for Bright Spots

As you go through your days (ideally a few of them), take note of things that you notice you're doing well that you didn't include in part 1, or things that you are doing okay, that you suspect you might be able to improve in easily. For example, perhaps you notice that when a student asked a random but interesting question, you found a way to respond that redirected the discussion, but honored her curiosity. That's a bright spot in your practice as a teacher. Maybe you notice that you are really good with helping students resolve minor conflict. Capture as many of these moments as you can.

Part 3: Scrutinize and Replicate

Now look at your lists of bright spots in your practice. What themes do you see? Perhaps you're really good at building relationships with and between students, or your bright spots are all about how you explain complex ideas or how you design engaging lessons. How can you build on those glimmers of potential? Where are there opportunities for you to share or maximize your skills and talents?

Savor the Little Moments

Researchers have found that the happiest people savor the good moments in life. By taking the time and spending the effort to appreciate the positive, we can experience more well-being.

Plan and Anticipate

Savoring little moments is a habit, and all good habits start with a plan. What will you savor this week? Make a list of at least 10 mundane but also enjoyable moments that you can anticipate savoring this week: Stretching in bed when you wake up, taking a shower, eating breakfast, listening to music on the way to work. Which moments in your day do you know you enjoy, but sometimes don't pay attention to? Start with those and then add a few others that you already anticipate will be good moments—the walk you have planned with a friend after school on Wednesday, the team meeting that you always enjoy, and so on.

Moments I Can Enjoy This Week

Notice and Enjoy

Now, when you experience those moments, the trick is to enjoy them. Because you've made a plan to enjoy them, your mind might remind you of your plan when you're in the moment. You might hear yourself saying, *Hey! I planned to enjoy my team meeting, and here I am in that meeting.* Catching yourself in the experience is the next key step.

From *The Onward Workbook: Daily Activities to Cultivate Your Emotional Resilience and Thrive* by Elena Aguilar. Copyright © 2018 by Elena Aguilar. Reproduced by permission.

Noticing—in the moment—what you enjoy and appreciate is the final component to this activity. You might recognize, for example, that during that team meeting, one member, whom you don't know very well, asks a question that is really insightful and moves the discussion along. Or you might notice that you feel that you're doing meaningful work with your team, or that you feel confident about challenging ideas. Savor each little moment that feels good—an interaction with a student, a glass of iced tea, the affection of a pet, and so on.

Reflect

At the end of each day, capture a reflection.

	What I Savored	What I Noticed
Monday		
Tuesday		
Wednesday		
Thursday		

From *The Onward Workbook: Daily Activities to Cultivate Your Emotional Resilience and Thrive* by Elena Aguilar. Copyright © 2018 by Elena Aguilar. Reproduced by permission.

Friday		
Saturday		
Sunday		

At the end of the week, reflect:

What did you learn about yourself from this activity?

How were mundane experiences different when you were aware of them and focusing on what you could appreciate about them?

Which moments stand out now as having been particularly enjoyable?

Share What You Savor

When you share with others what you savor, you reap double benefit from this activity: You've got the benefits of having paid close attention to mundane moments, and you get the benefit of connecting with another person and strengthening your relationship to him or her.

Invite a colleague or your entire team to "savor the little moments" with you one week, then share your reflections from the "Find the Bright Spots" activity at the beginning of this chapter and invite them to do the same.

Jot down a few of the moments that others savored—perhaps moments that you might also experience and savor.

Reflect and then discuss: What does it feel like to share your moments with someone else? To hear someone else's?

Feel the Feelings

The habit for this month is to focus on the bright spots, to find the silver linings, to search out strengths and assets in yourself and in others. But you can't do this if you are repressing or ignoring feelings. So take a few moments to examine a situation in its complexity, perhaps a situation about which you have strong or mixed feelings. What is the situation that you feel merits some reflection?

Use "The Core Emotions" in Chapter 2 to put words to those feelings. Let yourself sit with them for a little bit, feeling the different elements to them, noticing how your sense of the emotions intensifies and lessens. After you've spent some time with your feelings, if you want to you can poke around and look for any silver linings, but you don't have to.

Energy Check-In

Another way to consider your overall well-being is to reflect on the different energies you need in order to feel healthy, capable, engaged, and happy. These energies can be thought of as physical, emotional, cognitive, and spiritual energies that we all have, need, and can cultivate. When you don't feel well, it could be that you haven't tended to one of these areas and are out of balance.

Use this reflection tool every few months to check in on your energy. It can help you see where you're doing well in caring for your energy and which dimension might need some attention. You can also download it from www.onwardthebook.com.

Dimension		On a 1–5 scale, rate your agreement with the statement	Dimension Total
Body	I sleep for at least eight hours and wake up feeling rested.		
	I eat a nutritious breakfast almost every day.		
	I exercise at least three times a week.		
	I take little breaks during the day to recharge, and/or I stop work to eat lunch.		
Emotions	I usually feel calm, patient, and content at work.		
	I have enough time with my family and friends, and when I'm with them I feel fully present.		
	I have enough time in my life for the activities that I love doing the most.		
	I regularly stop to appreciate what I have and to relish my accomplishments.		

Mind	I am usually able to focus on the task in front of me, and I don't often get distracted.		
	My days usually go as planned, and I focus on valuable and high-leverage tasks.		
	I have regular time for reflection, planning, and creative thinking.		
	I rarely work in the evenings; I take almost the whole weekend off.		
Spirit	Most of my time at work is spent doing what I do best and enjoy the most.		
	The way I spend my time and energy reflects closely what is most important to me in my life.		
	My decisions at work are influenced by a strong, clear sense of my own purpose.		
	I feel that I'm making a positive difference in the world.		
	TOTAL		

Guide to Scores

68–80: You're doing great at managing your energies. You probably feel really good physically and emotionally.

54–67: You're doing okay at managing your energies. There are probably areas where you feel well and others where you know you need to make improvements.

31–53: You're struggling to manage your energies. You are approaching an energy crisis.

0–30: You're having a major energy crisis. Take action.

Reflect

What did your energy check-in tell you about yourself?

Which dimension is your strongest? Why do you think that is?

Which dimension do you want to care for a little more? What would you gain from focusing on that area?

What could you do today to tend to that dimension a little bit?

From The Onward Workbook: Daily Activities to Cultivate Your Emotional Resilience and Thrive
by Elena Aguilar. Copyright © 2018 by Elena Aguilar. Reproduced by permission.

Stop and Smell the Roses

Today, intentionally bring your senses into your moments of savoring. Perhaps start with focusing on smell. As you eat breakfast, drink coffee, and step outside your home in the morning, notice the smells. Notice the smell of rain or snow or trees or grass. Close your eyes and inhale.

At another moment in the day, bring your awareness to another sense and pay attention to sounds or touch or taste. When you're eating lunch, notice the textures and flavors. When you're walking through the hallways, pay attention to what you see—colors, light, shapes. When you greet your pets, your partner, or your own children, pay attention to sensations of touch. Try to engage just one sense at a time, and spend a few moments in that sensory experience before engaging a different sense.

The purpose of this activity is to expand your perception and to sense the elements of an experience that you otherwise miss.

At the end of the day, reflect:

What did you notice today when you engaged your senses?

What did you find surprising or enjoyable?

What was challenging about this activity?

According to many psychologists, burnout is simply the impaired ability to experience positive emotion. The interventions that are most effective at reducing burnout all have to do with improving a person's ability to perceive positive emotions. But our focus determines our reality, so if you're feeling down, it's hard to recognize the data pointing to what's going well. You literally won't see, hear, or register it.

Whether or not you're feeling burned out or are worried about preventing burnout, this exercise will help you hone your ability to experience positive feelings. For the next two weeks, every night before going to bed, write down a few good things that happened during the day. These can be little things—you enjoyed a TV show, finished your work by 6:00 p.m., or had a brief chat with a colleague—or bigger things. Then label them with 1 of these 10 positive emotions: joy, gratitude, serenity, interest, hope, pride, amusement, inspiration, awe, and love.

This process (which has been tried and tested among health care workers) helps you strengthen your ability to notice the good and to counteract a lot of the other demands that are put on your brain that force you to focus on the negative. It's really simple, takes only a few minutes, and can have a big impact.

If you want to extend the impact of this exercise: Share your good things with others. You could do this on an online forum or on poster paper that hangs in the faculty lounge, or you could email your three things to a buddy who is doing this exercise too. Also, note that this exercise is similar to "Three Good Things" in Chapter 3. You might compare this experience with that exercise and determine if you prefer one to the other. Honing awareness of the positive is so powerful that it's worth doing many times and in slightly different ways.

Create a Remember-lutions Jar

This activity is an alternative to creating New Year's resolutions, and you could do this at the start of a calendar or school year, or you could start at any time!

Over the course of a semester, school year, or calendar year, fill a jar with notes about your favorite memories and accomplishments. Find a jar, decorate it if you want, and then every day or every week, write a note and drop it in. Make sure to include notes about what you feel proud of having done.

At the end of the semester or year, sit back and read through the notes in your jar. You could even do this activity with students!

If you'd like, as a record of this activity, photograph your jar, paste that image in here, and then also glue on some of your favorite notes that you collected.

From The Onward Workbook: Daily Activities to Cultivate Your Emotional Resilience and Thrive by Elena Aguilar. Copyright © 2018 by Elena Aguilar. Reproduced by permission.

The Words of Others

The following quotes reflect the themes of this chapter.

In the middle of winter, I at last discovered that there was in me an invincible summer.
ALBERT CAMUS

All the world is full of suffering. It is also full of overcoming.
HELEN KELLER

When loss rips off the doors of the heart, or sadness veils your vision with despair, practice becomes simply bearing the truth.
DANNA FAULDS

Some people walk in the rain. Others just get wet.
ROGER MILLER

You never know how strong you are until being strong is your only choice.
BOB MARLEY

You do not become good by trying to be good, but by finding the goodness that is already within you, and allowing that goodness to emerge.
ECKHART TOLLE

Which ones resonate most for you? Pick two of these quotes that resonate most for you and illustrate them in the boxes here. Write the quote below the box. Try to capture the essence of the quote without holding yourself to any ideal of perfection. Color can help.

Joyful Anticipation

Here's another finding from the research on happy people: Those who practice joyful anticipation—imagining and looking forward to future happy events—are more likely to be optimistic and to experience more positive emotions.

Considering that research, let's plan! What can you look forward to today? This week? This month? List 5 things. Or 10. Or more!

Close your eyes and imagine a future event that you're looking forward to—this could be the end of a long week, the conclusion of a unit that you're teaching, a social event, the end of the school year, and so on. Conjure up feelings of excitement.

What did it feel like to imagine that event?

What could you plan now that you can look forward to in the future? Identify at least one thing, put it on your calendar, and put that plan in motion.

From *The Onward Workbook: Daily Activities to Cultivate Your Emotional Resilience and Thrive* by Elena Aguilar. Copyright © 2018 by Elena Aguilar. Reproduced by permission.

Repurpose Your Pain

Sometimes we have to create bright spots out of material that wasn't bright to begin with; we can transform our pain and moments of struggle into those that fuel our resilience. Resilient people are masters of innovation, resourcefulness, and improvisation. They take the raw materials of their life experiences and use them to create something beautiful.

Bricolage is an art form made with objects that have been repurposed and transformed. El Anatsui is a Ghanaian master of bricolage. He uses discarded metal caps of liquor bottles to make beautiful sculptures. These bottle caps are representative of postcolonial economic exchange with Africa, and symbolic of global inequalities, but he uses them to show how objects can be transmutable and shaped in many ways. His art pushes our thinking about what is trash and about how we can transform our painful or shameful histories to create something beautiful.

Activity

1. Google El Anatsui and look at some of his art. As an extension: His art is permanently displayed in many museums and galleries across the United States. If you're near one of those locations, plan a field trip for yourself to see his works in person.
2. Reflect on your own life and the elements of your experiences that you have transformed, or could transform, into a work of beauty. How could you reshape them? Cut them up? Reorganize those moments into something new? What form could that take?

Here's the image that comes to my mind: I can take threads of painful past experiences and create a blanket—a thread from the loneliness I experienced as a child in school, a thread from the grief I felt when my father left my mother, and another thread from the English teachers who told me I was a bad writer because I couldn't spell. I can take those threads from the experiences that were painful, and weave them into a blanket that I can use to cover myself or someone else.

Capture your reflections and ideas here. Of course, you're always welcome to sketch, draw, or sculpt!

From *The Onward Workbook: Daily Activities to Cultivate Your Emotional Resilience and Thrive* by Elena Aguilar. Copyright © 2018 by Elena Aguilar. Reproduced by permission.

Joyful Recollection

Here's more research on what makes for a resilient person: People who manage stress best are good at reminiscing about the past. They look back on happy times and rekindle joy from those memories. This is another habit to practice on our quest for resilience. This is a powerful activity to do in the morning before going to school.

1. Recall a happy time in your personal life. Remember it as if you were watching a movie. Pay close attention to the moments when you experienced joy. As you remember these moments, imagine that the joy is sinking into your body now. Jot down a few words about the memory you recalled.

2. Now recall another joyful memory, this time from your professional life—perhaps teaching. Again, feel yourself back in that time, taking in all the joy. Jot down a few words about the memory.

Do this as many times as you'd like. If you find yourself experiencing feelings of sadness or nostalgia, that's okay. You can also choose to shift the angle of your memory, turn the camera of your mind toward the moments of purer joy if you want to move away from sadness or nostalgia.

From *The Onward Workbook: Daily Activities to Cultivate Your Emotional Resilience and Thrive* by Elena Aguilar. Copyright © 2018 by Elena Aguilar. Reproduced by permission.

THINK Before You Speak

When trying to decide whether to say something to someone, ask yourself the questions that make up the acronym THINK:

T Is it **true**?
H Is it **helpful**?
I Is it **inspiring**?
N Is it **necessary**?
K Is it **kind**?

Sometimes I'm on the fence about the I—whether something *has* to be inspiring. Maybe there are times when we have to say things that may not be inspiring. I also feel some conflict about the H—because we might think we're being helpful to someone else, but the person doesn't experience it that way. So sometimes, when I'm in a quandary about whether to say something or not, I focus on the TNK: Is it true? Is it necessary? Is it kind?

In the space here, write these letters and their corresponding questions in colorful print. Decorate them if you want. Perhaps create something to post in your classroom. Of course, you could also engage your students in this exercise—I'm sure that they, too, could benefit from thinking before they speak.

Don't Worry, Be Happy

Actually, some say that "don't worry, be happy" is terrible advice. In this short video from big think, "How Forcing Positivity Can Create Despair" (https://youtu.be/-xA5xgAqj1I), Harvard psychologist Susan David shares her thoughts on this subject.

What do Dr. David's thoughts raise for you?

The Joy of Making Lists

It's hard for us to stay focused on the bright spots when our brains are cluttered with things to keep track of. Do you have a running, endless to-do list? Do you have ideas, dreams, and goals that pop into your mind and distract you?

Here are some other kinds of lists to keep that can free up space in your mind to be here now, stay focused, and notice the bright spots.

The Someday list. A Someday list is just what it sounds like: A list of things you want to do someday. These are bigger tasks like "Apply for a grant to take my kids on a field trip to the Grand Canyon" and "Reorganize the science supplies." What would you like to put on your Someday list to start with?

1.

2.

3.

4.

The Could-Do list. A Could-Do list is a list of stuff you could do if you felt like it: "Send out a monthly newsletter to parents" or "Send postcards in July to all my new students." What would you like to put on your Could-Do list?

1.

2.

3.

4.

The Later list. A Later list (a term coined by author of the *Together* books, Maia Heyck-Merlin) is for stuff you want or need to do but that you don't need to do right now. It's useful for when you're trying to get stuff done, but your mind keeps reminding you that you also might want to do this and that. The things on my Later list include learning about podcasting, reading some specific articles, and revising workshop materials. What would you like to put on your Later list?

1.

2.

3.

4.

I have each of these lists in a digital format. (I like using Evernote for this kind of organization.) And yes, there's also the Bucket list.

    Of these three kinds of lists, which one do you feel might be most useful?

Consider setting yourself up to use these lists—whether by creating them digitally or writing them in a notebook. See what happens if you use them for a week—whether your mind is better able to focus.

Reflecting on Sadness

What follows are a whole bunch of questions to help you reflect on sadness and gain a deeper understanding of it.

What's an important lesson you've learned from sadness?

When you're in a sad mood, what's something that can cheer you up?

What's something that makes other people sad that you don't care about? (For example: A TV show being canceled or bad weather)

What's an unconventional thing that makes you sad? (For example: Small talk, grammar errors)

Are you more susceptible to sadness during the day or at night? Is there a season when you feel more susceptible to sadness?

Check off the following common reactions to sadness if you experience them:

☐ Lethargy
☐ Crying
☐ Hopelessness
☐ Grumpiness
☐ Body tension

☐ Loss of appetite
☐ Increased appetite
☐ Uncontrollable laughter
☐ Stomachache

Are there things you won't do because they make you feel too sad—for example, read or watch the news, watch a sad movie, read sad books, or be alone?

From *The Onward Workbook: Daily Activities to Cultivate Your Emotional Resilience and Thrive* by Elena Aguilar. Copyright © 2018 by Elena Aguilar. Reproduced by permission.

Five Years in the Future

Try this activity when you find yourself stewing in frustration or anger at someone.

Think back three to five years ago and call to mind someone you were mad at. See if you can get yourself all worked up and angry at that person now. Some of us will be able to do this, but many of us can't. You might *remember* being mad at someone, but you won't be able to get all angry and worked up.

Depending on the severity of the situation you're dealing with now, imagine this: There will likely be a day when you will realize that you've let go of whatever it is that's bothering you. So whatever you're really angry about now, see if you can imagine that five years down the line it may not be as big of a deal. Sometimes, just imagining this loosens the claws of anger or frustration a little bit.

Learning to Settle Your Mind

It's hard for us to focus on bright spots when your mind is full of turbulence and anxiety. In order to refine the habit of this month, you need strategies to settle your mind when it gets off kilter. One habit that can help is to strengthen concentration, which steadies and focuses your attention so that you can let go of unhelpful thoughts—regrets about the past, worries about the future. These kinds of distracting thoughts drain your energy; concentration replenishes your energy.

Our mind often travels through arcs of anxiety: A little thing spurs a whole chain of regrets and worries. For example, let's say I've planned a unit for which I had to order some supplies. It's the day before I'm supposed to start the unit, and the supplies have yet to arrive. I ask someone in the office to look into what's happened with my order, and then my mind starts freaking out, thinking, *Now I won't be able to start tomorrow, or I'll have to start with an activity that won't be as exciting as the one I'd planned, and then this whole unit won't go that well, and I was planning on doing this one now, right before winter break so that I could keep kids engaged and focused, and I knew I should have ordered this earlier, but I was waiting for approval to use the funds, but I should have asked for those earlier . . .*

I suspect you've done this sort of thinking too. Most of us travel these anxious roads during moments of uncertainty.

Here's a phrase to help you regain clarity and balance:

Something will happen.

Maybe the order did arrive and it's at the warehouse, and I can go and pick it up. Maybe it'll arrive tomorrow. Maybe someone else has the supplies I need for tomorrow's lesson. Maybe I can get some of these at a local store. Maybe I can reorder the lessons and start with something else tomorrow. Something will happen. *I'll figure it out.*

When you find your mind spinning through an arc of anxiety, try saying this to yourself: *Something will happen.* You may be able to curtail some of the exhaustive rumination you go through, you might find your mind regaining concentration, and you might see that you can skillfully plan to deal with whatever is happening.

How might you remember to use this phrase?

In many traditions around the world, candles are symbolically lit in the shortest days of the year as a way to bring in light or to beckon back the sun. Gazing at a candle flame is also a meditation practice—focusing attention on the gentle flickers, shades and tones, and soft warmth that a candle emits.

Either in the morning or in the evening, or at both times, light a candle and spend time gazing at the flame. Reflect on what it means to you to "bring in the light"—perhaps to your thoughts, feelings, or spirit.

If you wish, capture those reflections here.

From *The Onward Workbook: Daily Activities to Cultivate Your Emotional Resilience and Thrive* by Elena Aguilar. Copyright © 2018 by Elena Aguilar. Reproduced by permission.

Gaining Perspective on Difficult Events

We typically think and talk about ourselves using first-person pronouns: *I, me, mine.* By using self-distanced language—*you* or *he/she* or *they*—we can cause a cognitive shift, allowing us to gain perspective on whatever is going on. Think about a challenging moment recently. Perhaps something like, *A student was really disruptive in class, and I lost my temper.* Now change the "I" to a third-person pronoun. Can you sense how just that shift might give you a different perspective on what happened or how you feel about it?

By using this kind of a self-distancing strategy, we can also think in more abstract terms. Rather than focusing on the concrete details and feelings involved in a particular event, we're more likely to have realizations, generate deeper understanding, and find closure. This allows us to deal with negative feelings constructively, without getting swept away by them.

When I recall a moment when I lost my temper with a student and feel a lot of shame for having done so, and I take a self-distancing perspective, I realize that my emotions that day were also fragile because of many challenging elements in that moment: There were two students from another class in my room, the front office staff had made several announcements through the intercom that disrupted the flow of class, and I hadn't had breakfast. I can see how all of these factors impacted my behavior, and I can both take responsibility for what I did as well as have some compassion for myself—which allows me to move on.

Take a moment to bring to mind a difficult experience you are dealing with: An event in the past that made you sad or angry, for example, or a worry you have about the future.

Try to understand your feelings using whatever pronoun you prefer or your own name as much as possible. If your name is Linda, for example, you might ask yourself, *Why does Linda feel this way? What are the underlying causes and reasons for her feelings? What are all the things that contributed to Linda experiencing these feelings?* Jot down some of the questions you can ask yourself here:

Imagine you're watching the event through the eyes of a distanced, third-party observer, rather than through your own eyes. The purpose is not to avoid or separate from your feelings, but to analyze them from a clearer and more helpful vantage point. Spend a few minutes reflecting in this way, writing down your thoughts if you want.

Although it may feel awkward to talk to yourself in the third person, it can help you confront difficult feelings without becoming overwhelmed by them. Eventually, you might be able to use this kind of self-talk during difficult events as they're unfolding. Repeat this exercise when you find yourself ruminating on a negative experience.

Uncovering Silver Linings

Focusing on the bright spots won't turn you into a Pollyanna or resign you to a situation that you might need to change. Most likely, it'll just help you balance your perspective of what's going on. Seeing silver linings can help boost your sense of self-worth, motivate you to pursue your goals, and heighten your enjoyment of life.

This is a practice that you need to repeat regularly. If it feels helpful, try doing it every day for two weeks to reap the greatest benefit.

List five things that make you feel like your life is enjoyable, meaningful, and/or enriching at this moment. These can be general, such as "I'm earning enough to pay my bills," or specific, such as "My partner teacher and I had a great conversation yesterday after school."

1.

2.

3.

4.

5.

Think about a recent time when you felt frustrated or upset. Describe the situation in a few sentences.

Identify a couple ways that you can see the bright side of this situation. For example, perhaps your prep period was cancelled yesterday. The following are a couple ways to see the bright side of this situation:

- *I had extra time with my students to finish the art project we'd started and hadn't had enough time to complete.*
- *I'll be compensated $26 for my missed prep, and I can use that to pay for a couple of yoga classes.*

If you can't find a silver lining, that's okay. Don't force it. Pick a different moment of upset and see if you can identify silver linings in that one.

Write your silver linings here:

Watch Your Thoughts, Again

Perhaps another reason to watch your thoughts and find the silver linings can be found in this passage that's attributed to a whole lot of different people, dating back to the teachings of Lao Tzu and the Buddha.

> Watch your thoughts, they become words.
> Watch your words, they become actions.
> Watch your actions, they become habits.
> Watch your habits, they become your character.
> Watch your character, it becomes your destiny.

Can you recall a thought you've had that became a word? Can you track how that word became action or even habit?

In the following chart, list some thoughts that you'd like to strengthen—they could be about your own strengths and assets or those of others—and predict how that thought could become action.

From *The Onward Workbook: Daily Activities to Cultivate Your Emotional Resilience and Thrive* by Elena Aguilar. Copyright © 2018 by Elena Aguilar. Reproduced by permission.

Thought	Words	Actions
Example: That student is trying to do his best.	"It's great to see you getting to work so quickly on your assignment. Good job!"	A note home to the students' mother; a comment to another teacher about how well he did in class today.

Photographing What Matters

Taking time to recognize and appreciate sources of meaning through photography can help you remember what matters most to you. (You probably already do this by taking pictures of your friends, family, or pets.) This activity also activates your visual thinking abilities. Although you could probably make a list right now of the 10 things that matter most to you, you can gain new insight by engaging in a search for images and using photography to capture them.

Over the next week, take photos of things that make your life feel meaningful or full of purpose. These can be people, places, objects, pets, and so on. If you are not able to take photos of these things, you can take photos of souvenirs, reminders, websites, or even other photos. Try to take at least 10 photographs. At the end of the week, print your photos out or collect them in one digital folder or slide show. You might want to include one in this workbook as a reminder of this activity. This is a great activity to share with colleagues.

Reflect

What does each photo represent to you?

Which themes run through your photos that might reflect what matters most to you?

In Search of Ordinary Good

Today at school, capture as many of the little good things that happen as possible. The challenge is to notice the ordinary: Your trash can is empty when you arrive, you easily find your favorite whiteboard marker, the front office staff person waves at you when you grab papers out of your mailbox, Denise arrives on time, Pablo has the novel he's reading, Marcus smiles. Nothing is too mundane. Look for things that have an emotional tone from neutral to good.

Give yourself a goal—to note 100 things. Or 50. Or 20. Whatever feels doable. Capture only enough words to remember the little things—write them in here, on sticky notes, or wherever you can. In the evening, respond to the prompts in the following exercise, "Reflecting on the Search for Ordinary Good."

Reflecting on the Search for Ordinary Good

After engaging in a day of noting ordinary good moments, reflect on these questions:

What did you learn from doing this activity?

What did you enjoy about this activity?

What was challenging about this activity?

Which was the best ordinary moment that you noticed?

From *The Onward Workbook: Daily Activities to Cultivate Your Emotional Resilience and Thrive* by Elena Aguilar. Copyright © 2018 by Elena Aguilar. Reproduced by permission.

A Letter to Sadness

The bright spots and joy in life exist with sadness. We can't fully appreciate joy without recognizing sadness. What would you like to say to sadness—in you, in the world, in others? Imagine that sadness, perhaps your sadness or sadness in general, is a person. Tell it whatever you'd like.

Here's a segment of my letter to sadness: *I'm slowly making peace with you. Around the edges of sadness, I can see the reverberations of tenderness, compassion, and wholeness. As long as we can be friends with each other, I accept you in my life. Please be patient with me—I still have a lot of fear of you, but I'm working on it.*

Artistic Depictions of Sadness

Go to your preferred online search engine and look for images of sadness—or another term that reflects sadness, such as grief, loneliness, or boredom (see "The Core Emotions" in Chapter 2 for these terms).

See what comes up, and then search for "depictions of sadness in art."

Look closely at a few of those images. Sit with them and spend some time getting to know them. Pay attention to how they make you feel and what thoughts go through your mind.

Reflect

What do you notice in the images that come up?

What have you learned about sadness through doing this exploration?

How did this exploration help you understand your own experience of sadness?

If you'd like, print out one (or more) of the images that particularly speak to you and stick them in here.

Destination Postcard: Focusing on Bright Spots

What would it look and sound like if you were able to focus on strengths, assets, and bright spots? Draw a picture of yourself with thought bubbles and labels to describe a you focusing on bright spots. If you'd like, draw this you at work, surrounded by kids and colleagues. How might you be in that space?

Chapter Reflection

What were your biggest takeaways from this chapter?

Of the different activities in this chapter, which were most useful?

Which activities would you like to revisit periodically? How might you get that habit going?

What implications do the ideas in this chapter have for the work you do?

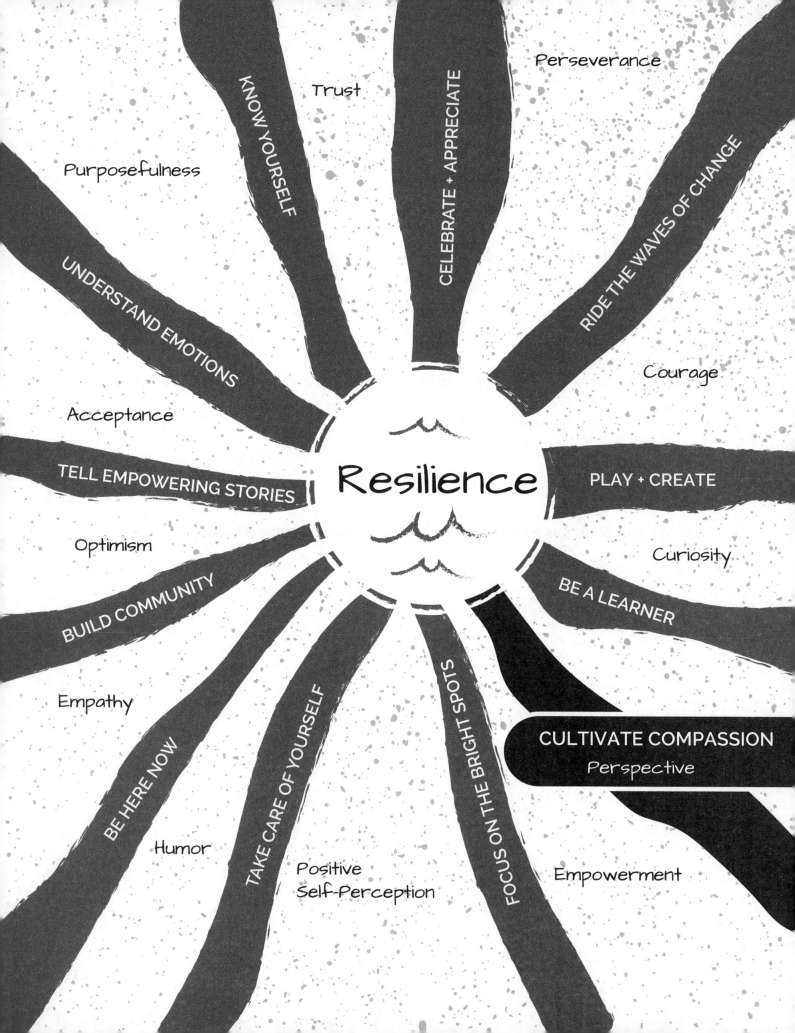

CHAPTER 8

Cultivate Compassion

Compassion for ourselves, as well as for others, helps us deal with the interpersonal challenges we face on a daily basis. Perspective allows us to recognize the complexity of a situation. Perspective allows us to empathize with others, see the long view, extricate ourselves from the drama of a moment, and identify a wider range of responses to an event.

January: Start the new year by strengthening your compassion for yourself and others, and unlock another resource for resilience.

Cultivate Compassion: Resilience Self-Assessment

The purpose of this self-assessment is to help you gauge the level of your resilience reservoir and to explore what might be draining or what could replenish it. The exercises that follow and the information in the corresponding chapter of *Onward* can boost your resilience by helping you activate feelings of empathy so that you can extend compassion to yourself and others.

Imagine each circle as a little *cenote* or reservoir within you, and fill it up according to how much each statement reflects a source of resilience. If you need something more concrete, imagine marks at ¼, ½, and ¾ full.

Before you start the exercises in this chapter, take this self-assessment and fill in the date. At the end of the month, take the assessment again. (You might even cover up your original markings with a strip of paper.) Is your resilience reservoir a little more full? If so, which practices do you want to keep up? If not, what else do you want to try?

Statement	Date:	Date:
I understand the difference between pity, sympathy, empathy, and compassion.	◯	◯
I understand what it means to have compassion for myself, and I understand the importance of self-compassion.	◯	◯
I know how to offer compassion to others.	◯	◯
I know how to offer compassion to myself.	◯	◯

I understand how compassion helps me strengthen social relationships.	◯	◯
I understand how forgiveness is connected to compassion, and how it is critical for resilience.	◯	◯
I have strategies to forgive others.	◯	◯
I can set boundaries around how other people treat me.	◯	◯
I know what envy is, and I have strategies to deal with it in myself.	◯	◯
I understand how having perspective helps cultivate resilience, and I have strategies to widen my perspective on things that happen.	◯	◯

New Year's Activities

If you're going through this workbook according to the calendar of learning that I've suggested, then you might be starting this chapter around New Year's Day. Here are some activities to help you reflect on last year and launch this new one. These can be alternatives or additions to resolutions. Of course, you could also engage in these activities around the start of the school year too!

- Choose one word that will set the tone for the new year. Think of it as a chapter heading for the book that is your life. Print this word out (you might even do a quick Google search and find it written in a cool font!) and place it somewhere you will see it every day.
- Write a New Year's letter to yourself. Consider reflecting on the best and hardest parts of last year, anything from last year that you want to let go of, hopes for the new year, and visions for how you want to feel this year.
- Enter in your calendar one day per month when you'll do something that brings you joy. Go through the whole year, identify that date, and block it out. You can decide now or later what you'll do on that day.

Make Those Resolutions Stick

Although 44% of Americans make resolutions every year, only a tiny fraction carry them out. Here are some tips to make your resolutions stick:

- **Be specific.** Make concrete resolutions—for example, "I will exercise 30 minutes a day, four times a week" rather than "I will get more exercise."
- **Write them down**—and track your progress in writing.
- **Review your resolutions** every day or at least several times a week.
- **Hold yourself accountable.** Tell other people what your resolutions are, find others who share those resolutions, engage together in the activities you want to be doing, and track your progress in writing.

What do you resolve to do this year?

How will you hold yourself accountable? Who can you enlist to support you in your resolutions?

From *The Onward Workbook: Daily Activities to Cultivate Your Emotional Resilience and Thrive* by Elena Aguilar. Copyright © 2018 by Elena Aguilar. Reproduced by permission.

This is a powerful and basic meditation to cultivate compassion for yourself and others. It's like the multivitamin for compassion—if you're going to regularly engage in only one practice, do this one. Try doing it every morning before work for a week—or a month!—and see how it changes you and your experience of the day. Of all the exercises in this chapter, it's the one I hope you'll spend the most time exploring. You can spend three minutes a day in this meditation, or longer if you like; what makes it most effective is doing it regularly. You can also hear it on the website, www.onwardthebook.com.

Lovingkindness Meditation

Sit or lie down comfortably, with your eyes closed or open. Say to yourself, *May I be safe. May I be happy. May I be healthy. May I live with ease.*

Repeat the phrases to yourself slowly, bringing your attention to each one as you say it.

Call to mind someone who has been kind to you. Picture the person, get a sense of him, and then say these phrases to him: May you be safe. May you be happy. May you be healthy. May you live with ease.

Call to mind someone who is having a difficult time. Picture the person, get a sense of her, and then say these phrases to her: May you be safe. May you be happy. May you be healthy. May you live with ease.

Call to mind someone you see fairly often, but don't know very well; someone about whom you have neutral feelings. Picture the person, get a sense of him, and then say these phrases to him: May you be safe. May you be happy. May you be healthy. May you live with ease.

Call to mind someone you have trouble getting along with. Picture the person, get a sense of her, and then say these phrases to her: May you be safe. May you be happy. May you be healthy. May you live with ease.

If you have a hard time sending this person loving kindness, then go back to sending loving kindness to yourself. In that moment, you're suffering and you deserve compassion.

Finally, offer loving kindness to all beings everywhere, known and unknown: May all beings be safe. May all beings be happy. May all beings be healthy. May all beings live with ease.

During the day, when you notice yourself feeling distressed about something that's going on, see what happens if you repeat these phrases—perhaps just offering yourself loving kindness in a difficult moment, or offering these thoughts to your students or others.

From *The Onward Workbook: Daily Activities to Cultivate Your Emotional Resilience and Thrive* by Elena Aguilar. Copyright © 2018 by Elena Aguilar. Reproduced by permission.

Reflect

After engaging in this meditation at least a few times, what do you notice about how you feel when doing it?

Which phrase or phrases feel easiest?

To whom is it easiest to say these phrases?

Which set feels hardest?

What do you notice about your days on the mornings in which you engage in this practice?

Kindness and compassion are communicated through simple, small actions. This morning, set an intention to become more aware of how you communicate care in small actions throughout your day—for example, how you greet students, how you communicate with the office staff or your supervisor, or how you address parents. Then bring your attention to those interactions throughout the day.

Which of your behaviors will you pay attention to today?

How might you communicate care in those interactions?

At the end of the day, reflect: What happened? What did you notice?

Acknowledging Your Teachers

Mentally acknowledge those who have helped you become who you are at work, those who have taught you what you know and who have helped you learn what to do. Today, as many times as you can, acknowledge those people quickly in your mind as you go about your work. Just send a simple mental message of thanks, such as "Thank you, Liz, for being a compassionate coach" or "Thank you, Jamis, for showing me how to make double-sided copies!"

Right now, before you head off to work, call to mind a few people whom you might think about and thank during the day. Jot their names down:

At the end of the day, reflect on these questions:

Whom did you acknowledge and for what?

How did it feel to engage in this activity?

Six Ways to Forgive Someone

It's likely that there are many people in your life who have hurt you. In this set of exercises, I encourage you think first about people in your work world who you feel have harmed you, and whom you might want to forgive. Some of these harms could be minor—the student's parent who was relentlessly critical of your teaching approach, the principal who barked orders at you and everyone, the student whom you spent endless hours tutoring only to hear him mocking you one afternoon. Many people carry around a lot of resentment and anger at school. If you are also tempted to use these practices to forgive people from your personal life, of course go ahead. But by strengthening your forgiveness muscles first with people to whom you have less attachment, such as your principal, you'll be more prepared for those tougher cases.

What follows are six exercises to help you forgive someone. Try them all—if only to see which ones are most helpful. But to be honest, when I wanted to forgive someone who I felt had really hurt me, it wasn't until I'd finished the final forgiveness exercise that I felt truly relieved of that pain. You may want to spread these out over the course of a week or two.

1. Remember Being Forgiven

Recall a time when you hurt another person and you were forgiven. Jot down a few words about what happened.

How did this person communicate his or her forgiveness to you?

From *The Onward Workbook: Daily Activities to Cultivate Your Emotional Resilience and Thrive* by Elena Aguilar. Copyright © 2018 by Elena Aguilar. Reproduced by permission.

How did you respond?

Why do you think this person forgave you?

How did his or her forgiveness change your relationship?

How did that experience change you?

2. Forgiving Yourself

Write a letter of apology to someone you harmed in the past or present, in your professional or personal life. In remembering and accepting that you've hurt others, you can cultivate empathy and insight into people who may have hurt you.

In the letter, describe what you did, why it was wrong, and how it harmed the other person and your relationship. Apologize for your behavior, affirm the value of your relationship, and express your desire to restore the relationship. You could ask, "What would it take to reestablish our relationship?" You could pledge to change your behavior or offer a way to make amends.

Whether or not you send the letter is up to you. It may not be possible to send it, or it may not even be wise to send it. The power of this activity comes from writing it, from the space it opens up inside you.

From *The Onward Workbook: Daily Activities to Cultivate Your Emotional Resilience and Thrive* by Elena Aguilar. Copyright © 2018 by Elena Aguilar. Reproduced by permission.

Write your letter somewhere else, and then if you want to tape or staple it in here, that's your choice.

3. Forgiving Someone Else: Imagine the Other Person as a Kid

Think of the person who hurt you as a little kid. Imagine what she might have looked like. As you recall the harm that this person did to you, think of her acting out of fear, attempting to deal with her pain and suffering and complex emotions in the only way she knows how. Sit with this image for a few moments. Jot down your reflections if you want.

4. Imagine Forgiveness

Sit down or lie down somewhere where you feel safe. Close your eyes or keep them open, and imagine a person who you feel mistreated you. If you feel that there are many people in your life who have mistreated you, start by thinking about someone whose actions toward you were less harmful than those of others. Again, you may want to start with someone from your professional life.

Now, empathize with that person. Try to see through his eyes and ears. Trying seeing that person as a whole person with many sides to him—he is more than his offending behaviors.

Imagine forgiving this person. Imagine exactly what you'd say. Imagine your facial expressions as you forgive him. Imagine how you'd feel in that moment.

Remember: Forgiving someone doesn't mean that you excuse or tolerate the hurtful behavior. It means that you try to let go of some of your own hurt and anger.

5. Write a Letter of Forgiveness

Write, but don't send, a letter of forgiveness to a person who has hurt or wronged you. Describe that hurt, how it affected you, and how it continues to hurt you. Tell the person what you wish she had done instead.

From The Onward Workbook: Daily Activities to Cultivate Your Emotional Resilience and Thrive by Elena Aguilar. Copyright © 2018 by Elena Aguilar. Reproduced by permission.

End with an explicit statement of forgiveness and understanding. For example: "I realize now that what you did was the best you could do at the time, and I forgive you."

6. Write the Letter You Want to Receive

Imagine that the person who has harmed you receives the letter you wrote in the previous exercise granting forgiveness, and writes you back. What would her letter say? What do you want her to say? What explanation do you want for her behavior? Write the letter you want to receive.

Bridging Differences

Human beings have a deep propensity to be kind and generous, but one of the greatest barriers to altruism is our perception that others are different from us. We are much less motivated to help someone who we don't feel is part of our group. In fact, we can even feel hostile toward members of an "out-group." But who we see as part of our "in-group" can change. We can increase our altruism by recognizing commonalities with someone else, even if those similarities aren't immediately apparent.

This exercise will help you expand your sense of shared identity with others.

1.   Write down the name of a person in your life who seems to be very different from you in every way that you can imagine—or someone you feel distanced from, someone about whom you think, *We have nothing in common.* Perhaps this person has different religious or political beliefs, life experiences, or interests. He or she may be someone with whom you have had a personal conflict, or who belongs to a group that has been in conflict with a group to which you belong.

2.   Make a list of things that you imagine you share in common. Perhaps you both work at the same school or in the same city. Maybe you both have children or a significant other. Probably you have both lost a loved one or had a broken heart. At the most basic level, you both belong to the human species. What else do you have in common?

3. Review your list of commonalities. How do they help you see this person differently?

4. What did it feel like to do this activity? What did you learn?

It's Not Personal

This is an activity to do every day for a few days or a week. If it helps, continue doing it longer.

The goal is to notice and catalogue everything that happens that you take personally—the annoying attitude of a student who pushes your buttons, a snarky comment from a colleague, a terse text from a parent. Each time you feel a personal sting, notice it; say to yourself, *It's not personal;* and as soon as you can, write down a few words that capture the event that felt personal (such as "snarky comment"). Write these in this workbook or on sticky notes that you can put in here.

At the end of each day, reflect on the questions here:

What did you take personally?

What themes or patterns do you notice in what you took personally?

How did it feel to say to yourself, *It's not personal*? Did you believe it?

From The Onward Workbook: Daily Activities to Cultivate Your Emotional Resilience and Thrive by Elena Aguilar. Copyright © 2018 by Elena Aguilar. Reproduced by permission.

How to Apologize

It's really hard to be a human being and never hurt someone. Therefore, we all need to make apologies at some point. Apologizing for the hurt we've inflicted on others is also necessary for us to forgive ourselves. The following suggestions for how to apologize can contribute to healing and reconciliation.

To whom do you owe an apology? Can you think of someone you recently wronged in a small way? Start by practicing apologies for small harms that you've inflicted and then work your way up to bigger ones.

Steps to a Good Apology

1. **Acknowledge the offense.** Demonstrate your recognition of who was responsible, who was harmed, and the nature of the offense. Say, "I made a mistake" rather than "Mistakes were made," which fails to allocate responsibility. Acknowledge that harm occurred and be specific. Say, "I'm sorry that I snapped at you in our team meeting yesterday," rather than "I'm sorry for whatever I said yesterday" or "I'm sorry if I hurt you." Vague statements such as that last one aren't as effective.

2. **Provide an explanation.** Sometimes it helps to explain yourself, but be very careful that your explanation doesn't sound like an excuse or like blaming the other person. Say, "I'd had a tough sixth period and hadn't slept well, but there's no excuse for my behavior."

3. **Express remorse.** When you hurt someone, it's natural to feel shame or remorse. Sharing these feelings communicates that you recognize and regret the suffering you caused. Acknowledge your disappointment in yourself by saying something like, "I regret the way I spoke to you." State your commitment to improve: "I'm going to be more aware of my mood and communication in our meetings." However, be careful that this expression of remorse doesn't become a way for you to seek consolation for a tough day. Make your statements crisp and to the point, and keep your attention focused on the other person.

4. **Make amends.** Ask the other person, "What can I do repair this dent in our relationship?" Offer to make amends.

Here's how this could sound all together. This was my apology to a student to whom I'd spoken harshly: "Henry, I'm sorry that earlier today when I asked you to sit down my tone of voice was mean. I was getting stressed because the bell had rung five minutes earlier and so many people were still out of their seat, but there's no excuse for my behavior.

I could have said it in a clear but kind way. I don't want to be a teacher who yells, and I'm working on this. Is there anything I can do to help you feel better?"

Practice writing apologies and saying them when you're alone, and you'll feel more confident and able when you need to deliver them in the moment or soon after. Apologize for the little things you do that hurt other people—those little hurts can tear the fine threads of our relationships, and they all need to be strong.

Apologies that include the four elements listed here can meet the psychological needs of the hurt person. They can restore his or her sense of dignity and validate that he or she is not to blame and did not deserve to be hurt. They can give the offended person an opportunity to express his or her feelings and even offer forgiveness. A sincere apology can also reassure others that they are safe from further harm, making them more likely to trust you again.

We can all improve our ability to apologize. Know that you'll likely feel vulnerable, but it will be worth it.

Now practice writing an apology:

The Self-Compassion Break

Any time you feel overwhelmed by stress or pain, take a self-compassion break. There are three parts to this break:

1. **Be mindful.** Without judgment or analysis, notice what you're feeling. Say to yourself, *This is a moment of suffering* or *This hurts* or *This is stress*.
2. **Remember that you're not alone.** Everyone experiences deep and painful human emotions, although the causes might be different. Say to yourself, *Suffering is a part of life* or *We all feel this way* or *We all struggle in our lives*.
3. **Be kind to yourself.** Put your hands on your heart and say something like, *May I give myself compassion* or *May I accept myself as I am* or *May I be patient*.

For each of these steps, write down the phrase that feels most comfortable for you to say in that moment. You can select from one of the examples given, or craft your own phrase that feels like something you'd say, but that keeps the essence of the meaning.

Be mindful:

Remember that you're not alone:

Be kind to yourself:

How Would You Treat a Friend?

Here, you compare how you respond to your own struggles—and the tone you use—with how you respond to a friend's. Often, this comparison unearths some surprising differences and valuable reflections: *Why am I so harsh on myself, and what would happen if I weren't?*

1. Think about a time when a close friend felt bad about himself or herself and was struggling in some way. How did you respond to your friend? Write down—or record a short voice memo on your phone—what you typically do and say to a friend who is having a hard time.

2. Now think about times when you feel bad about yourself or are struggling. How do you typically respond to yourself in these situations? Write down—or record a short voice memo on your phone—what you typically do and say. Also note the tone in which you talk to yourself.

3. Read back over what you wrote or listen to the voice memos you recorded. What differences do you notice between how you talk to a friend and how you talk to yourself? What factors do you think lead you to treat yourself differently than you treat others?

4. How do you think things might change if you responded to your suffering in the same way you typically respond to a close friend?

5. Next time you are struggling with something, what do you want to say to yourself? If you wish, record yourself saying these words the way you'd want to hear them. You might even play it back to yourself in the moment!

Self-Compassion Letter

Once you start to develop a kinder attitude toward yourself, you can express that feeling toward yourself in a self-compassion letter. Spend some time writing words of understanding, acceptance, and compassion toward yourself about a specific struggle that you feel ashamed of—for example, being disorganized, not being as patient as you want with others, or feeling envious of a colleague. In the letter, you might remind yourself that everyone struggles and that you aren't solely responsible for this shortcoming. You could also consider constructive ways to improve your habit or disposition.

Exploring Cynicism

Cynicism is an emotion that can completely shut off our ability to feel empathy or compassion for another. It may be the result of being hurt and disappointed, but its effect on us is counterproductive. Caitlin Moran, author of *How to Build a Girl* (2015), has this to say: "Cynicism is, ultimately, fear. Cynicism makes contact with your skin, and a thick black carapace begins to grow—like insect armor. This armor will protect your heart, from disappointment—but it leaves you almost unable to walk. You cannot dance in this armor. Cynicism keeps you pinned to the spot, in the same posture, forever" (p. 263).

When have you felt cynical? What was happening?

What effect did your cynicism have on your relationships with other people?

When have you perceived someone else's cynicism? How did it make you feel?

From *The Onward Workbook: Daily Activities to Cultivate Your Emotional Resilience and Thrive* by Elena Aguilar. Copyright © 2018 by Elena Aguilar. Reproduced by permission.

The Quest for Good

When you're dealing with someone you don't like, look for the good in him or her. Start by remembering that everyone wants to be happy and to feel a sense of belonging. Even if someone's actions seem to be leading him or her away from that goal, he or she does want to be happy and to belong. If you can't find one good attribute about someone, maybe there's been too much hurt or history. Don't force yourself or feel guilty that you can't find something good about this person; direct your attention to someone else and stay open to the idea that someday, there might be something good in the first person.

Who could you start with right now? What good might lie within this person? Don't force yourself, but be open. Jot down any thoughts.

Just Like Me

Call to mind a student, student's parent, colleague, or supervisor with whom you've really struggled.

Then say to yourself, or say aloud:

Just like me, this person has suffered in life.
Just like me, this person has made mistakes and has regrets.
Just like me, this person wants to be happy.

We often take other people's actions personally, yet most of the time, it's not personal. Saying these phrases cultivates an appreciation of that person as someone trying to do the right thing, even if you don't like his or her behavior. This can also make his or her behavior feel less personal.

In the space here, draw a stick figure to represent the person you called to mind. Add a couple of details to identify the person. Then write the "just like me" phrases in the space around your drawing. If you want to include the person's name, go ahead.

The Fly on the Wall

Sometimes when something happens that makes us feel bad, we get caught up in the details about how we were wronged and how someone else's words or actions made us feel. In these moments, we're acting from what psychologists call a *self-immersed perspective*. We are seeing the situation from inside. If we can shift to a *self-distanced perspective*, observing the situation objectively from the outside, we can often find the clarity and insight necessary to move past our hurt.

When you're discussing a difficult situation, if you can adopt a self-distanced perspective, you may have a keener understanding of your reactions. You might also experience less emotional distress and fewer physiological signs of stress. (There's actually research to suggest that different parts of our brains, those less associated with strong emotions, are activated when we recollect experiences from a self-distanced perspective.) Weeks or months later, when you think back to that event, you may also feel less reactive if you've taken a self-distanced perspective.

Think of a current or past challenge. Visualize the situation as you were dealing with it—perhaps talking with a student after school about his or her behavior, or a tense meeting with an administration.

Now, visualize an observer—perhaps a fly on the wall, or a thoughtful and trusted friend. What does this observer see? What does he or she understand about the situation?

What advice does this observer have for you? How would this observer deal with your situation?

When we're experiencing a challenging event, it's easy to get sucked into its power. We ruminate over what's happening, the unfairness of things, and the way we are treated; we talk to others about the situation and our distress; we lie awake at night going over and over it. Our ruminations are often unproductive; they only make us feel more distressed. And we don't sleep. This is why it's so useful to have self-distancing strategies—so here's another one.

To create some temporal distance between the challenging event and yourself, ask, *How might I feel about this one week from now or 10 years from now?* This kind of mental time travel can direct your attention away from your immediate situation. Also, when we're in a difficult moment, the situation can feel permanent. Reminding yourself that the future exists and that you might feel different at some point can be calming.

Now try it. Recall a moment recently when you were upset about something—it could be a big thing or a small incident.

Distressing event:

How you might feel in a week:

How you might feel in one year:

From *The Onward Workbook: Daily Activities to Cultivate Your Emotional Resilience and Thrive* by Elena Aguilar. Copyright © 2018 by Elena Aguilar. Reproduced by permission.

How you might feel in 10 years:

One of the ways that envy can be our teacher is for us to pay attention to what it might be saying about what we want in our life. Envy is uncomfortable and can be very painful, but it may be giving us a clue about the changes we need to make in our life so that we can be happier.

Whom do you envy? What do you envy about this person's life?

What insight do you get into your life, and what you're missing or wanting in your life, from the envy you feel?

What could you do to bring those elements into your own life? What action could you take now to make those things happen?

From *The Onward Workbook: Daily Activities to Cultivate Your Emotional Resilience and Thrive* by Elena Aguilar. Copyright © 2018 by Elena Aguilar. Reproduced by permission.

Recognizing Bids for Attention

For several decades, Dr. John Gottman and Dr. Julie Schwartz Gottman have been studying what fosters happy and committed relationships. They lead the Gottman Institute, which focuses on research-based ways to strengthen relationships. One such way is to notice and respond appropriately to *bids*. A bid is any attempt by one person toward another to cultivate positive connection—attention, affirmation, affection.

A bid can be simple, such as a smile, or more complex, such as a request for help. Often, there is subtext that is easy to miss if we're not looking for it. For example, "I had a terrible conversation with a parent this afternoon" could mean "Will you help me process my emotions?" Or, "Let's get this meeting started" could really mean, "Will you help me?" If we regularly disregard these bids, either because we don't notice them or don't want to respond to them, the relationship weakens and the bids become less frequent.

Take a few minutes to think about the bids you make and the bids others make for your attention and affirmation at work (or elsewhere!). Consider:

What's one bid someone made to you today? How did you respond? What was the impact of that response?

What's one bid you made to someone else today? How did they respond? What was the impact of that response?

What do you know about how you make bids?

Could or should you get better at making bids? How?

How good are you at recognizing the difference between text and subtext? What helps you pay attention to subtext?

The Self-Compassion Journal

Part 1: Take 2–3 minutes to write about something you did that you feel bad about or for which you have judged yourself. For example, perhaps you snapped at a student and afterward felt ashamed. Be honest about your feelings.

Part 2: Imagine a fantasy friend who is unconditionally loving, accepting, kind, and compassionate. This friend sees all your strengths and weaknesses and loves and accepts you just as you are, with all your human imperfections. Take just a moment to close your eyes and imagine being in the presence of this kind and forgiving friend.

Part 3: In the space provided, write a journal entry from the perspective of your friend. How does your friend view your actions from his or her perspective of unlimited compassion? How does your friend convey his or her compassion for the pain you feel when you judge yourself harshly? If you think your friend would suggest changes you might make, how would these suggestions embody feelings of unconditional compassion?

Part 4: After writing the journal entry, put it down for a while. Come back after a few hours or even a few days and read the entry again, really letting the words sink in. You might even read it aloud. Feel the compassion pouring into you. Notice that compassion doesn't preclude change and understanding. You can still resolve to behave better and also take in compassion.

What did it feel like to do this exercise? What did you learn about yourself?

Cultivating Compassion for Difficult People

If you really want to transform how you experience a difficult person, you can. You always have the freedom to choose your attitude. This exercise is based on the Buddhist meditation known as *metta,* or loving kindness.

Start cultivating compassion for difficult people by beginning with a person with whom you're in a small conflict, or by whom you feel mildly bothered. This way you'll build compassion muscles, and later, down the road, you can work on compassion for the really difficult people in your life. Remember to be patient with yourself as you work to build your compassion. As meditation teacher Sharon Salzberg says in her book, *Real Happiness at Work,* "Sending loving-kindness to a difficult person is a process of relaxing the heart and freeing yourself from fear and corrosive resentment. We are working on our own timeline (2014, p. 97)."

You can find an audio recording of this exercise at www.onwardthebook.com.

Sit somewhere quiet, where you can draw your attention inward. Close your eyes or find a place to rest your gaze. Take a few deep and slow breaths.

Bring to mind someone by whom you're feeling challenged or bothered, or with whom you have a conflict. Now, bring your attention to the other person's suffering. Take a moment to recognize that like you, this person also suffers.

Say the following phrases to yourself, directing them toward the other person:

May you have happiness, clarity, and kindness.
May you be filled with loving kindness.
May you be free of suffering and the causes of suffering.
May you be free of anger and bitterness.

After you've sat with these feelings for a bit, capture a short reflection on your experience of this meditation.

From *The Onward Workbook: Daily Activities to Cultivate Your Emotional Resilience and Thrive* by Elena Aguilar. Copyright © 2018 by Elena Aguilar. Reproduced by permission.

"The Awesome Anthem"

Sekou Andrews is a spoken word poet, playwright, musician, and the creator of "The Awesome Anthem." You can find it here: www.theawesomeanthem.com.

Watch it. Right now. Seriously. Share it with kids, colleagues, friends, and neighbors.

What would you like to say to yourself that's inspired by this video? In the space provided, draw a mirror and you looking at yourself in the mirror. Add speech bubbles to say whatever you want to say to yourself.

Nonviolent Communication

Nonviolent communication is a method developed by Dr. Marshall B. Rosenberg intended to increase our sense of choice, meaning, and connectedness. It offers a four-step process both to express *how you are* and to empathetically receive *how others are.*

1. **Observations:** What can be perceived by the senses that may, or may not, be contributing to my own or another's well-being
2. **Feelings:** The feelings that emerge in response
3. **Needs:** What is needed or valued that causes that feeling
4. **Requests:** The concrete action I or you would like taken

By including all four steps in our communication, we invite connection and resolution without blaming or criticizing. Here is an example. Expressing *my own experience* might sound like this:

> Tony, when I see you looking at your phone while I'm talking during our department meeting (*observation*), I feel hurt (*feeling*) because it feels like my contributions to the team aren't valued (*need*). Would you be willing to keep your phone put away during our meetings or just to let me know if you need to be checking it for personal reasons, so I don't interpret it as you disregarding what I'm saying (*request*)?

Acknowledging *someone else's experience,* such as that of a student who blows up after receiving a poor grade, might sound like this:

> Denise, seeing that D (*observation*), it looks like you feel frustrated and maybe disappointed (*feeling*) because you worked hard on this project and want to do well in this class (*need*). Would you like to look over it together after school to see what revisions you might make so you can resubmit it on Friday (*request*)?

Now it's your turn! Think about a recent challenging interaction with someone at work (or not), one where perhaps both you and the other person were not having your needs met. Practice a nonviolent way to communicate those unmet needs and the requests that follow from them. Trying expressing your own experience. Then practice

From *The Onward Workbook: Daily Activities to Cultivate Your Emotional Resilience and Thrive* by Elena Aguilar. Copyright © 2018 by Elena Aguilar. Reproduced by permission.

responding to the other person's experience of the situation. Script these here, then practice saying them aloud.

If you're interested in learning more, check out www.nonviolentcommunication .com. In many communities in the United States and around the world, there are individuals who offer training in this method. You can study it on your own or in partnership with others.

Nonverbal Communication of Compassion

Animals, who can't talk of course, have many nonverbal ways to communicate care and compassion for each other. The great apes, for example, spend hours every day grooming each other, even when no one has lice. They use grooming to resolve conflicts and reward each other's generosity. Perhaps inspired by studying your own cat or dog, or reflecting on conflict resolution among apes, consider your own nonverbal communication of compassion.

How do you communicate care and compassion nonverbally to others?

What could you do today, when you go to work, to show others nonverbally that you care about them?

Of course, use your judgment if you're a hugger! Some people might not feel comfortable with physical affection, or it may not be appropriate. But perhaps if you see a colleague who's looking sad, you could say, "Could I give you a hug? Would that be okay?"

The People Who Support Me

When you're feeling stressed, threatened, or insecure, but you want to feel caring and connected to others, this exercise can help. Just thinking about the people we turn to when we're distressed can make us feel more compassionate toward others.

1.   Write down the names of one or two people to whom you turn when you feel stressed or upset.

2.   Write down three to five positive qualities that are common to these people. Maybe they are both good listeners, or they have a sense of humor.

3.   Recall a specific situation in which you felt worried or upset and one of these people helped you. Visualize that time.

4.   Write a brief description of that situation and the way you felt.

Four Minutes of Eye Contact

In 2016, Amnesty International in Europe was concerned about how Europeans were responding to the refugee crisis. They noted that when discussing the "problem" of refugees, people often used dehumanizing language and reduced human tragedies to statistics and numbers.

Amnesty conducted an experiment in Berlin in which they invited two strangers to sit down together—a European and a refugee who had been in Europe for less than a year—and just make eye contact with each other for four minutes. They found that these four minutes of eye contact brought people closer together than anything else.

Watch this video of the experiment: https://youtu.be/f7XhrXUoD6U

If you want to be really brave and bold, invite a colleague to engage in this activity with you. Just sit and look at each other for four minutes. You could also invite your team or staff to do this activity—it's a powerful community builder and cultivates empathy for one another in a unique way.

What implications for your work might there be from this idea?

Thirty-Six Questions to Fall in Love with Someone

In the mid-1990s, psychologist Arthur Aron identified 36 questions that when followed by four minutes of eye contact could make two strangers fall in love. In 2015, the writer and professor Mandy Len Cantron organized these questions a little, modified them just a bit, and conducted her own experiment with an acquaintance—and they fell in love. You can find her entertaining reflection on this experience online.

As I read the 36 questions, I thought about how discussing these could build intimacy and caring between any two people; falling in love didn't need to be the end goal. Conversations about these topics could strengthen our understanding of and compassion for each other. It would be easy to include 10 minutes of sharing time in a team meeting or longer in a staff retreat to discuss a set of these questions. Some of these questions could even be appropriate for students to talk about with each other.

As you read through the questions, check the ones that you'd like to ask a friend or colleague as a way of getting to know him or her better. And of course, if you're seeking to fall in love, try them all out! Don't forget that the original experiment included four minutes of silent eye contact following the hours discussing these questions. So if falling in love is your goal, be sure to include that part.

The Questions

Set I

1. Given the choice of anyone in the world, whom would you want as a dinner guest?
2. Would you like to be famous? In what way?
3. Before making a telephone call, do you ever rehearse what you are going to say? Why?
4. What would constitute a "perfect" day for you?
5. When did you last sing to yourself? To someone else?
6. If you were able to live to the age of 90 and retain either the mind or body of a 30-year-old for the last 60 years of your life, which would you want?
7. Do you have a secret hunch about how you will die?
8. Name three things you and your partner in this conversation appear to have in common.
9. What do you feel most grateful for in your life?
10. If you could change something about the way you were raised, what would it be?

From *The Onward Workbook: Daily Activities to Cultivate Your Emotional Resilience and Thrive* by Elena Aguilar. Copyright © 2018 by Elena Aguilar. Reproduced by permission.

11. Take four minutes and tell your partner your life story in as much detail as possible.
12. If you could wake up tomorrow having gained any one quality or ability, what would it be?

Set II

1. If a crystal ball could tell you the truth about yourself, your life, the future, or anything else, what would you want to know?
2. Is there something that you've dreamed of doing for a long time? Why haven't you done it?
3. What is the greatest accomplishment of your life?
4. What do you value most in a friendship?
5. What is your most treasured memory?
6. What is your most terrible memory?
7. If you knew that in one year you would die suddenly, would you change anything about the way you are now living? Why?
8. What does friendship mean to you?
9. What roles do love and affection play in your life?
10. Alternate sharing something you consider a positive characteristic of your partner. Share a total of five items.
11. How close and warm is your family? Do you feel that your childhood was happier than most other people's?
12. How do you feel about your relationship with your mother?

Set III

1. Make three true "we" statements each. For instance, "We are both in this room feeling . . ."
2. Complete this sentence: "I wish I had someone with whom I could share . . ."
3. If you were going to become a close friend with your partner, share what would be important for him or her to know.
4. Tell your partner what you like about him or her; be very honest.
5. Share an embarrassing moment in your life.
6. When did you last cry in front of another person? By yourself?
7. Tell your partner something that you like about him or her.
8. What, if anything, is too serious to be joked about?
9. If you were to die this evening with no opportunity to communicate with anyone, what would you most regret not having told someone? Why haven't you told them yet?

10. Your house, containing everything you own, catches fire. After saving your loved ones and pets, you have time to safely make a final dash to save any one item. What would it be? Why?

11. Of all the people in your family, whose death would you find most disturbing? Why?

12. Share a personal problem and ask your partner's advice on how he or she might handle it. Also ask your partner to reflect back to you how you seem to be feeling about the problem you have chosen.

Eat Together

Some of my favorite memories of connecting with students' parents during my years as a teacher were when we had potlucks. Parents would bring foods they'd lovingly prepared from their cultural traditions, parents who didn't speak the same language would show delight at tasting each other's foods, and without words, they'd connect. Students would feel pride in seeing their parents' being appreciated. We'd simply come together and joyfully share a meal.

This is such a simple way to build connection and compassion with one another. There's something very primal about eating together. Break bread with colleagues, students, and students' parents. In fact, the word *companion* is Latin for "with bread." Sit around on a picnic blanket or at a table and share stories as you eat.

How could you act on this suggestion? When and where might you have an opportunity to gather people for a meal?

A Meditation to Boost Equanimity

Equanimity is one of the more challenging states to cultivate, because it can often feel nebulous. Try this meditation for a series of days and see if it helps you understand what equanimity is or could be. You can also find a recording of it on www.onwardthebook.com.

Sit comfortably and close your eyes. Take a few deep breaths. Let your awareness move slowly throughout your body, inviting each area to relax.

Silently say to yourself, *May I be centered in this moment.*

Imagine feeling balanced and grounded.

Just notice if thoughts arise that wish for things to be different than how they are in that moment.

Don't try to push away confusion or agitation. Just breathe and imagine yourself resting between wanting to change things and pushing the present away.

Between desire and aversion is where equanimity lives.

Imagine that equanimity exists, and imagine that you can rest there, even for just a second.

Preventing Empathic Fatigue

When we completely take on other people's suffering as our own, we risk feeling personally distressed, threatened, and overwhelmed. In some cases, this can even lead to burnout. Rather than being a sponge when you experience other people's distress, try to be receptive to their feelings without adopting those feelings as your own.

When I'm with someone who is in distress, I often visualize myself inside a big bubble, and the other person is in his bubble. I can hear what he says, I can see him, and I can communicate care and concern, but his distress stays contained within his space. Our bubbles don't cut us off from each other; they simply contain our energies.

Can you recall a time when you were with someone who was really distressed and you sensed yourself taking in his or her feelings?

Try drawing yourself here, inside a bubble, standing next to the other person, who stands inside his or her bubble. Add speech or thought bubbles if you want.

A Letter to Envy

What would you like to say to the envy that exists within you? What would you like to ask your envy? What would you like to request of it? Write a letter to the envy inside of you.

Here's part of my letter to envy: *I am so ashamed of you that I don't even know where to start. I'm afraid to look at you. I'm afraid of what you want to say to me. But someone I trust suggested that I get to know you, suggested that I could learn from you, so I'm here.*

Artistic Depictions of Envy

Go to your preferred online search engine and look for images of envy—or another term that reflects envy, such as jealousy, resentment, or competitiveness (see "The Core Emotions" in Chapter 2 for these terms).

See what comes up, and then search for "depictions of envy in art."

Look closely at a few of those images. Sit with them and spend some time getting to know them. Pay attention to how they make you feel and what thoughts go through your mind.

Reflect

What do you notice in the images that come up?

What have you learned about envy through doing this exploration?

How did this exploration help you understand your own experience of envy?

If you'd like, print out one (or more) of the images that particularly speak to you and stick them in here.

Destination Postcard: Compassion

What would it look and sound like if you had far greater levels of compassion? Draw a picture of yourself with thought bubbles and labels that depict a compassionate you. If you'd like, draw this you at work, surrounded by kids and colleagues. How might you be in that space?

Chapter Reflection

What were your biggest takeaways from this chapter?

Of the different activities in this chapter, which were most useful?

Which activities would you like to revisit periodically? How might you get that habit going?

What implications do the ideas in this chapter have for the work you do?

CHAPTER 9

Be a Learner

If we see challenges as opportunities for learning, if we engage our curiosity whenever we're presented with an obstacle, we're more likely to find solutions. This habit and disposition help us not just survive adversity but thrive in the aftermath.

February: Around midyear, you may have the bandwidth to reflect on how you learn and to return to your beginner's mind, because learning is a path to growth and resilience.

Be a Learner: Resilience Self-Assessment

The purpose of this self-assessment is to help you gauge the level of your resilience reservoir and to explore what might be draining or what could replenish it. The exercises that follow and the information in the corresponding chapter of *Onward* can boost your resilience by helping you see challenges and failures as opportunities for growth and new learning.

Imagine each circle as a little *cenote* or reservoir within you, and fill it up according to how much each statement reflects a source of resilience. If you need something more concrete, imagine marks at ¼, ½, and ¾ full.

Before you start the exercises in this chapter, take this self-assessment and fill in the date. At the end of the month, take the assessment again. (You might even cover up your original markings with a strip of paper.) Is your resilience reservoir a little more full? If so, which practices do you want to keep up? If not, what else do you want to try?

Statement	Date:	Date:
I understand how taking the stance of a learner can help me manage difficult moments.	◯	◯
I have ways to think about myself as a learner that help me grow in the areas in which I want to grow.	◯	◯
When I can't do something I want to do, I can clearly identify why I can't do it.	◯	◯
I know how to get myself into the state of mind of a learner.	◯	◯

I can guide and direct my own learning when there's something I want to do or to do better.	◯	◯
I can evaluate the conditions in which my learning occurs, and I do what I can to create optimal conditions in which to learn.	◯	◯
I have strong time management strategies.	◯	◯
I manage my time in a way that allows for time to learn and to develop my practice.	◯	◯
I value and appreciate curiosity.	◯	◯
I have ways to cultivate my own curiosity.	◯	◯

How Writing Helps You Learn

Writing helps us clarify and organize thoughts, see our growth and progress, achieve goals, and perhaps even feel happier. Writing also keeps us honest and allows us to remember what our faulty memories often forget. This month, consider using writing as a tool to help you reflect on who you are as an educator, make growth, and cultivate resilience.

Here are some topics you could write about. Select one and then build in writing as much as possible this month.

Goals. Committing goals to paper helps you realize and accept your hopes, dreams, and desires and helps you make decisions when you're stuck. You don't have to achieve all your goals, nor will they always stay the same, but you're more likely to follow through on goals if you've written them down.

Ideas. Keep a notebook, use sticky notes, find an app you like, and record your ideas about units, lessons, blogs to write, field trips to take, and so on. Teaching is about creating learning experiences, and this creativity requires lots of ideas. You most likely have them—now capture them.

Anxieties. Writing about your worries can help you feel calmer, especially if you designate a time to do this. For example, during the day if you find yourself worrying about something, remind yourself that Worry Time is 5:00–5:15 and that you'll write down all your worries then. Writing down anxieties is also useful because you can later look back at them and see that many expected catastrophes did not happen. As Mark Twain said, "I've had a lot of worries in my life, most of which never happened." Writing down your anxieties will clear out space for learning.

Experiences. Keep a journal. The process of recording the experience may give you insight into what happened and enables you to see a record of events. And who knows? Perhaps in 20 years you'll have material for a book!

Ask a Question

This is a simple morning meditation to help you anchor yourself in curiosity, the disposition of the month. Set your timer for three to five minutes. Simply sit quietly, close your eyes, take a few slow breaths, and ask a question that you want answers to or are working on. Here are some of the questions I've asked:

- How can I be more patient with _____ (a particular student)?
- How can I notice the bright spots today?
- Where can I find joy in teaching today?
- How do I know I'm in the right job?

Then sit quietly and see where your mind takes you. Every so often, or whenever you need to re-anchor in curiosity, repeat the question to yourself.

When you finish this mediation, jot down a few insights you gained, if any.

This morning, draw yourself as a superhero. This is meant to be a quick activity to help prime your mind before going to work. Superheroes are heroic, self-sacrificing at times, and tremendously courageous—and that's what I'm hoping to wake up in you this morning. Do you want a costume, cape, or mask? Do you want to enhance your body or your brain? Add speech and thought bubbles, or if you want to draw a short comic strip, go ahead.

The Million-Dollar Question:
What Can I Learn?

This chapter's habit, Be a Learner, is a stance to embody. At its core, this stance is an invocation to remember that whenever you're in a difficult moment, you can ask yourself, *What can I learn right now?* After a parent yells at you, a kid throws his books on the floor and bolts from the room, or an unplanned fire drill goes off in the middle of the final rehearsal for the spring play, ask yourself: *What can I learn right now?*

Asking this question catapults you into a learning stance from which you can see challenges as opportunities for growth, rather than as threats. Asking yourself this question can subtly shift you away from identifying too closely with the emotion you feel. The trick is to remember to ask yourself the question when strong emotions are triggered.

Write this on a piece of paper—*What can I learn right now?*—and post it on the wall. How many times can you ask yourself this today?

Action Research: What and Why

Action research is a transformational approach to professional learning that any educator can engage in alone or with others. It's a way of guiding your own learning around a student-centered dilemma that really matters, such that you will more quickly uncover solutions to your problems. It honors the intellect of teachers, invites us to rigorously and productively participate in our classrooms, and produces results.

When I started teaching sixth-grade humanities, I discovered that the majority of my students didn't like reading. I identified a simple and authentic question for my inquiry project: How can I get my students to love to read? I began my inquiry by seeking a deeper understanding of their attitudes. Without judgment and with only the intent to learn more, I interviewed students, conducted surveys, observed my students, and listened to them talk to each other. As I did this, I immediately got ideas about methods I could try the next day. Sometimes my research illuminated what I didn't know, and I sought out additional resources. As I implemented new routines and designed new lessons, my students' attitudes shifted and their skills improved.

Action research made me feel engaged in the classroom in a new way. Every day I learned something about teaching, and every day I could see positive changes in my students. I'd hear revealing comments from students like Vincent, who, at the start of Sustained Silent Reading, reached into his desk and said to Stephan, "When we came in this morning I saw this book on the shelves about deep sea creatures, and I snagged it," and I'd note that as a positive indicator of his attitude, as well as of the genre that he wanted to read. On the day that Anthony loudly expressed his dislike of reading—"It's so boring! What's the point?"—I thought, *Oh! That's a good question!* And I saw an opportunity to explore the purpose of reading, which became a lesson later that week.

Inquiry helped me know my class of sixth-grade students better than any I'd ever taught before. Paying acute attention to everything they said helped me appreciate and connect more fully with them. It also helped me see bright spots and successes. And, with my inquiry lens on, there was something to celebrate every day. I hadn't seen it when I focused on deficits and shortcomings. Action research showed me that if I paid attention to my students in the right way and listened to them carefully, I could find ways to help them make reading growth. This gave me a sense of power that I'd never felt before as a teacher, but had always yearned for.

What thoughts come up for you as you read this description of my inquiry project?

How do you think action research could be useful to you?

When you think about teaching and your students, what would you like to know more about?

Mini Inquiry Cycle

You can try an inquiry project for a month, a semester, or a year. Try it alone, with a partner teacher, or with your department, and see how you feel. Here are some guidelines for using inquiry.

1. Brainstorm a list of questions. They should be open ended and could start with *What* or *How.* For example: How can I get my students to love reading? What gets my students interested in polynomials? How can I help cultivate a school environment where a student can feel comfortable on a social and emotional level, while lowering the affective filter that he or she experiences in the classroom? How can I increase verbal participation of girls during whole-class discussions of literature?

2. Create a plan. Try different things in the classroom. Do things you've never done before that might offer insight into your question. Ask colleagues for their ideas. Consult other resources—books, articles, and experts.

3. Implement that plan. Do these things. Pay close attention to what happens.

4. Collect data. Take notes on the results of what you try and what you hear and notice in your students. Survey your students. Look at their work.

5. Adjust your plan. Let the data direct you to actions that could help you continue to answer your question.

That's pretty much it. If you are intrigued and want to go deeper into inquiry, you can find resources in Appendix F in *Onward,* "Resources for Further Learning."

Lessons on Learning from Merlin

T. H. White's novel *The Once and Future King*, based on the legend of King Arthur, offers us a provocative passage related to learning. In it, the wizard, Merlin, who has been entrusted with educating the future king, is speaking to the young Arthur at what we'd call a "teachable moment":

> "The best thing for being sad," replied Merlin, beginning to puff and blow, "is to learn something. That's the only thing that never fails. You may grow old and trembling in your anatomies, you may lie awake at night listening to the disorder of your veins, you may miss your only love, you may see the world around you devastated by evil lunatics, or know your honor trampled in the sewers of baser minds. There is only one thing for it then—to learn. Learn why the world wags and what wags it. That is the only thing which the mind can never exhaust, never alienate, never be tortured by, never fear or distrust, and never dream of regretting. Learning is the only thing for you. Look what a lot of things there are to learn."

What connections can you make with this passage? What does it raise for you?

Get Rid of Uncomfortable Clothes

Being slightly uncomfortable in your clothes will drain your resilience. I'm serious. That little drain of energy all day as you register that your pants are just a bit snug or that your shoes pinch your baby toes will add up day after day. Uncomfortable clothes do not belong in the closet of the resilient. Get rid of them.

And if you're wondering what this has to do with the theme of the month, Be a Learner, it's only remotely connected. I just really wanted to put this activity in this book. Maybe the connection is that it's important for you to learn about your body and what it needs and what feels comfortable. So much of what we wear emerges from our distorted notions of how society thinks we should look. What do you love to wear? What do you feel good in? Consider that a mini inquiry for the month.

Go fill up a bag full of uncomfortable clothes and take it to a donation center. And now, draw a picture of what you love to wear. Feel free to draw multiple pictures if you like!

Get Rid of Some More Things

The habit of this month, Be a Learner, is really only possible if you have space in your head to take in new things. We all live with all kinds of clutter in our minds and inboxes and houses.

What clutter can you clear out? Here are a few suggestions:

- Unsubscribe from email mailing lists that you don't read and that clutter your inbox—the email lists you never joined and the ones you did sign up for but now realize you just don't have time to read.
- Get rid of an app that distracts you, that doesn't make you feel good, or that sucks your soul. You can always reinstall it, but you also might find that you don't miss it.
- Do a task on your "I don't have time for this" list—the kind of task that you don't like to do and never want to do, but that's always lingering in the back of your mind, nagging at you. Get that blood test done; make a dentist appointment; respond to that email you really don't want to deal with. This stuff takes up so much energy in the back of your mind. Check one off.
- Try reducing clutter with the one-minute rule: Don't put off anything that takes less than a minute. Take junk mail straight from the mailbox to the recycling bin; put your work bag directly in its place when you get home; return whiteboard markers to their tray at the end of class.

Piggyback Behaviors

What's a learning habit that you'd like to build? It could be one that you read about in *Onward* or that appeared earlier in this chapter. According to Thaler and Sunstein in their book *Nudge* (2009), a good way to build in a new behavior is to tack it on to an existing habit.

Want to start taking vitamins every day? Identify the already existing habit, such as eating breakfast, and attach vitamin taking to it. As your brain learns to associate the two behaviors, the new behavior becomes unconsciously integrated. Think of a new habit as an add-on to something you already do routinely.

What's a learning habit that you'd like to develop with which you could practice this behavior-changing trick?

Parker Palmer's Words on Learning

You may not like what you learn about yourself or the world. But if you learn it well, it might help you become an agent of transformation—even when (to quote Merlin) you are seeing "the world around you devastated by evil lunatics."

PARKER PALMER

What does this quote raise for you? What does it imply?

Whom Do I Want as a Mentor?

According to Dr. Anders Ericsson, the professor who came up with the "10,000 hours" theory of expertise, the first step in getting better at anything is to find a mentor. This needs to be someone whom you admire, who is doing something in a way that you might eventually like to do it. A mentor can help you identify what you might need to learn and the steps involved in acquiring the skill set that he or she has.

A mentor has experienced what you're going through and offers guidance and emotional support. A mentor also often acts as a role model, giving you something to emulate and aspire to. For the first couple of years that I was an instructional coach, every time I faced a challenge, I would think of Liz, my phenomenal coach, and I'd ask myself, *What would Liz do?* I was surprised how often this helped me identify new options when I was stuck.

Make a list of people you would like as a mentor. You are welcome to include unrealistic possibilities (Merlin, Professor Dumbledore, John Lennon) as well as realistic ones.

How to Find a Mentor

To find a mentor, you first need to know yourself and what you need. Look for someone with resilience, someone who, as Dan Coyle says, "scares you a little," and who seems relatively content in his or her profession. You'll want and need many mentors over the course of your life, so be on the lookout. Find someone who has done things you think you want to do.

To connect with a potential mentor, reach out in an email and share uncommon commonalities. Ask good questions—not the kind you can find an answer to in Google. (Never ask this kind of question; it says that you aren't respecting the person's time.) Do everything you can do within your power to get better, and a potential mentor will see that and want to support you. Show that you're resourceful. When you meet, ask good questions and listen. This isn't your time to share your opinions or extensively process. You want to glean insights from this potential mentor. Make the person feel that he or she has unique value.

Here's an example of what this could sound like:

Last year, when I saw you present at our district training, you mentioned your love of horse-back riding. Although I don't ride myself, I was raised among women who rode horses, and felt a connection with you. I wondered whether for you, riding is a way of relaxing and rejuvenating from this work we do; I'm always seeking insight into how we deal with the stressors of teaching. I am wondering if you'd be willing to have a cup of coffee together and share your reflections on thriving in our district. I can see that you've acquired some healthy strategies to do so, and I aspire to be here for a long stretch, too.

Take the first action, right now, to connect with a mentor. Identify a couple of people you might approach, and draft an email.

How to Receive Feedback

Seeking feedback is a key way to increase self-awareness. We all have blind spots, aspects of ourselves that we can't see but others can. To see ourselves as we are, not just as we *think* we are, we must seek feedback. If we're really lucky, there'll be people in our lives who see our blind spots and have the courage to share them with us in a way that we can truly hear the feedback. We need to develop a crew of these people who are willing to hold up the mirror, who see our blind spots and care about us enough to skillfully let us know what's up. In order to find and keep these people, you need to be good at asking for and receiving feedback.

Stone and Heen's book *Thanks for the Feedback* (2014) is a comprehensive and helpful guide to seeking and learning from feedback. One of my favorite chapters has to do with how to dismantle our distortions of feedback. Here, the authors recommend:

1. **Be prepared; be mindful.** Consider how you typically respond to less-than-favorable feedback. Do you start by accepting it and then dismiss it with time? Do you get defensive? Do you blame, chatter, get very quiet? Ask yourself, *How do I typically react?*
2. **Separate the strands: Feeling, story, feedback.** It can be helpful to tease apart your emotions and interpretations from the actual feedback. Simply ask yourself, *What do I feel? What's the story I'm telling? What's the actual feedback?*
3. **Contain the story.** When we distort feedback, we tend to do so in predictable ways. Specifically, we generalize shortcomings to see them as overly personal ("I messed up" becomes "I'm a bad person"), overly permanent ("I messed up this time" becomes "I always mess up"), or overly pervasive ("I did this wrong" becomes "I do everything wrong"). Again, ask yourself, *What's the actual feedback?*
4. **Change your vantage point.** If our interpretation is distorted, perhaps we need to view the feedback from a different perspective—that of a friend or sibling, or ourselves 10 to 20 years in the future. Ask yourself, *How might my sister/my colleague/the future me interpret this feedback?*

Consider a piece of feedback you recently received, either solicited or not. How did the feedback sit with you? As you consider the distortions noted here, do any stand out for you? How else might you interpret the feedback you received? Jot your reflections here.

How to Give Feedback

Sometimes we are called to *offer* feedback to someone else. If you work in education, chances are good that it's part of your job to give feedback—to students, to staff, to people you supervise. When it's your turn to offer feedback, you'll find it helpful to keep in mind your own challenges receiving and acting on feedback. It can also be helpful to distinguish among three types of feedback.

1. **Appreciation.** "I'm so glad you're on this committee. Your insight this afternoon really moved the discussion forward." Although this kind of feedback may seem to be the least helpful, it's essential to building relationships and creating inclusive learning environments. And let's be honest, it's often what we want when we ask for feedback. We all need appreciation and validation from time to time.

2. **Coaching.** "When you said that, it seemed to me you were feeling frustrated, and others in the group stopped listening. Is that what you saw?" Coaching can help us learn and grow by focusing our attention and energies. However, it requires that both parties be clear on the role of the person offering feedback. For example, well-intended administrators often offer coaching feedback following an observation, when teachers are expecting evaluation and hoping for appreciation.

3. **Evaluation.** "This assignment asked you to contrast two poems, but you analyzed only one. You'll have to redo it if you want a passing grade." Evaluative feedback tells us where we stand. Although this type of feedback can leave us feeling judged, if we *don't* receive a clear message on our standing, we go looking for it in appreciation and coaching feedback, which doesn't always give us an accurate reading on our performance.

Before offering feedback, take a moment to check in with the recipient about the kind of feedback he or she is wanting or expecting. You might ask, "I'm intending to give you coaching; is that how you're hearing it? From your point of view, is that what you need right now?"

Think about the people to whom you offer feedback in the course of your job. What type of feedback are you usually offering? How do you deliver it?

What type(s) of feedback might they have been needing or wanting? How might you offer it?

The One-Sentence Journal

If you don't really like writing, but I'm starting to get to you with my frequent injunctions that you should write, try keeping a one-sentence journal. That's all you need to do each day—just script one sentence with a few juicy details about your day, a light reflection, or a statement about your mindset or heart. Here's my one-sentence entry from yesterday: *Meeting with X reminded me of how much I love coaching and must make sure I get to coach every week—I learn so much each time I coach and it's mutually rewarding.*

Just do one sentence. Try it here for this week, and then if you want to continue, get yourself a little notebook or journal to continue.

Monday:

Tuesday:

Wednesday:

Thursday:

Friday:

From *The Onward Workbook: Daily Activities to Cultivate Your Emotional Resilience and Thrive* by Elena Aguilar. Copyright © 2018 by Elena Aguilar. Reproduced by permission.

Indicators of a Learning Organization

This activity can help you reflect on the degree to which your organization is a learning organization. It can be very hard to push your own learning to a really deep place if you're in an organization that is a weak learning organization. Rate the following indicators of a learning organization on a 1–5 scale (1 = low; 5 = high) as they apply to you and as you perceive them applying to your colleagues.

Element	Indicator	Rating (1–5)	Evidence, Comments, Reflections
Learning Environment			
Psychological Safety	We can disagree with colleagues or supervisors; we can ask any kind of question; we can make mistakes; we can express divergent opinions.		
Appreciation of Differences	Our discussions surface differences in ideas; we have healthy disagreements about ideas.		
Openness to New Ideas	We are encouraged to take risks and try new things, and we do so.		
Time for Reflection	We take time to pause, thoughtfully reflect on our processes, and learn from our experiences.		
Feedback	We get feedback on our work from multiple sources (including from colleagues and supervisors).		
Purpose	We feel that our work matters to us personally and is connected to something bigger than us.		

Element	Indicator	Rating (1–5)	Evidence, Comments, Reflections
Learning Processes and Practices			
Orientation	Our learning is connected to and in support of the organization's core purpose.		
Generation	We learn together.		
Interpretation	We make sense of our learning together.		
Dissemination	We share what we learn with each other and outside of our group and organization.		
Leadership			
Listening and Questioning	Leaders prompt dialogue and debate.		
Ensuring Process	Leaders ensure time for reflection, generation, interpretation, and dissemination.		
Openness	Leaders are willing to entertain alternative points of view.		
Modeling	Leaders make their learning visible and model the practices of a learner.		

Source: Adapted from Garvin, D., A. Edmondson, and F. Gino, "Is Yours a Learning Organization?" *Harvard Business Review,* March 2008, 109–116.

Reflect

What insights did this activity give you into your organization?

How do you think the state of your organization, in terms of its being a learning organization, affects your ability to learn?

The Power of Yet: A Musical Interlude

Go to YouTube and look for a song called "The Power of Yet" sung by Janelle Monae. Listen, watch, and sing along. This is another one to share with kids. It's the lyrics of a growth mindset. If you want, draw a picture that reflects a big takeaway from this song or how it relates to your life.

From *The Onward Workbook: Daily Activities to Cultivate Your Emotional Resilience and Thrive* by Elena Aguilar. Copyright © 2018 by Elena Aguilar. Reproduced by permission.

Expanding Your Learning Community

As I discussed in Chapter 4 of *Onward,* we are social creatures, we need each other to learn, and there's nothing like good colleagues to help you manage the stress of teaching, as well as to find joy.

Do whatever you can to create a healthy community of collegial learners—go outside your grade level or school setting, find folks online, and then learn together. Start a book club. Share videos of yourself teaching (or leading or coaching). Ask questions and listen to each other.

What's the state of your learning community now? With whom do you learn? In what structures?

Where are there gaps in your learning community? For example, do you have people who teach the same thing you teach with whom you can learn about that content? Or do you wish you had more opportunities to learn with others in person, rather than just virtually? What else would you like in your learning community as far as structures, routines, and people?

With whom would you like to learn? Do you have specific ideas of people you'd like in your learning community? What would you like to learn?

What could you do right now to expand or strengthen the community of adults with whom you learn? Could you send an email to a colleague inviting her to read an article together? Could you ask your principal if you could attend a workshop? Could you get onto www.onwardthebook.com and join us there for a discussion of this chapter? Do it. Now.

From The Onward Workbook: Daily Activities to Cultivate Your Emotional Resilience and Thrive by Elena Aguilar. Copyright © 2018 by Elena Aguilar. Reproduced by permission.

Cultivating Curiosity: The Art of Noticing

Curiosity is like a muscle: It gets strengthened with use and can atrophy from neglect. If you are fortunate enough to have small children in your life, then you know that humans are curious by nature. As we age, our increasing sense of responsibility can alienate us from the innate desire to explore and understand the world around us.

Today, make a point of noticing. Set an intention to "see" the world through fresh eyes, perhaps a child's eyes. You might make this intention broadly, or commit to noticing in a particular way. For example:

- Follow the color red (or any other color). Let red objects trace a path through your day.
- Look up or down instead of straight ahead as you walk. What lies just beyond your usual view?
- Study the space between. Look for the negative space—the holes, the space between columns, the line created by the edge of a lamp . . .

At the end of the day, use this space to jot down—or sketch!—some of what you noticed.

Growing Brains

In the space here, draw a large picture of what you think your brain looks like. (You can interpret this literally or figuratively.) Fill your drawing with some of the plethora of things your brain holds—knowledge, skills, memories, words, intuitions, emotions.

Now, in the space around your brain, write in some of the things you'd *like* your brain to hold. Redraw the outline of your original brain to include everything you've added. Try to imagine your own brain growing larger to hold these new things.

Cultivating Curiosity . . . by Knowing More

We shall not cease from exploration, and the end of all our exploring will be to arrive where we started and know the place for the first time.

T. S. ELIOT

The more we know about something, the more we *want* to know. Sometimes the best way to spark curiosity about a topic is just to dip our toes in the water. Find a way to expose yourself to new ideas on a daily basis. Here are some ideas:

- Follow the blog *Brainpickings,* by Maria Popova, described as "an inventory of cross-disciplinary interestingness, spanning art, science, design, history, philosophy, and more."
- Subscribe to a monthly magazine that covers a wide range of topics, such as the *Smithsonian* or the *Atlantic.*
- Read any book by Bill Bryson, an author with a miraculous ability to weave seemingly unconnected topics together into a compelling narrative. (A personal favorite of mine is *Home: A Short History of Private Life.*)
- Spend an hour or two hopping hyperlinks on Wikipedia—the modern-day equivalent of flipping through an encyclopedia.
- Pick up a catalog from your local community college and skim through the community classes available next term. Always wanted to learn photography? French? Guitar? Pick something.
- Visit a specialty museum you've never been to before. Many counties also have historical societies with collections on local history.
- Subscribe to TedX on YouTube. Watch one talk a day for a month. Make a point of watching videos on unfamiliar topics.

Now decide—right now. What can you commit to doing for the next week, month, or year, to expose yourself to new ideas?

> I commit to . . .

Three Kinds of Curiosity

In his book *Curious: The Desire to Know and Why Your Future Depends on It* (2014), Ian Leslie argues that curiosity takes one of three forms.

1. **Diversive curiosity** encourages us to seek out new places, people, and things. This attraction to novelty is what leads some people to continually update their smartphone, peek behind the door that says No Entry, or attend a conference.
2. **Epistemic curiosity** is a quest for deeper knowledge, the kind that requires sustained attention and cognitive effort. According to Leslie, "it's what happens when diversive curiosity grows up" (p.11). It's hard work, but it's also more rewarding.
3. **Empathetic curiosity** leads us to wonder about the thoughts and feelings of others. It is a conscious practice. Leslie writes, "Diversive curiosity might make you wonder what a person does for a living; empathic curiosity makes you wonder *why* they do it" (p. xxi).

Take a moment to reflect on these three types of curiosity.

Which do you think you demonstrate most often? How does that curiosity show up?

How has that curiosity served you in the past? Can you think of a specific time when demonstrating one of these kinds of curiosity made a situation (or your perception of it) better?

Which are you most interested in cultivating? Why? What difference might it make in your life if you demonstrated more of that type of curiosity?

Cultivating Curiosity: Backwards

Play is a wonderful way to reconnect with our inner child and draw out our innate curiosity. Look for ways to add interest by creating games out of mundane tasks. Change your setting, switch up your method, try working backward or upside down.

Sit with this idea for a while, then envision yourself turning a mundane task into a game. For myself, I chose to turn laundry into a basketball game. Pair of socks—two points! Jeans—two points! Yoga pants—rim shot from the doorway, three points!

Draw yourself engaged in this activity. (Stick figures welcome!)

Now go out and do it! Come back here to record a few thoughts about how it felt. Did you notice anything new about the task or about how you felt doing it?

Beliefs and Assumptions About Time

What do you believe about time? What do you find yourself saying about time? (For example, *I wish I had more time; there's never enough.*)

Where do you think your notions of time come from? Can you identify any dominant messages about time from your childhood family, culture, or religious traditions?

What are some other ways of thinking about time that you'd like to try using?

What do you feel like you have time for right now in your life?

What don't you have time for now that you'd like to have time for?

What do you spend time on that you could use for a different purpose?

Tracking My Time

Keep track of your time this week. How do you use it? What do you do? You could do this here or on a calendar. The more detail the better. Pay close attention to unstructured time—before and after school, prep time, and lunch.

	Before School	Lunch and Prep	After School to Bedtime
Monday			
Tuesday			
Wednesday			
Thursday			
Friday			

What do you notice about how you use your time throughout the day?

Are there any ways you'd like to shift these patterns?

What Else Could This Mean?

Most misunderstandings in the world could be avoided if people would simply take the time to ask, "What else could this mean?"
SHANNON L. ALDER

Think of a time when you *have* stopped to ask yourself the question *What else could this mean?* What were the circumstances?

What did your second look reveal that you missed the first time? How did that second look change what happened after the event? Write about that experience here—or draw it!

What would you like to say to the shame inside you? What would you like to ask it? What would you like to tell it? Here's how my letter starts: *Get the fuck out of me!* And then I get all compassionate and reflective.

Artistic Depictions of Shame

Go to your preferred online search engine and look for images of shame—or another term that reflects shame, such as guilt, humiliation, or regret (see "The Core Emotions" in Chapter 2 for these terms).

See what comes up, and then search for "depictions of shame in art."

Look closely at a few of those images. Sit with them and spend some time getting to know them. Pay attention to how they make you feel and what thoughts go through your mind.

Reflect

What do you notice in the images that come up?

What have you learned about shame through doing this exploration?

How did this exploration help you understand your own experience of shame?

If you'd like, print out one (or more) of the images that particularly speak to you and stick them in here.

Destination Postcard: Being a Learner

What would it look and sound like if you took the stance of a learner every day? Draw a picture of yourself with thought bubbles and labels to describe a you in the mindset of a learner. If you'd like, draw this you at work, surrounded by kids and colleagues. How might you be in that space?

Chapter Reflection

What were your biggest takeaways from this chapter?

Of the different activities in this chapter, which were most useful?

Which activities would you like to revisit periodically? How might you get that habit going?

What implications do the ideas in this chapter have for the work you do?

From *The Onward Workbook: Daily Activities to Cultivate Your Emotional Resilience and Thrive* by Elena Aguilar. Copyright © 2018 by Elena Aguilar. Reproduced by permission.

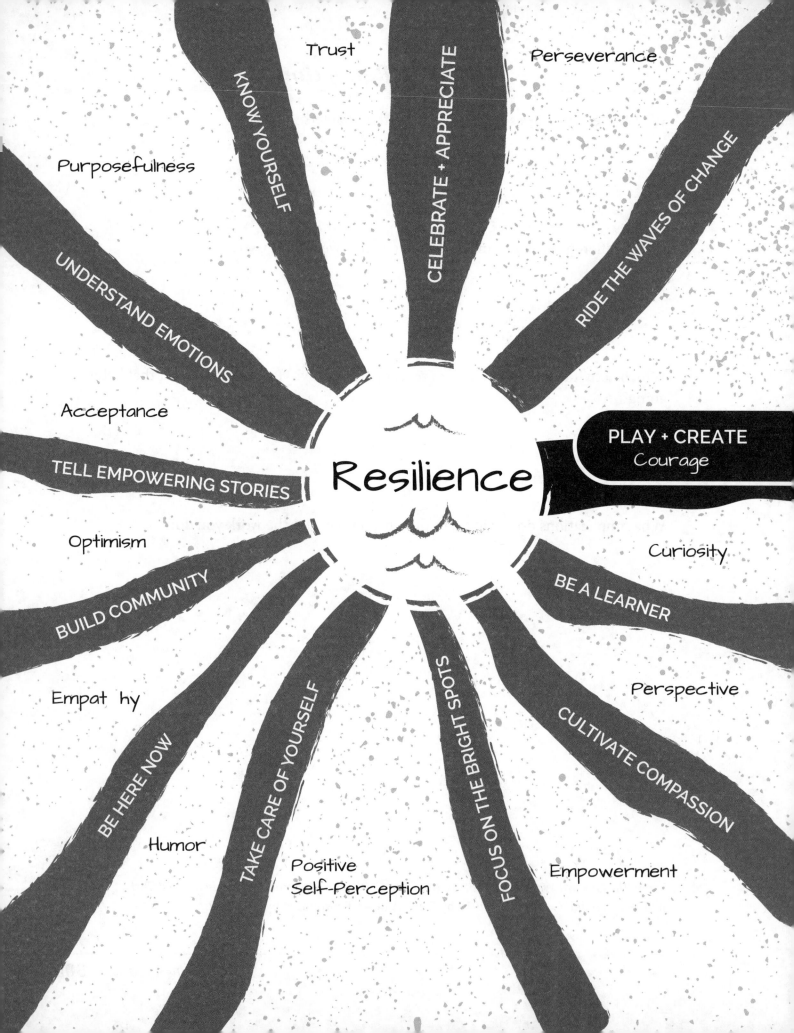

CHAPTER 10

Play and Create

Creativity and play unlock inner resources for dealing with stress, solving problems, and enjoying life. When we are creative, we are resourceful, and we problem-solve in new and original ways, which fuels our courage. Our thinking expands, and our connections with ourselves and others deepen.

March: Spring break brings an opportunity to explore play and creativity so that you can integrate these activities into daily life. Resilience arises from creation.

Play and Create: Resilience Self-Assessment

The purpose of this self-assessment is to help you gauge the level of your resilience reservoir and to explore what might be draining or what could replenish it. The exercises that follow and the information in the corresponding chapter of *Onward* can boost your resilience by inviting your inner maker-creator out to play for a while.

Imagine each circle as a little *cenote* or reservoir within you, and fill it up according to how much each statement reflects a source of resilience. If you need something more concrete, imagine marks at ¼, ½, and ¾ full.

Before you start the exercises in this chapter, take this self-assessment and fill in the date. At the end of the month, take the assessment again. (You might even cover up your original markings with a strip of paper.) Is your resilience reservoir a little more full? If so, which practices do you want to keep up? If not, what else do you want to try?

Statement	Date:	Date:
I understand what play is and why it's important.	◯	◯
I understand how creativity cultivates resilience.	◯	◯
I know many ways to play, and I engage in them sometimes.	◯	◯
I appreciate how experiencing and/or creating art helps people explore and process emotions.	◯	◯

I understand the many aspects of creativity and the many ways that it can be expressed.	◯	◯
I'm not afraid of doing art.	◯	◯
I know how to boost my creativity.	◯	◯
I can access my courage when I need to, and I feel that I have a deep reserve of it.	◯	◯
I know how to boost my courage.	◯	◯
I recognize and appreciate the role that art plays in a healthy, resilient society.	◯	◯

Your Play Personality

Stuart Brown, author of *Play* (2010), identifies eight "play personalities":

1. The joker: Makes people laugh, plays practical jokes
2. The kinesthete: Loves to move, dance, play sports, hike, bike
3. The explorer: Meets new people, seeks out new experiences
4. The competitor: Loves all forms of competition, loves to keep score
5. The director: Has fun planning and executing events and experiences
6. The collector: Revels in the thrill of collecting objects and experiences
7. The artist/creator: Finds joy in working with his or her hands or making things
8. The storyteller: Uses his or her imagination to create and absorb stories

Which is your most dominant play personality or combination of play personalities?

Which play personality would you like to explore?

Think of your close friends. What are their play personalities?

From The Onward Workbook: Daily Activities to Cultivate Your Emotional Resilience and Thrive by Elena Aguilar. Copyright © 2018 by Elena Aguilar. Reproduced by permission.

Six Ways to Water Your Creativity

We've all got the seeds of creativity inside us; some of us just have parched soil that requires intensive watering. Whether you want to cultivate your creativity when you're working on lesson planning, cleaning your classroom, or building a memorial to all the pets you've loved, there are steps you can take to find flow and to fall into creative expression.

Although I appreciate metaphor, I also like specific directions, so here are six tips to get your creative juices going.

1. Prepare the ground. Your creativity will be more likely to emerge if you're feeling relaxed. Especially if you have art anxiety, do something (run, breathe, drink tea) to calm your nerves.
2. Put your perfectionism in a box and seal it away. Visualize this. Write down your intention to create without the pressure of being perfect. Put that paper in a box. Or in a drawer. Or burn it.
3. Ask questions. It's said that at the age of five, children ask 120 questions a day, and at age six, they ask only 60; at age 40, adults ask four questions a day. Embrace a beginner's mind and ask questions. Pay attention to questions other people ask. Collect questions you find compelling.
4. Be curious. Collect scraps of ideas, fragments of words, leaves and petals, images and scents. Put them in a drawer or a little box in your mind. Don't look for connections, but be open to allowing these scraps to form together in new ways. Combining ideas and making connections are key practices of creativity.
5. Experiment, fail, and take notes. As Thomas Edison said, "I make more mistakes than anyone else I know, and sooner or later, I patent most of them." Edison was a prolific inventor and innovator and a master at learning from failed experiments. When he died, he left 3,500 notebooks containing details of his ideas and thoughts. If you follow your curiosity, experiment with ideas, and learn from your mistakes, the quality of your creativity will vastly improve.
6. Use your hands. Get them dirty.

What does this list spark in you? What does it make you think about or want to do?

What can you do, right now, to increase your creativity?

The Closet in My Classroom

Two of my favorite books as a child were *The Lion, The Witch and the Wardrobe* and *The Secret Garden*. The possibility that within an ordinary and familiar space there could be a door that opened into another world was endlessly enticing. Don't we all yearn for a portal into a different place when we're stressed or bored or afraid?

Try this activity on a day when you don't feel like going to school. Imagine that in the back of the closet (or a cabinet) in your classroom there is a door leading to another place. In the space here, draw that door, open, revealing the other land, room, space, or place.

Now, go to school. During the day, when you're feeling stressed or that you don't want to be there, look at your closet or cabinet door. Activate your imagination and sense that other land. Notice how this moment of imagination and distraction makes you feel.

Create a Logo

Create a unique symbol for yourself. It doesn't have to be literal or represent anything, but should be something you enjoy drawing.

Start by giving yourself permission to play and brainstorm and draft at least four to six different logos. Use these boxes if you'd like, or play on bigger paper.

Then select one to refine, and draw it here.

From *The Onward Workbook: Daily Activities to Cultivate Your Emotional Resilience and Thrive* by Elena Aguilar. Copyright © 2018 by Elena Aguilar. Reproduced by permission.

As an extension of this activity, with a group of colleagues, you can create a large drawing with each person's logo. Try to combine the symbols in a way that creates a cohesive composition. This might involve overlap, connection, or repetition of some of the symbols. If you want, take a photo of the creation or make a photocopy of it, and paste it here.

Thank You, Courage

What can you thank your courage for? When has it shown up and guided you, pushed you, carried you?

    Complete these statements. You might run out of ideas after the first few, but stick with it and see if you can complete all nine. You might be surprised by what comes up!

Thank you, courage, for . . .

Thank you, courage, for . . .

Thank you, courage, for . . .

Thank you, courage, for . . .

Thank you, courage, for . . .

Thank you, courage, for . . .

Thank you, courage, for . . .

Thank you, courage, for . . .

Thank you, courage, for . . .

Sisu, Ikigai, and Gigil

Our language says so much about how we experience emotions. In English, for example, we have lots of words for the uncomfortable or negative emotions we experience—you may have noticed this when you looked at "The Core Emotions" in Chapter 2. Without language, we can't express our emotional states. I think we'd have far more positive emotions if we had more words to describe them and their fine nuances.

In other languages, we can find inspiration for how words can communicate the complexity of feelings. Perhaps you know this because you speak another language. When I'm speaking in English, there are times when I incorporate words in Spanish (in which I'm fluent) or in Yiddish (which my grandparents spoke) because there are just no other words that communicate the feeling I want to express.

Tim Lomas, at the University of East London, has a goal to bring language into our daily lexicon that captures the many flavors of good feelings found around the world. His Positive Lexicography Project is compiling hundreds of words from around the world that are untranslatable into English and that might allow us to better understand ourselves and better communicate with others. Lomas suspects that familiarizing ourselves with the words might change the way we feel, by drawing our attention to sensations we've ignored.

Here are some of my favorite words from other languages that describe experiences or emotional states for which we have no word in English:

Sisu: In Finnish, an extraordinary determination in the face of adversity. According to Finnish speakers, the English ideas of "grit," "perseverance," or "resilience" do not come close to describing the inner strength encapsulated in their native term.

Ikigai: In Japanese, a reason to get up in the morning, a reason to live.

Mbuki-mvuki: In Bantu, the irresistible urge to shuck off your clothes as you dance.

Gigil: In Filipino, the urge to pinch or squeeze something that is irresistibly cute.

Natsukashii: In Japanese, a nostalgic longing for the past, with happiness for the fond memory, yet sadness that it is no longer.

Mamihlapinatapei: In Yagan, an indigenous language from Tierra del Fuego, this is the wordless yet meaningful look shared by two people who both desire to initiate something but are both reluctant to start.

Uitwaaien: In Dutch, the revitalizing effects of taking a walk in the wind.

Dadirri: In an Australian aboriginal language, a deep, spiritual act of reflective and respectful listening.

From *The Onward Workbook: Daily Activities to Cultivate Your Emotional Resilience and Thrive* by Elena Aguilar. Copyright © 2018 by Elena Aguilar. Reproduced by permission.

Saudade: In Portuguese, the feeling of longing for something or someone that you love and that is lost.

Litost: In Czech, a state of agony and torment created by the sudden sight of one's own misery.

Iktsuarpok: In Inuktitut, (the language spoken by the Inuit who live in Canada) the feeling of anticipation when you're waiting for someone to show up at your house and you keep going outside to see if he or she is there yet.

Tartle: In Scottish, the panicky hesitation just before you have to introduce someone whose name you can't quite remember.

Duende: In Spanish, this was originally used to describe a mythical, spirit-like entity that possesses humans and creates the feeling of awe of one's surroundings in nature. It's meaning has expanded, and it has come to refer to the mysterious power that a work of art has to deeply move a person.

Bilita Mpash: In Bantu, an amazing dream. Not just a good dream; the opposite of a nightmare.

Wabi-Sabi: In Japanese, a way of living that focuses on finding beauty in the imperfections of life and accepting peacefully the natural cycle of growth and decay.

Tingo: In Pascuenese, a language spoken on Easter Island, this is the act of taking objects one desires from the house of a friend by gradually borrowing all of them.

Ya'arburnee: In Arabic, the hopeful declaration that you will die before someone you love deeply, because you cannot stand to live without the person. Literally, "may you bury me."

If you speak another language, which words describe emotional states for you that are unique?

What do you wish there was a word for? For example: I want a word to describe the joy I feel when a former student accomplishes something that I had hoped he'd accomplish, but had worried that he wouldn't. I want another word that describes the feeling I get when I meet someone and just know that she will become a friend.

Which emotional experiences do you want words for? Make a list, and if you'd like to take a stab at creating a word, go ahead! This is a chapter on creativity—so see what happens!

How to Be Courageous

Create a list of as many ways as you can possibly think of to be courageous. Spend a few days building this list.

Then identify 15–25 ways that most speak to you, and make a poster with these phrases or words on them. Consider ways to place the words so that they communicate a message with their size, placement, direction, and type. Use color if you want. You could also create this poster out of collaged words. Or explore different types and prints. Make it yours.

Street Interviews

Break up into pairs or groups, or head out on your own, to interview people in and around your community. You might want to ask questions concerning the perceptions of your school or specific issues affecting education. Use the audio-recording features of your phone to record respondents' replies, and take several photos of each person. Ask a colleague to take a photo of you engaged in this activity as well, or take some selfies. Combine the photos in a slide show and incorporate the audio interviews. You can share this slide show with a team, a colleague, or friends or family.

In this space, paste in one photo of you on this adventure. Draw thought bubbles around your head in which to write what you were thinking.

What did you learn from this activity?

From The Onward Workbook: Daily Activities to Cultivate Your Emotional Resilience and Thrive by Elena Aguilar. Copyright © 2018 by Elena Aguilar. Reproduced by permission.

Create Your Alter Ego

An alter ego is a second self distinct from your normal personality. An alter ego could represent the shadow side of yourself (like Dr. Jekyll's Mr. Hyde) or a superhero side of you. In the *Calvin and Hobbes* comic strip, Calvin has multiple alter egos, including Spaceman Spiff, a space explorer constantly exploring planets and fighting aliens; Stupendous Man, a superpowered being with self-narrated adventures; and Tracer Bullet, a private eye in a world of classical noir.

What kind of alter ego would you like to have?

Give it a name. Perhaps give it all the dispositions, habits, and capacities that you're working on developing. Perhaps it's a super-resilient alter ego! Describe your alter ego here.

When you're stuck, call on your alter ego and ask, *What would _____ do right now?*

From *The Onward Workbook: Daily Activities to Cultivate Your Emotional Resilience and Thrive* by Elena Aguilar. Copyright © 2018 by Elena Aguilar. Reproduced by permission.

Play Hide-and-Seek

Part 1: Play

Share a childhood game, such as hopscotch or hide-and-seek, with a small group. Or play a childhood game that you might have never played as a child, such as Duck, Duck, Goose. Consider activities that involve being outdoors and that are as inclusive as possible. Make the objective of the game to be as silly as possible.

Part 2: Reflect

What was it like to play childhood games?

What was challenging?

What did you learn about yourself?

What did you learn about your colleagues?

From *The Onward Workbook: Daily Activities to Cultivate Your Emotional Resilience and Thrive* by Elena Aguilar. Copyright © 2018 by Elena Aguilar. Reproduced by permission.

Create a Monster

Lynda Barry is a cartoonist, a teacher, and the author of a number of unique and inspiring books that defy definition. Here's an activity that she designed that is especially fun to do alone or with others.

First, recall that monsters follow no rules—they can have eight legs or 16 horns or wings coming out of their feet. Let this serve as permission to send your creativity wherever it wants to go.

Part 1: Monster To-Do List

1. Take an 8½-by-11 piece of paper and fold it in half twice so that it's divided into four quadrants.
2. With pencil or pen, make a squiggle in one quadrant.
3. In another quadrant, make a closed shape, like a square or an octagon.
4. In the third quadrant, make another squiggle.
5. Set a timer for two minutes and turn that first squiggle into a monster. Add eyeballs, teeth, claws, and so on. Repeat for all three chambers.
6. In the fourth quadrant, make a list of 10 things you have to do that you're not doing (plan a lesson, clean the classroom, do laundry, go to the dentist, so on).
7. Look at your list and figure out which monster has to do what.
8. Write those tasks above those monsters.

Part 2: Monster Parenting

1. On another sheet of paper, take any one of those monsters and draw that monster's parents.
2. Think about the tasks the monster has to do—such as going to the dentist. Make one parent who loves the monster say, "Honey, those teeth aren't important; what matters is you're happy." Make another parent critical and mean to the monster, saying things like "You always procrastinate. Of course you're not going to the dentist."
3. Just let the parents talk about the problem.
4. There is no purpose to this part of the activity other than just to explore your playful and fun side.

From The Onward Workbook: Daily Activities to Cultivate Your Emotional Resilience and Thrive by Elena Aguilar. Copyright © 2018 by Elena Aguilar. Reproduced by permission.

Part 3: Reflect

What did this activity raise for you?

What did you learn about yourself?

Nondominant Hand Monsters

I like monsters, but if you want, you could substitute a real creature (such as a butterfly, flower, bird, or person) for a monster in this activity.

Drawing with your nondominant hand is a common beginning practice in art classes. It helps you shake off your art anxiety a bit because what you create is unlikely to be a perfect masterpiece, and it helps you pay close attention to what you see. What you draw will most likely be messy and funny looking, so put on a silly hat or just remind yourself that it's okay to be playful, and pick up a pen or pencil with your nondominant hand.

Now, draw a monster or other creature. You can draw it from your imagination. Or, if you're drawing something real, you can find an image of it—a bird, dog, tree—and try copying it with your nondominant hand. If you want, you can color it in after. (If you want to use your dominant hand for coloring, that's okay!) You could also give it a name. Or add speech or thought bubbles to it.

Reflect

How did it feel to create something with your nondominant hand?

How did your experience change as you continued drawing?

What might this reveal about your own creative process?

The Four-Minute Diary

This is another Lynda Barry activity (see "Create a Monster") that can get your creative juices flowing. You'll need a composition book or a journal, and you'll want to do this for at least one week to reap the full benefits.

Fold a page of your journal in half vertically so that you have two columns. On one side, at the top, write REMEMBERED. On the second side, write SAW.

In the first column, for just two minutes, write everything you can remember from the day before. In the second column, for just two minutes, write everything you remember seeing from the day before.

After doing this for a number of days, your observational powers will heighten and you'll find yourself mentally noting what you're seeing and experiencing in the moment itself.

Making the Familiar Strange

Do we know our environments as well as we think we do? This is another photography exercise, which is so easy now, given that most of us have cameras on our phones.

Take photos of your classroom, campus, and offices, but in such a way that others might not be able to identify the location. Do this by taking photos of places that most people don't know about or by using nonconventional angles such as extreme close-ups and bird's-eye or worm's-eye points of view. Then compile these into a slide show.

With a team or group of colleagues, share your images and see if others can identify the location or object. This turns the activity into a game.

Afterward, reflect: What was your favorite part of this activity? In taking this approach, what did you see that you might not otherwise have noticed?

Discovering Creativity in Your Community

Venture out on a hunt to find creativity in your community, and photograph that creativity when you find it: A creative hairstyle, an interesting facade of a building, a nice garden, a mural, or detailing on a car. Keep your mind open to creativity. Print out one of your favorite images and paste it in the space provided. This can be a great activity to do alone or with colleagues at school, or do it in the community in which you live.

A Play List

Create a list of activities that you've found enjoyable and playful. (You can see my list here.) Add to your list whenever you get another idea, and then when you're itching to play, select an activity from the list.

Elena's Play List

- Doodle
- Finger paint
- Make a vision board
- Sketch
- Collect rocks and sticks and make a sculpture
- Color a meditation coloring book
- Play Ping-Pong
- Fly a kite
- Sing karaoke
- Host a game night
- Throw a dress-up party
- Sew pillowcases
- Knit scarves

- Build a model plane
- Build a ship inside a glass bottle
- Play with a dog
- Read poetry to someone else
- Make a new recipe or an old family one
- Play Frisbee
- Take photos
- Join a choir
- Build a mud, sand, or snow creature
- Play charades
- Go for a bike ride with no destination in mind

Elevate the Ordinary

Take an everyday object in your surroundings, such a stapler, textbook, or eraser, and make it extraordinary by decorating it with glitter, gluing other objects onto it, and so on. Make sure to retain the functionality of the object. As a record of this activity, photograph your creation and paste that image in the space here.

What feelings come up as you look at your "new and improved" object? How might you be seeing it differently now?

Map Your Day

Depict your day visually by using pictures, words, lines, and arrows. Try selecting moments from your day that might feel small, but that stand out. For example, my map for today would start with a raindrop—I awoke to the sound of rain. Then I'd have a picture of a cup of coffee, an important part of my day. Later, I took a walk, and the sun was shining as I sat on a bench; I'd draw a sun and my walking shoes. I'd also draw a stick figure of me sitting at my kitchen table and talking to my son about his homework—because that was a special part of my afternoon.

Use colored pencils if you'd like. If you repeat this exercise a number of times, you'll notice that you pay attention to your day differently; you'll attend to visuals and glean new insights into what you experience.

Create a Community Sketchbook

This is a long-term activity that can span a month, a semester, or even the entire school year.

Buy a new sketchbook, decorate it, and do a drawing on the first page. On the last page, write: "When every page has been filled, please return to _____." Make sure to put your name, school, and email address.

Now pass it along—to another colleague in your department, to another department, or even to another school in your district or network. Instruct the person or group to draw in it and then pass it along, trying to reach as many people in the community as possible.

When you pass the sketchbook along, offer prompts such as "Share the highlight of your day" or give them a line from a poem or song to illustrate. Let them know that when they pass along the sketchbook, they can offer their own prompt—which could be the same as the one they responded to or a different one.

After the book is filled, be sure to get it back so that you can look at it. And then re-circulate it so that everyone else can see the sketchbook.

This activity fosters creativity, community, and connection.

Ai Weiwei's Shoes

The artist Ai Weiwei took a pair of shoes, cut them in half, and then stitched the two halves together. Do a quick search online and you'll easily turn up an image of this work.

Take an ordinary object or objects, break them apart, and piece them back together in creative ways. This could be a fun activity to do in a staff meeting to promote creative thinking about how to deal with situations that seem fixed.

In the space here, sketch the object you created.

Create Your Cheerleading Squad

What if you could have your own squad of cheerleaders to support, encourage, and cheer you on whenever you need them to? You can create them! You might want to do this activity on a piece of paper that you can post in your classroom, or of course you can do it here.

You'll need a thin black ink pen and watercolor paints or an ink pad to do this.

Steps to Creating Your Squad

1. Paint or ink your fingertip and press it onto the page. Make as many prints as you want in your squad.

2. After they dry, add faces, arms, legs, and accessories. You might want to have creatures among your squad, maybe a few cats, birds, or bugs—that's fine too! Give them the characteristics that they need to become the creatures you want them to be.

3. Then give them speech bubbles—what do you want them to say to you? Here's what one of my cheering creatures says to me (it's a winged horse): "Elena! You can write this book! You were born to write it!" Another one says, "Take a break when you need. You've gotta rest!"

If you don't create the cheerleaders in the space provided in this workbook, then take a photo of them and paste it in here as a record.

Ice Cube Street Art

Using ice cubes and gloves, work in pairs to create creative public sculptures with the cubes. Make sure the melting ice drains into a place that can handle water. For fun, add food coloring to the water before freezing the cubes. The trick to getting them to stick together is to rub a little warm water on one cube before pressing another against it for 15–20 seconds. The water will freeze, and the cubes will be stuck together!

Remember to take photos and include them here. This could also be a fun activity to incorporate into a staff meeting, PD day, or back-to-school retreat.

A Collage of Student Voices

Today when you're at school, listen to what your students say, with an ear to collecting fragments of their words for a collage. When you hear interesting phrases, jot them down. Here are the fragments of dialogue that I captured recently in a fifth-grade classroom:

- 17 salami sandwiches
- It was magnanimous
- How old is your lizard?
- Soup on her head
- Frustrating, frustrating fractions
- Danced at recess
- When? When? When?!

This evening, fill in the speech bubbles with the phrases you collected—perhaps just your favorites if you found many.

From *The Onward Workbook: Daily Activities to Cultivate Your Emotional Resilience and Thrive* by Elena Aguilar. Copyright © 2018 by Elena Aguilar. Reproduced by permission.

Banksyfy Yourself

Banksy is a famous anonymous graffiti artist, political activist, and filmmaker. His art is often satirical and presented in a distinctive stencil technique. Google him and look at some of the street art he's done.

Choose an artist street name for yourself. Then do legal street art by rearranging or placing objects in creative places in the real world. Sign your works with your street name.

You can make objects out of recycled materials or objects found in garage sales or thrift stores. In Figure 10.1, you'll see a piece of my street art that I left in a local park—a violin that I transformed into a winged creature. You can't see my artist name, however—I'll keep that a secret!

Figure 10.1 Elena's Street Art

Document your street art adventure and include an image of it here.

From *The Onward Workbook: Daily Activities to Cultivate Your Emotional Resilience and Thrive* by Elena Aguilar. Copyright © 2018 by Elena Aguilar. Reproduced by permission.

Transforming the Ordinary

The artist Marcel Duchamp took a urinal, flipped it on its side, and titled it *Fountain*.

Take an ordinary object, reposition it if necessary, and ascribe to it a different designation, role, or function. Duchamp used the name R. Mutt. You can give yourself a new name if you like, and sign your artistic creations.

Take a picture and insert it here, or sketch what you did.

A Family Tree of Courage

You get to identify and select a lineage of courage from which you've emerged. On this tree, you might have ancestors or family members, fictional or historical characters, or even entire communities to which you belong or would like to belong. Among dozens on my family tree of courage, I have the Dalai Lama, musician Victor Jara, writer Cheryl Strayed, my grandmother, and Wonder Woman.

Draw a family tree and put yourself in the trunk. Then draw branches and leaves on the tree and label them with the names of the people from whom you draw courage. You could use the space here, or you could do this on a larger piece of paper and paste in a photo here.

On Creative Resilience and Resistance

Many people felt dispirited following the political turmoil of 2016. Writer Courtney E. Martin drafted a short passage, which her illustrator friend, Wendy McNaughton, transformed into a stunning graphic. I encourage you to look it up—just Google their names. It's visually powerful and the words are moving. Here's an excerpt of those words:

> This is your assignment. Feel all the things. Feel the hard things. The inexplicable things, the things that make you disavow humanity's capacity for redemption. Feel all the maddening paradoxes. Feel overwhelmed, crazy. Feel uncertain. Feel angry. Feel afraid. Feel powerless. Feel frozen. And then FOCUS.

What does this passage bring up for you?

What does it make you want to do?

From *The Onward Workbook: Daily Activities to Cultivate Your Emotional Resilience and Thrive* by Elena Aguilar. Copyright © 2018 by Elena Aguilar. Reproduced by permission.

A Letter to Courage

Write a letter to courage—perhaps to the courage that's within you or the courage that exists in the universe. What would you like to ask from courage? What do you need to say to courage in yourself as well as to courage in the universe?

Here's a selection of my letter to courage: *Hello, my friend. My trusty companion. You have been present from the beginning, haven't you? I'm so grateful for the moments when you've stood up tall and spoken, acted, and cared for me. I may not have acknowledged your hard work all the time, but I'm so grateful and committed to thanking you more often. Now, one request, okay? I'm afraid to ask this of you, but with your strength, I will. There are some times when I need you more . . .*

From *The Onward Workbook: Daily Activities to Cultivate Your Emotional Resilience and Thrive* by Elena Aguilar. Copyright © 2018 by Elena Aguilar. Reproduced by permission.

Artistic Depictions of Flow

Go to your preferred online search engine and look for images of flow—or perhaps a closely related state, such as satisfaction, full concentration, or absorption.

See what comes up, and then search for "depictions of flow in art."

Look closely at a few of those images. Sit with them and spend some time getting to know them. Pay attention to how they make you feel and what thoughts go through your mind.

Reflect

What do you notice in the images that come up?

What do you learn about flow through doing this?

How did this exploration help you understand your own experience of flow?

If you'd like, print out one (or more) of the images that particularly speak to you and stick them in here.

Destination Postcard: Play and Create

What would it look and sound like if you were always able to summon forth your playful and creative self? Draw a picture of yourself with thought bubbles and labels that depict a playful and creative you. If you'd like, draw this you at work, surrounded by kids and colleagues. How might you be in that space?

From *The Onward Workbook: Daily Activities to Cultivate Your Emotional Resilience and Thrive* by Elena Aguilar. Copyright © 2018 by Elena Aguilar. Reproduced by permission.

Chapter Reflection

What were your biggest takeaways from this chapter?

Of the different activities in this chapter, which were most useful?

Which activities would you like to revisit periodically? How might you get that habit going?

What implications do the ideas in this chapter have for the work you do?

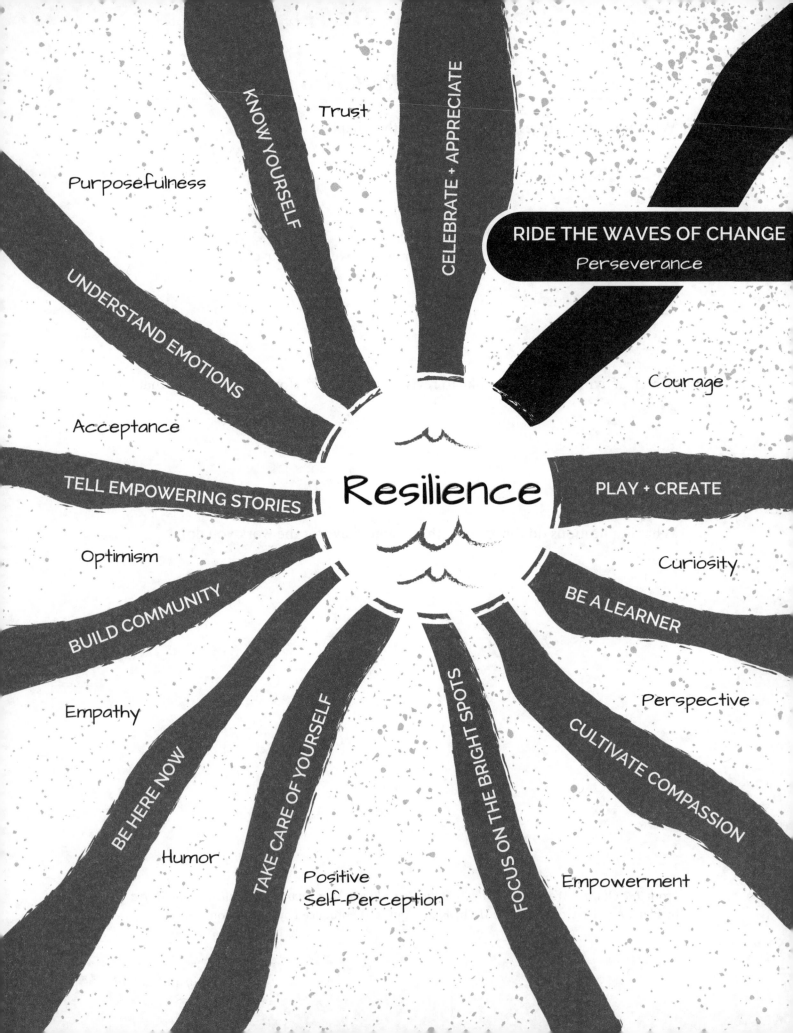

CHAPTER 11

Ride the Waves of Change

Change is one thing we can count on, and when we encounter it, we can harness our physical, emotional, mental, and spiritual energies, and direct them where they will make the biggest difference. Perseverance, patience, and courage help us manage change.

April: Although change is constant, spring brings especially high levels of change to schools. Learn to ride those waves of change with focus, patience, persistence, and courage.

Ride the Waves of Change: Resilience Self-Assessment

The purpose of this self-assessment is to help you gauge the level of your resilience reservoir and to explore what might be draining or what could replenish it. The exercises that follow and the information in the corresponding chapter of *Onward* can boost your resilience by helping you understand and manage the psychological and social processes of change.

Imagine each circle as a little *cenote* or reservoir within you, and fill it up according to how much each statement reflects a source of resilience. If you need something more concrete, imagine marks at ¼, ½, and ¾ full.

Before you start the exercises in this chapter, take this self-assessment and fill in the date. At the end of the month, take the assessment again. (You might even cover up your original markings with a strip of paper.) Is your resilience reservoir a little more full? If so, which practices do you want to keep up? If not, what else do you want to try?

Statement	Date:	Date:
I have many ways to think about change.	◯	◯
I know that the way I think about change has a great deal to do with how resilient I am.	◯	◯
I am able to distinguish between things I can influence or control and those I can't.	◯	◯
I can direct my energy to the places that count the most—to the areas where I can have the greatest influence or control.	◯	◯

From *The Onward Workbook: Daily Activities to Cultivate Your Emotional Resilience and Thrive* by Elena Aguilar. Copyright © 2018 by Elena Aguilar. Reproduced by permission.

I have strategies to deal with unwanted change.	◯	◯
I am able to stay open to outcomes even when I have strong ideas about what should happen.	◯	◯
I have strategies to lead change.	◯	◯
I understand that all change involves loss and have strategies to cope with that loss (or support others in doing so).	◯	◯
I understand the role that perseverance plays in cultivating my resilience.	◯	◯
I know how to increase my tenacity.	◯	◯

Make a Vision Board

When big changes come beating down on us, we lurch into reactive mode, responding only to what is in front of us, dog-paddling to stay afloat. A lot of energy is used in that effort. This is an optimal time to shift your attention to what you want in life.

Because our minds think in images, a vision board is a fun way to generate thoughts about what we want to see, feel, experience, and have. You simply cut out pictures from magazines of places you'd like to be, experiences you want in your life, people you want around you, and so on—and paste them on a board and hang it somewhere that you'll see every day.

Of course, you could do this activity at any point during the year—it's a great New Year's or end-of summer/back-to-school activity because it pushes you to think about what you want to manifest.

If you've never made one of these boards before and are a little skeptical about trying it—I hear you. I felt the same. Then I tried it, and it worked. Try it—what have you got to lose?

Start collecting magazines. Think about both your personal and professional life—so save some of those education-related catalogues that you'd otherwise recycle right away. Collect for a while and then find yourself a space on a rug, at a big table, or out under an oak tree, and cut, place, and paste without giving it too much thought. Perhaps paste a photo of your vision board here as a record.

The Roots of Our Attitude Toward Change

As we have with other mindsets, we've acquired our attitude toward change over the course of our life—perhaps from our family of origin, our culture, and the organizations with which we've been affiliated. Reflect on these origins.

Where do you think your thoughts and feelings about change come from?

Were the adults in your family of origin patient people?

How did that patience—or lack thereof—manifest?

What attitudes about change surrounded you as a child?

Was change something to be avoided and feared, or was it exciting and to be sought out?

Face Your Fears

What's the worst that can happen?

This is a useful question to ask yourself when you're facing a change or afraid of the unknown. Push yourself to explore your fears—all of them. See where they take you. This is a kind of emotional preparation. Thinking about the worst thing that can happen can help you stay calm and rational.

So, right now: What are you afraid of? What's the worst that can happen? Write those fears down here. Face them on the page.

Reflecting on Hope and Change

Here are a few quotes related to hope and change that speak to me.

Hope, in this deep and powerful sense, is not the same as joy that things are going well, or willingness to invest in enterprises that are obviously headed for early success, but, rather, an ability to work for something because it is good, not just because it stands a chance to succeed.

VACLAV HAVEL, CZECH PLAYWRIGHT AND POLITICAL LEADER

Things don't always change for the better, but they change, and we can play a role in that change if we act. Which is where hope comes in, and memory, the collective memory we call history.

REBECCA SOLNIT

History says, don't hope
On this side of the grave.
But then, once in a lifetime
The longed-for tidal wave
Of justice can rise up,
And hope and history rhyme.

SEAMUS HEANEY

What do these quotes bring up for you? What connections can you make?

Which Changes Do You Desire?

Imagine that you have a magic wand. Draw it right here. (If you're a Harry Potter fan, you can also imagine what it has as its core.)

Now imagine that you can wave this wand, and any of the changes you want to make have happened. What would those changes be? Consider sorting them into the categories of personal and professional changes.

Personal Changes I Want to Make	Professional Changes I Want to Make

From *The Onward Workbook: Daily Activities to Cultivate Your Emotional Resilience and Thrive* by Elena Aguilar. Copyright © 2018 by Elena Aguilar. Reproduced by permission.

Reflecting on Perseverance

Who are your role models of perseverance? They could be people you know personally or famous or historical figures.

Where do you think your attitudes about perseverance and tenacity come from? Did you see these dispositions modeled when you were a child?

When have you been tenacious in your life? What happened?

In which areas would you like to boost your tenacity? Where do you feel a desire to persevere?

"Maybe," Said the Farmer

The following is a classic Zen parable.

Once upon a time, there was an old farmer who had worked his crops for many years. One day, his horse ran away.

Upon hearing the news, his neighbors came to visit. "Such bad luck," they said sympathetically. "Maybe," the farmer replied.

The next morning, the horse returned, bringing with it three other wild horses. "How wonderful," the neighbors exclaimed. "Maybe," replied the old man.

The following day, his son tried to ride one of the untamed horses, was thrown, and broke his leg.

The neighbors again came to offer their sympathy for his misfortune. "Maybe," answered the farmer.

The day after, military officials came to the village to draft young men into the army. Seeing that the son's leg was broken, they passed him by.

The neighbors congratulated the farmer on how well things had turned out. "Maybe," said the farmer.

Reflect

Can you think of an incident in your own life that may have seemed bad at first, but turned out to have an unexpected positive outcome?

Is there anything right now in your life that you are thinking of as good or bad, toward which you'd like to try having a "maybe" attitude?

How do you think a "maybe" view could affect your feelings about the situation?

What might be possible in this situation if you adopted a "maybe" attitude?

What might you do differently if you held a "maybe" view? What actions would you take—or not take?

The Monster in the Closet

Few would disagree that change can be scary. It brings uncertainty and unpredictability, which in turn can summon deep-rooted fears about failure, self-worth, and purpose.

It makes me think of the children's story *There's a Monster at the End of This Book.* In the book, Sesame Street's most loveable monster, Grover, tries to convince the reader, page after page, to stop reading for fear of reaching the monster at the end of the book—only to discover that the monster is himself, "loveable, furry old Grover." The monster we can't see is always scarier than the one we can.

So we're going to try a little exercise. Think of the biggest, scariest change facing you right now. It can either be one in progress or one that you've been reluctant to get started. It could be from work, such as agreeing to teach a new course, or from outside of work, such as deciding to buy a house.

In the space provided, depict that change as a little monster. Draw and label every detail—the fangs of failure, the claws of confusion! Don't worry about the quality of your drawing; this is about the emotions we're calling forth through visual symbolism. When you've finished, sit with your drawing for a bit.

Then invite the monster to show its silly side. Give it a tutu or purple toenails or ridiculously long eyelashes. What aspects of the change might these details represent?

Finally, imagine this monster—the change you're facing—out and about in the world, fully alive and free. Is it as scary as it seems to you right now, hiding in the shadows?

Honoring What You've Lost

One of the reasons I think we're so afraid of change is that we don't take the time to grieve our losses. We're not really afraid of change—we're afraid of *loss*. And even though we know that loss is inevitable—whether it's the end of a vacation or the loss of a friendship—we struggle to accept it.

So let's back up in this conversation about change. I suspect we could accept change and loss more easily if we had more rituals and ways to honor what has come and gone.

What have you lost that you wish you could honor? What do you feel nostalgic for? What do you miss? Whatever comes to mind is fine.

I miss the ability that my body once had to run six miles. I feel nostalgic for the ease of college friendships. I grieve for the children I wasn't able to have. I am always trying to honor my mother and the unconditional love she gave to me.

What have you lost?

How could you honor what you've lost? This is a challenging question, because what does it mean *to honor* experiences, abilities, people, hopes and dreams? Sometimes just feeling the feelings is a way of honoring the loss—noticing them, naming them, allowing those feelings to exist. What comes to mind?

There's a connection between honoring something you've lost and appreciating it. What could you say or do to express your gratitude for what you've lost? (We'll explore gratitude further in Chapter 12.)

What has this activity raised for you? Which feelings? What thoughts?

Keep a Promise to Yourself

Keeping a promise to yourself, say the experts, is a surefire way to boost your morale and self-esteem. When you make a commitment and stick to it, you'll also feel encouraged to make additional or bigger commitments.

What promise to yourself could you make today? To eat lunch? To chat with a colleague with whom you've felt some tension? To sleep eight hours or walk for 20 minutes?

Make a promise right now. Write it here:

At the end of the day, jot down a note to yourself in appreciation of the promise that you kept. Write it here:

Detachment Meditation

When you feel overwhelmed by stress or you experience high levels of anxiety, imagine what it would be like to look at the situation from the outside. Imagine you're behind a two-way mirror, the kind you may have seen on TV when detectives watch their suspects. The situation that's causing you stress is in the interrogation room, and you're on the other side of the glass, observing it.

Do a little sketch of this here. To depict what you see in the interrogation room, select a few symbols to represent that stressful situation, and perhaps add a couple of labels.

Now, close your eyes and imagine watching this situation for a few moments. Pay attention to what you notice, hear, and see.

After this short meditation, jot down any reflections you have or thoughts that came to mind about the situation.

Reflecting on Energy

Your decisions about what to change in your life can be informed by what is already working in your life. The following questions will help you surface the sources of energy that fuel you so that you can gain more clarity on what you might need to change in your life.

Think of a time at work in the last few months when you felt effective, absorbed, fulfilled, and inspired. What specifically energized you?

Which of your skills and talents were you using?

How might you do more of this at work?

Identify some moments at work when there's a discrepancy between what's important to you and what you actually do. Jot down a few words to describe that discrepancy.

How can you draw boundaries around what you do to preserve more energy for what's important? What actions do you need to take to preserve your energy for what's important?

From *The Onward Workbook: Daily Activities to Cultivate Your Emotional Resilience and Thrive* by Elena Aguilar. Copyright © 2018 by Elena Aguilar. Reproduced by permission.

Transformation and Decay

From *A Field Guide to Getting Lost,* by Rebecca Solnit (2006, p. 81):

> In her novel *Regeneration,* Pat Barker writes of a doctor who "knew only too well how often the early stages of change or cure may mimic deterioration. Cut a chrysalis open, and you will find a rotting caterpillar. What you will never find is that mythical creature, half caterpillar, half butterfly, a fit emblem of the human soul, for those whose cast of mind leads them to see such emblems. No, the process of transformation consists almost entirely of decay."

What thoughts and feelings does this quote raise for you?

In what ways has your own journey of change reflected a caterpillar's transformation? What have your moments of decay been like?

Metaphors for Patience

Consider metaphors for patience:

What color is patience?

What season is it?

What animal best embodies patience?

What does patience sound like?

Reflect

What does thinking about patience in this way call to mind for you?

What feelings do the representations you called to mind evoke in you?

How the Light Gets In

The theme for this month is change, and sometimes change is painful. Some changes in life can feel as though they are breaking us. That's how I felt when my mom died: As though I was broken, as though I would never feel whole again. It took me a while, but I slowly gained an appreciation for how the experience of being broken could allow for other things to come that otherwise wouldn't have happened. These two quotes speak to this experience for me.

> *There is a crack in everything. That's how the light gets in.*
> LEONARD COHEN, SINGER AND SONGWRITER

> *The wound is the place where the light enters you.*
> RUMI, THIRTEENTH-CENTURY SUFI POET

What connections can you make to these quotes? Is there one that you'd like to draw in the space here?

From The Onward Workbook: Daily Activities to Cultivate Your Emotional Resilience and Thrive by Elena Aguilar. Copyright © 2018 by Elena Aguilar. Reproduced by permission.

Silence

In the end, we will remember not the words of our enemies,
but the silence of our friends.
DR. MARTIN LUTHER KING JR.

What does this quote raise for you?

Whose silence are you noticing now? Do you have friends who you wish would speak up?

Do you have friends who might wish you would speak up about something? What might they want you to say?

Scream and Yell

When you're dealing with change that straight-up sucks, and when it's unfair and infuriating, it's okay to scream and yell and cry. It's okay to have anger, and you can express it in a way that won't harm yourself or others.

Go somewhere alone, or with someone else who supports you, and scream whatever you want to scream. If you want to throw things or smash things, you even have permission to do that too (of course as long as you're safe and so are other people and important things).

There are a couple of key things to know about this activity. First, don't make it a regular habit—if you scream and yell every day, even alone, you solidify the neural pathways through which your anger runs. You can make your anger stronger, rather than move it through your system. Second, as you scream and yell, visualize that you're releasing your anger. Imagine that with each bellowing curse, a quantity of rage or frustration departs from your system. If you don't feel a sense of relief at the end of this exercise, it might not be for you.

If you feel the need to scream and yell, go do so. Then come back here and, in the space provided, write about what that felt like and what you released. This might also be a fun reflection to illustrate.

From *The Onward Workbook: Daily Activities to Cultivate Your Emotional Resilience and Thrive* by Elena Aguilar. Copyright © 2018 by Elena Aguilar. Reproduced by permission.

Patience

What thoughts, feelings and associations do you have with the word *patience*?

Do you think of yourself as a patient person? How so? Why or why not?

What are the conditions in which you feel you can be more patient?

When have you wished you had more patience?

When would you like to have more patience?

What makes it hard to feel patient?

Rumi, a thirteenth-century mystic and poet, wrote: "When you're anxious or worried, be patient. The key of patience opens the door of happiness." What connections can you make to these words? Do they ring true to you?

George Jackson was a Black Panther who wrote, "Patience has its limits. Take it too far, and it's cowardice." What do you think of his words? Where is the boundary between patience and resignation or cowardice for you?

From *The Onward Workbook: Daily Activities to Cultivate Your Emotional Resilience and Thrive* by Elena Aguilar. Copyright © 2018 by Elena Aguilar. Reproduced by permission.

Accepting Fragility

Xavier Le Pichon is a geophysicist and an expert in plate tectonics. He explains how evolving systems—be those geological or human—must have the capacity to accept and accommodate fragility. Geological faults that allow for movement and flow are good faults, he explains. By contrast, earthquakes happen when weakness in the faults cannot be expressed. This, of course, is powerfully symbolic for thinking about weaknesses in ourselves or in our communities.

Le Pichon expands on this connection: "Communities which are rigid, which do not take into account the weak points of the community—people who are in difficulty—tend to be communities that do not evolve" (quoted in Krista Tippett's *Becoming Wise*, 2016, p. 131).

What connections can you make with these ideas?

It's All Right to Cry

Just as anger is okay when you're facing an unwanted change, crying is also all right. Often, below our anger is a deep well of sadness. We don't fear change; we fear loss—and whenever there is change (both wanted and unwanted), there is loss.

I was raised in the 1970s by a feminist mother who sought to validate and affirm my feelings. The album *Free to Be You and Me* was the soundtrack to my childhood. If you missed the experience of this album, it's not too late. Right now, go to YouTube and look up the song "It's Alright to Cry," sung by Rosey Grier. It might make you feel better.

And then cry if you want to. And if you can't just cry spontaneously, perhaps consider doing something to make yourself cry! Watch a movie or listen to a piece of music that gets those tears rolling—a good cry can be very cathartic.

Afterward, if you want to jot down some words about how it felt to cry, go ahead.

Strengthening Your Intuition

In 2011, Nobel Prize–winning economist Daniel Kahneman published a book called *Thinking, Fast and Slow,* based on research from the field of behavioral science. Kahneman argues that our brains bounce between two distinct modes of thought. "System 1" is fast and largely automatic, governed by emotion and intuition—solving 2 + 2 or driving on an empty road. "System 2" is slow and deliberative, governed by logic and rational thought—comparing the value of two differently priced products or parking in a tight spot.

Whereas most of what we think of as "thought" falls under the purview of System 2, Kahneman shows that it is System 1 that controls most of our decision making and thus our behavior. System 1, largely comprising a set of heuristics or rules of thumb, evolved to help us make the split-second decisions that can determine life or death, such as slamming on the breaks when a deer runs in front of the car. Often, our brain sends signals to our body before we are even consciously aware of what's happening. Our bodies are acutely attuned to sensory information—both sensations that come from the traditional "five senses" and information that comes from subtler sources that science is just starting to understand, such as the electromagnetic field of the heart.

All of this information is filtered through Systems 1 and 2 to generate some kind of reaction—a feeling, an action, an impulse, and *intuition*. We all have intuition, whether we choose to heed it or not. That intuition is a powerful doorway to acting on the less readily obvious information that our brains and bodies are constantly taking in.

Take a few minutes to reflect:

How much stock do you put in your own intuition?

When have you made a decision based purely on intuition? How did it turn out?

When have you ignored your intuition? What were the consequences?

Are you interested in cultivating your intuition? Here are a few things that research suggests can help:

- Meditate. Cultivate nonattachment to your rational thoughts and see what bubbles up to take their place.
- Get creative. Put pencil or brush to paper with no image in mind. What emerges?
- Notice and name sudden feelings.
- Do something repetitive. See what comes up when you let yourself go on autopilot for a bit.
- Try to anticipate outcomes. Try to predict when the stoplight will change or who will be first to this afternoon's meeting.
- Feel, don't think. Try taking a drive without setting a destination.
- Test your hunches. Got a sense that it will rain tomorrow? Write it down and see what happens.
- Pay attention to your dreams. When the rational mind is busy, it can override the intuitive mind. When reason sleeps, sometimes intuition speaks.

Inspiration to Fight the Good Fight

Go to YouTube and look for Sekou Andrews's "Revolution 101." It's an inspiring piece of spoken word poetry.

As you listen, jot down words or phrases you hear that resonate. Doodle your feelings. Consider the actions you feel compelled to take after watching this video.

From *The Onward Workbook: Daily Activities to Cultivate Your Emotional Resilience and Thrive* by Elena Aguilar. Copyright © 2018 by Elena Aguilar. Reproduced by permission.

Tackle Your Complaints

The concept of spheres of influence and control (illustrated in Figure 11.1) can be invaluable during times of change and also for making changes in your life.

Figure 11.1   The Spheres of Influence

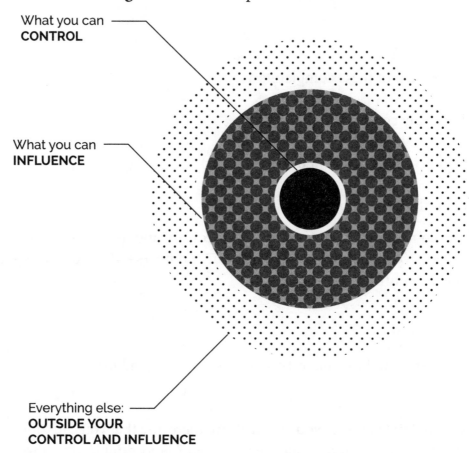

What you can **CONTROL**

What you can **INFLUENCE**

Everything else: **OUTSIDE YOUR CONTROL AND INFLUENCE**

From *The Onward Workbook: Daily Activities to Cultivate Your Emotional Resilience and Thrive* by Elena Aguilar. Copyright © 2018 by Elena Aguilar. Reproduced by permission.

Think about your work or personal life and list as many complaints as you can. For example: I don't exercise enough, my rent is high, I hate waking up at 5:30 a.m., and so on.

Then code each of these complaints as

- Within my control (C)
- Within my influence (I)
- Outside of my control and influence (O)

Reflect on these questions:

Read the complaints that are outside your control and influence and notice how your body feels as you read them—perhaps your shoulders tighten or your breathing shallows. What do you notice?

Which category did the majority of your complaints fall into?

Of the complaints outside your control, are there any that you can look at differently so that you can have more influence over them? For example, if you were just told that as the head of the English Department you will be required to attend a twice-monthly evening meeting on new assessment procedures, you might feel as though you have no control over this mandate. But perhaps you could talk to your principal about a rotating schedule where you'd attend some, but not all, of the meetings. Or perhaps you could request a stipend for attending. Sometimes we can find ways to influence what feels like something outside our control, or at least to have a voice in it. What could you do?

From *The Onward Workbook: Daily Activities to Cultivate Your Emotional Resilience and Thrive* by Elena Aguilar. Copyright © 2018 by Elena Aguilar. Reproduced by permission.

Of the complaints outside your control, are there any that you'd like to let go of? Imagine putting them into a helium-filled balloon and then watching the balloon rise into the sky and disappear. Draw a balloon here. Inside of it, write the complaint that you want to let go of. Draw as many balloons as you want.

Look at the complaints that are within your spheres of influence and control. What concrete action can you take to address one of these complaints? For example, I haven't been eating enough vegetables lately. If I signed up for a veggie box to be delivered each week, I'd probably eat more because they'd be in my refrigerator already. Identify actions you could take to address at least three of your complaints.

How to Worry Less

Here are three ways to worry less:

1. Schedule worry time. Give yourself a dedicated time each day when you are allowed to worry, perhaps 4:30–5:00 p.m. During the day, if you find yourself worrying, tell yourself, *No, you have to wait,* and then return to the worry during your allotted time. What's your worry time?

2. Identify what you can and can't influence and control. Go back to the "Tackle Your Complaints" exercise to recall those things that are within and outside of your influence or control. Print out the Spheres of Influence and post it somewhere visible.
3. Practice accepting uncertainty. Tell yourself, *Right now, there's nothing you can do about this. Take a deep breath, and hold on.*

Which of these strategies might be most effective for you?

Can you think of any others that have worked for you in the past?

Which would you like to try for the next few days?

From *The Onward Workbook: Daily Activities to Cultivate Your Emotional Resilience and Thrive* by Elena Aguilar. Copyright © 2018 by Elena Aguilar. Reproduced by permission.

Plan for Change: Observe Others

Over a decade ago, when I was still a teacher, I attended a workshop facilitated by master presenters. I marveled at how they engaged us in learning, the way they responded to questions, and their humor and calm presence. Those of us participating in this PD experience learned a great deal, and our connections to each other deepened. At the end of those three days, I wrote in my journal, "I now know what I want to do when I grow up"; I was referring to the ability to facilitate transformational learning experiences. This workshop was profound in leading me to where I am now, for this is what I believe I now offer in the workshops and trainings that I present around the world. Sometimes I wonder if I would have gotten here if I hadn't seen others doing this and gotten the notion that I, too, could do it.

If you feel dissatisfied with your work (or other areas of your life), one step on your journey to change is to stay alert to people whose work or life appeals to you. Stay attuned to that feeling in your gut that says, *I want that too!* And then study those people.

What is it about what they're doing that's calling to you? Get specific about the things in their lives that are attractive to you. Maybe you're drawn to what the science teacher's life looks like because she gets to do lots of cool and exciting experiments with kids all the time. Maybe you're envious of your roommate who teaches special ed because he's always talking about how incredible it is to see kids make leaps and bounds who otherwise might not make growth. Maybe every time your school's tech coach talks about her work you think, *That would be a great way for me to use my knowledge of technology.* Stay attuned to your feelings of curiosity, envy, and attraction toward other people's work and lives.

Who comes to mind right now? Whose life (or professional role) are you attracted to? What is it about his or her life or work that draws you?

Crisis and Opportunity

I'm sure you've heard it said that crisis can be an opportunity to evaluate your circumstances, to make a change that is ultimately better for you, or to have a breakthrough. When big and scary things happen—your position is consolidated, your principal is fired, you are involuntarily assigned a different grade level—look for the opportunity to reevaluate things: The school or district you work in, the career path you've chosen (remember—there are many career paths within education), and the people you're around.

Ask yourself whether you are truly happy where you are and whether you can think of any ways to take advantage of the crisis to become happier. Ask yourself whether the people around you—your colleagues and supervisors—are nurturing your development and contributing to your sense of purpose and joy. Could there be another place where you'd find this same support or even more? Ask yourself whether the role or situation you're in is tending to your whole self—to your body, mind, spirit, emotions, and social self.

Sometimes a crisis is the perfect opportunity to make a big change. And even if you're not in the midst of a crisis, if you're reading this, reflecting on these questions, and realizing that you want to make a big change, that's great! We don't need to have crises to make big changes.

What do these suggestions bring up for you? What connections can you make with these ideas?

Dragonflies

Dragonflies offer us a metaphor for how to deal with change. They begin their lives in the water and then move into the air to fly. They seem to glide with ease, light and able to adapt to the wind's direction.

When you're in an uncertain situation, visualize yourself as a dragonfly, gliding above the water—and the uncertainty—rising easily, moving with the winds toward a good outcome. The dragonfly is flexible and adaptable. As it flies, it gains new perspective, and it can change direction if necessary. It has a light spirit and an ease that we might try adopting when we're managing change.

Draw a picture of a dragonfly here. If you want, make its face your face. Dragonflies are very pretty, so you might also use color.

Your Own Change Management Model

There are a lot of change management models out there (including, for example, those described in the books *Switch, Nudge,* and *Immunity to Change*). All of the models have suggestions about how to help our psyches navigate the risk implicit in change.

On the spot, come up with your own change management approach. Pretend you're a speaker who gets paid millions of dollars a day to help others navigate the turbulent waters of change. What's your foolproof method?

If you need help getting started, pick a word that speaks to you, such as *onward,* and assign each letter in the word to a principle: O—own your purpose, N—navigate conflict, W—walk every day, A—act now, R—rest, D—dive into emotions.

This exercise can help you reflect on all you've learned in *Onward* and in the course of using this workbook, as it'll push you to think about what's been most helpful.

A Letter to Patience

Write a letter to patience. What would you like to say to patience? To the patience in yourself? What would you like to ask of it or appreciate it for?

Here's a selection from my letter: *Patience, I'm completely aware of a paradox as I write to you—I am impatient to get to know you. I have a hundred questions I want to fire away at you, but I'm not sure I want to listen to you. I just want you to do as I say, to serve me. Because I need you. I need more of you. What mother of a teenager doesn't need patience? How can I get more of you? Tell me!*

Artistic Depictions of Patience

Go to your preferred online search engine and look for images of patience—or another term that reflects patience, such as perseverance, serenity, or endurance (see "The Core Emotions" in Chapter 2 for these terms).

See what comes up, and then search for "depictions of patience in art."

Look closely at a few of those images. Sit with them and spend some time getting to know them. Pay attention to how they make you feel and what thoughts go through your mind.

Reflect

What do you notice in the images that come up?

What have you learned about patience through doing this exploration?

How did this exploration help you understand your own experience of patience?

If you'd like, print out one (or more) of the images that particularly speak to you and stick them in here.

From *The Onward Workbook: Daily Activities to Cultivate Your Emotional Resilience and Thrive* by Elena Aguilar. Copyright © 2018 by Elena Aguilar. Reproduced by permission.

Destination Postcard:
Riding the Waves of Change

What would it look and sound like if you felt confident riding the waves of change? Draw a picture of yourself with thought bubbles and labels to depict a you who is skilled at managing change. If you'd like, draw this you at work, surrounded by kids and colleagues. How might you be in that space?

Chapter Reflection

What were your biggest takeaways from this chapter?

Of the different activities in this chapter, which were most useful?

Which activities would you like to revisit periodically? How might you get that habit going?

What implications do the ideas in this chapter have for the work you do?

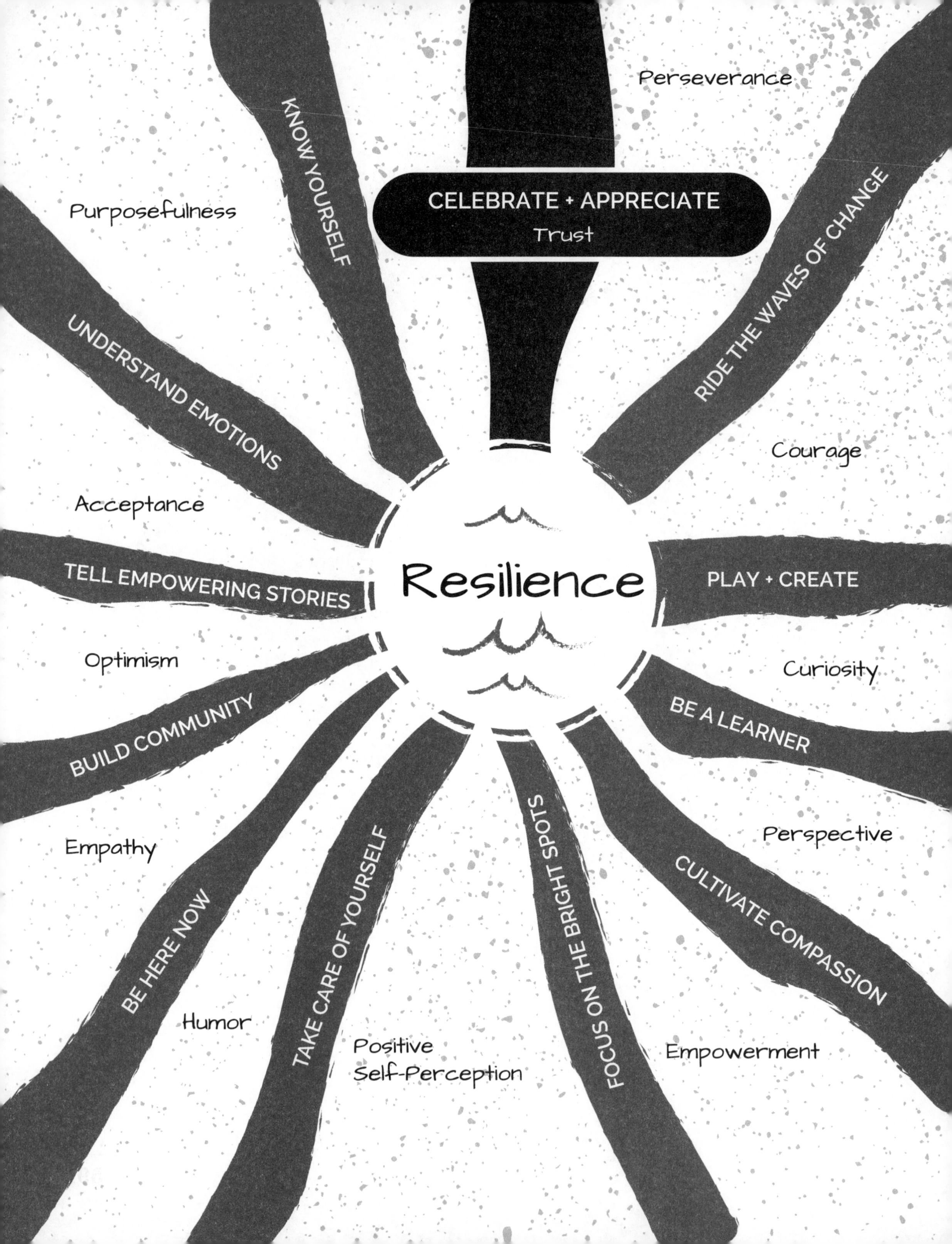

CHAPTER 12

Celebrate and Appreciate

Individual and collective celebration, as well as the practice of gratitude, is the capstone to the habits in this book. Even during hard moments, if we can shift into a stance of appreciation, we'll build our resilience. Appreciation cultivates our trust in ourselves, in a process, and perhaps in something greater, which helps us respond to the inevitable challenges of life.

May: Endings are times for celebration and appreciation, which lay the foundation for resilience in the days ahead.

Celebrate and Appreciate:
Resilience Self-Assessment

The purpose of this self-assessment is to help you gauge the level of your resilience reservoir and to explore what might be draining or what could replenish it. The exercises that follow and the information in the corresponding chapter of *Onward* can boost your resilience by catalyzing your sense of gratitude and helping you recognize moments worthy of appreciation and celebration.

Imagine each circle as a little *cenote* or reservoir within you, and fill it up according to how much each statement reflects a source of resilience. If you need something more concrete, imagine marks at ¼, ½, and ¾ full.

Before you start the exercises in this chapter, take this self-assessment and fill in the date. At the end of the month, take the assessment again. (You might even cover up your original markings with a strip of paper.) Is your resilience reservoir a little more full? If so, which practices do you want to keep up? If not, what else do you want to try?

Statement	Date:	Date:
I understand the role that appreciation plays in cultivating resilience.	○	○
There are many ways that I practice appreciation and gratitude.	○	○
I recognize the connection between practicing gratitude and the strength of a community.	○	○
I know that appreciating myself is important, and I do it.	○	○

From *The Onward Workbook: Daily Activities to Cultivate Your Emotional Resilience and Thrive* by Elena Aguilar. Copyright © 2018 by Elena Aguilar. Reproduced by permission.

I'm aware of my thoughts and feelings when I receive gratitude, and I'm able to accept appreciation.	◯	◯
I understand how gratitude can help me gain clarity into areas of my life that I want to change.	◯	◯
I understand the role that spirituality plays in cultivating resilience, and I have ways of tending to my spirit.	◯	◯
I have ways to cultivate a sense of trust in myself, in others, and in a process.	◯	◯
I know why celebration is important and how it cultivates resilience.	◯	◯
I celebrate my own successes and those of others.	◯	◯

Gratitude Journals

I bet you anticipated that somewhere in this workbook, I'd suggest you keep a gratitude journal. That's because it's one of the most effective and researched ways to provoke a positive shift in your overall mood.

A gratitude journal pushes you to pay attention to the good things in life that you can take for granted and helps you become more attuned to the everyday sources of joy around you. It's not enough just to call these moments to mind—*you must write them down.* When you translate thoughts into concrete language, you're more aware of those thoughts, and they have a deeper emotional impact.

The basic idea behind a gratitude journal is to capture a written record of what you feel grateful for. You don't need to write every day; in fact, some research suggests that writing occasionally (one to three times per week) is more beneficial than daily journaling.

How to do it: Write down five things for which you feel grateful. They can range from small in importance ("First period was calm today") to relatively large ("I have a supportive, fun, skilled partner teacher"). You can list things from your professional life, your personal life, or both.

These tips will help you get the most from this exercise:

- Be specific. For example, write "I'm grateful that I responded calmly to José when he came into first period shouting and that the whole class settled down quickly," rather than "I'm grateful that first period was calm today."
- Go for depth over breadth. Elaborate about something you're grateful for—describe it in detail. That's more beneficial than making a superficial list of many things.
- Think about people. Describe the people you are grateful for more than the things.
- Reflect on what your life would be like without certain people or things.
- Be grateful for what you have avoided, prevented, escaped, or turned into something positive; try not to take good fortune for granted.
- Be sure to capture positive events that were unexpected or surprising. These elicit higher levels of gratitude. You can write about them as they happen, and you can write your memories of them.
- Write about the same people and things over and over if you want, but each time you write about them, describe a different aspect in detail.
- Avoid snarkiness. ("I'm grateful that my principal didn't yell at me today like he does every day"; "I'm grateful that Miguel was absent.")
- Write regularly. Commit to a regular time to journal, and honor that commitment.

From *The Onward Workbook: Daily Activities to Cultivate Your Emotional Resilience and Thrive* by Elena Aguilar. Copyright © 2018 by Elena Aguilar. Reproduced by permission.

A Visual Gratitude Journal

If you're visually inclined, and want an alternative to writing a gratitude journal, try an app called 365 Gratitude to capture an image each day of something you're grateful for. I did this one year and quickly found myself literally looking for something every day because I wanted to fulfill my assignment. I often found that thing to be grateful for before I'd left the house in the morning—and then all day I'd think, *Maybe I should take a photo of this and use that instead?* The result was an abundance of gratitude, every day. It became a habit.

From *The Onward Workbook: Daily Activities to Cultivate Your Emotional Resilience and Thrive* by Elena Aguilar. Copyright © 2018 by Elena Aguilar. Reproduced by permission.

Everyone I'm Grateful For

On this page, write the names of everyone you're grateful for. Include people from your past and people you don't know but who have contributed to your life. Include pets if you wish. Use colors if you want, or write names in different sizes. How many names can you fit on this page?

A Flurry of Appreciations

This week, set a goal to share a certain number of appreciations for those with whom you work. This could include students, their parents, colleagues, supervisors, and so on. Set an ambitious goal right here:

Then, go about offering them. Send emails and text messages, offer them in person, even make some anonymously—leave notes on people's desks or doors. See how it feels to make specific appreciations ("Thank you for helping me prepare sub plans when I was sick last week") and general ones ("I'm so grateful that you're in my life").

At the end of the week, reflect on this experience.

How did it feel? Did any part of this experience surprise you?

How did others react to your appreciations?

From *The Onward Workbook: Daily Activities to Cultivate Your Emotional Resilience and Thrive* by Elena Aguilar. Copyright © 2018 by Elena Aguilar. Reproduced by permission.

Which offerings of appreciation felt especially good?

What did you learn about yourself?

From *The Onward Workbook: Daily Activities to Cultivate Your Emotional Resilience and Thrive* by Elena Aguilar. Copyright © 2018 by Elena Aguilar. Reproduced by permission.

Honoring the Ancestors

In many cultures around the world, there are practices to honor the ancestors. These are ways to acknowledge those who have gone before and to express appreciation for, at the very least, the gift of life. In many of these traditions, there's a distinction made between the act of honoring the ancestors and approving of their actions—because most likely, we all have family members whose actions may have been, at times, less than noble. Honoring the ancestors can involve extending appreciations or can simply be a recognition that they existed.

If you want, you can also practice retroactive compassion for them—considering that they may have tried to do their best, given who they were, where they were, and what they had available to them. This doesn't mean that you condone their behaviors. It simply means that you try to expand your sense of who they were beyond specific actions they may have taken.

Having a sense of our ancestors and appreciating aspects of who they were can contribute to our resilience. We can cultivate a sense of connection to others, to other communities, and to the struggles of those who went before us.

How could you honor your ancestors?

One practice found in many cultures is to say your name and their names aloud. Here's what this sounds like for me: "Elena, daughter of Linda and Gilbert, granddaughter of Lil and Frank and Adelia and Azarias, great granddaughter of Tsyvia and Harry, of Yochewet and Fissel, and of . . ."

Say first names and last names if you want, or just first names—whatever makes you feel connected to these people who went before.

Could you find and display photos of your ancestors? Or create an altar space where you could display a photo and perhaps some objects that belonged to them or that they enjoyed?

You can also honor your ancestors by learning more about them: Learn about the cultural groups to which they belonged; travel to the regions from which they came. Although many people may not know exactly to which cultural groups they belong, many do have a general sense.

As you learn about your ancestors and their cultures, what can you appreciate? Appreciation is a way of honoring who they were.

What other ideas do you have about how you can honor your ancestors? Jot down some ideas and reflections here.

From *The Onward Workbook: Daily Activities to Cultivate Your Emotional Resilience and Thrive* by Elena Aguilar. Copyright © 2018 by Elena Aguilar. Reproduced by permission.

Deep Gratitude

A desire to kneel down sometimes pulses through my body, or rather it is as if my body has been meant and made for the act of kneeling. Sometimes, in moments of deep gratitude, kneeling down becomes an overwhelming urge, head deeply bowed, hands before my face.

ETTY HILLESUM

What makes you feel the kind of deep gratitude that Etty Hillesum describes?

Describe a time when you felt this kind of gratitude. Where were you? Who were you with? What happened? How did you feel physically? What did you do to express your gratitude?

How does it feel to remember that moment of deep gratitude?

The Power of the Positive Phone Call Home

In 2012, I published the following article on Edutopia, where I frequently blog. It has become one of the most widely read articles on the site and continues to resonate with readers. If you are not a teacher, you can still implement these ideas—you might just be sending a note of appreciation to someone who cares for the person you supervise. One former principal I know used to send letters to her teacher's partners and parents at the end of every school year sharing her appreciation. Think about how you might adapt these ideas to your context.

The Power of the Positive Phone Call Home

When I first started teaching and was overwhelmed by the demands and complexity of the job, my survival strategy was simply to take all the advice that came my way and implement it. So when my wise mentor suggested that after the first day of school I call all of my second graders' parents, I did so.

In spite of my exhaustion, I called each family and introduced myself. I asked a few questions about their child. I said that their kid had had a good first day. I said I looked forward to working together.

Throughout that year, and the years that followed, I continued this practice—I had an intuitive feeling that it was key: The positive phone call home. After the first days, as soon as I'd identified the kids who might be challenging, I made it a goal to call home with positive news every week. I'd share this goal with my students, greeting them at the door with something like: "I'm so excited to see you this morning, Oscar! I am going to be watching you really closely today to find some good news to share with your mom this evening. I can't wait to call her and tell her what a good day you had!"

When I taught middle school, this strategy made the difference between an unmanageable group of kids and an easy group. You'd be surprised, perhaps, how desperately an eighth-grade boy wants his mom (or dad or grandma or pastor) to get a positive call home. On the first day of school I'd give students a survey that included this question, "Who would you like me to call when I have good news to share about how you're doing in my class? You're welcome to list up to five people and please let them know I might call—even tonight or tomorrow!"

First, I'd call parents of the kids who I knew would be challenging, those I suspected rarely got positive calls. When an adult answered the phone, I'd say, all in one long breath, "Hi Mrs. _____? I'm calling from _____ Middle School with great news about your son, _____. Can I share this news?" If I didn't immediately blurt out the "great news" pieces, sometimes they'd hang up on me or I'd hear a long anxious silence.

Some of these kids were difficult, extremely difficult. However, I was always able to find something sincerely positive about what he or she had done. As the days followed, I kept calling—"I just wanted to share that today when _____ came into my class he said 'good morning' to me and opened his notebook right away. I knew we'd have a good day!" Sometimes I'd stop in the middle of class and in front of all the students I'd call a parent. The kids *loved* that. They started begging for me to call their parent too. It was the first choice of reward for good behavior—"just call my mama and tell her I did good today."

What shocked and saddened me were the parents who would say, "I don't think anyone has ever called me from school with anything positive about my child." I occasionally heard soft sobbing during these calls.

I'd first used this phone call thing as a strategy for managing behavior and building partnerships and it worked. However, after ten years of teaching I became a parent and my feelings shifted into some other universe. As a parent, I now can't think of anything more I want a teacher to do—just recognize what my boy is doing well, when he's trying, when he's learning, when his behavior is shifting, and share those observations with me.

I know how many hours teachers work. And I also know that a phone call can take three minutes. If every teacher allocated 15 minutes a day to calling parents with good news, the impact could be tremendous. In the long list of priorities for teachers, communicating good news is usually not at the top. But try it—just for a week—try calling the parents of a few kids (and maybe not *just* the challenging ones—they all need and deserve these calls) and see what happens. The ripple effects for the kid, the class, and the teacher might be transformational.

Exploring Attitudes Around Celebration

These prompts will help you explore the beliefs and attitudes you hold around celebrations and, in particular, celebrating your own accomplishments.

When you were a child, how did you see others celebrate? How did they celebrate or acknowledge the accomplishments of other people as well as their own?

What values did your family of origin hold around celebration—both celebrating others and oneself?

When you accomplish something big—such as graduating from a program, getting a new job, or a personal success—how do you want to be acknowledged? How do you acknowledge yourself?

What were you taught about modesty and humility growing up? How did you see others reacting when someone talked about his or her accomplishments or strengths?

From *The Onward Workbook: Daily Activities to Cultivate Your Emotional Resilience and Thrive* by Elena Aguilar. Copyright © 2018 by Elena Aguilar. Reproduced by permission.

Talk About People Behind Their Backs

The only reason to talk about people behind their backs is if you're singing their praises. Today, share with others what you appreciate about individual students, colleagues, and supervisors. Be specific when talking about what you appreciate and name the actions they take that you are grateful for. You may need to go out of your way a little—for example, stop your principal in the hall and tell him how much you have been appreciating your assistant principal this year, how this AP has ironed out some key systems at school that are making your daily life much easier.

Be careful that there's no chance that this can slip into gossip or talking negatively about someone. If you share that you are loving one of your new students, and a colleague starts saying something like, "Well, that wasn't my experience of her at all; in fact, when she was my student . . .," feel free to stop your colleague right there in the middle of the sentence and say, "Maybe at some other point we can talk about how you experienced her. Today I'm just singing the praises of the people in my life. Is there anyone you're feeling grateful for today?"

Now go. Talk beautifully about others behind their backs. And at the end of the day, capture your reflections on this experience.

How did this exercise feel? What was challenging? What did you enjoy?

From *The Onward Workbook: Daily Activities to Cultivate Your Emotional Resilience and Thrive* by Elena Aguilar. Copyright © 2018 by Elena Aguilar. Reproduced by permission.

One Little Thought: My Life Is Very Blessed

In his book *Awakening Joy* (2010), James Baraz offers a simple exercise to help us increase our gratitude. He suggests that each time we find ourselves worrying or complaining, we add this phrase to the end of the thought: *and my life is really very blessed.* For example, I may complain about having to do yard duty before school, but I can remind myself that my life is really very blessed.

Try this today. When you find yourself feeling frustrated, annoyed, or challenged, see what happens if you add *and my life is really very blessed* to your thought. At the end of the day, jot down a short reflection on what you noticed.

The Heartbreak of Teaching

Small wonder, then, that teaching tugs at the heart, opens the heart, even breaks the heart—and the more one loves teaching, the more heartbreaking it can be. The courage to teach is the courage to keep one's heart open in those very moments when the heart is asked to hold more than it is able.

PARKER PALMER

In your life as an educator, when has your heart been asked to hold more than it is able? When, during your teaching career, has your heart been broken?

From where do you draw the courage to keep your heart open?

A Gratitude Letter

Select one person you feel grateful for (living or dead) and write a letter appreciating the ways that he or she has enriched your life. If you can, read it to the person face-to-face. In addition to the people who may have just come to mind, you could also write a letter to a former student, a colleague, a mentor, or a teacher you had as a child.

What Sets Your Soul on Fire?

A couple years ago, a friend shared this quote (attribution unknown):

Be fearless in the pursuit of what sets your soul on fire.

I loved the power of these words; I loved how reading the words made me feel. I wrote the quote in purple marker on a piece of paper and posted it above my desk, where I'm contemplating it right now. If this quote resonates for you, you might want to do the same—print these words and let them find a place to perch and talk to you.

Reflect

What comes to mind when you read these words?

What sets your soul on fire?

Where does your soul feel on fire?

From *The Onward Workbook: Daily Activities to Cultivate Your Emotional Resilience and Thrive* by Elena Aguilar. Copyright © 2018 by Elena Aguilar. Reproduced by permission.

What dampens your soul?

Which fears arise when you think about pursuing those things that set your soul on fire?

How can you manage those fears?

What would it be like to spend the majority of your life doing something that sets your soul on fire?

Enlisting an Accountability Buddy

Find a friend who wants to commit to emailing back and forth every day—or a few times a week—to share what you're grateful for. Some of us feel more motivated and accountable if we have an audience. Be a buddy to each other to listen to and share what you're grateful for.

Time Traveling to Deliver Appreciations

Here is a time-traveling machine: I am offering it to you—just reach out your hand and grab it. Now, jump in, buckle up, and travel back to any time when you wish you had appreciated someone, or perhaps when you'd wanted to offer another appreciation.

There are many moments in my life when I wish I'd appreciated someone; or I now recognize that something that person did, which at the time I didn't appreciate, was actually a gift. I wish I could go back and say, "Thank you for giving me that hard feedback" or "Thank you for being my friend."

In the space here, plan your course of time travel. Write the names of the people you'd like to thank. What year(s) do you need to travel to? What will you say? And once you have a plan, visualize yourself doing this.

What are you grateful for today? Decorate the letters of GRATITUDE if you want, and then add words, phrases, and images for things you are grateful for that are represented by each letter.

G
R
A
T
I
T
U
D
E

From *The Onward Workbook: Daily Activities to Cultivate Your Emotional Resilience and Thrive* by Elena Aguilar. Copyright © 2018 by Elena Aguilar. Reproduced by permission.

What's at Risk?

And the day came when the risk to remain tight in a bud was more painful than the risk it took to blossom.

ANAÏS NIN

In what ways have you lived tight in a bud? How have you held back from being your full, expansive, and authentic self?

What have been the unintended consequences of living tight in a bud—of not fully expressing yourself or fully being yourself?

What risk do you run from continuing to live tight in a bud, of not blossoming?

What holds you back from being who you are and offering what you have to offer?

Who in your life would appreciate it if you would blossom into your authentic, expansive, full self? What words of appreciation might they say?

From *The Onward Workbook: Daily Activities to Cultivate Your Emotional Resilience and Thrive* by Elena Aguilar. Copyright © 2018 by Elena Aguilar. Reproduced by permission.

Awe Boosts Your Immune System

Feeling awe is good for your physical health. Researchers[1] have linked positive emotions—especially the awe we feel when touched by the beauty of nature, art, and spirituality—with lower levels of inflammatory cytokines, proteins that signal the immune system to work harder. People who experienced awe more frequently in their daily lives showed lower tissue levels of interleukin-6, an inflammatory cytokine associated with heart disease risk. Remarkably, awe predicted lower levels of interleukin-6 more than other positive emotions, including joy, contentment, and amusement.

Part of the experience of awe is a sense of smallness, not the kind associated with shame or self-doubt, but rather the sense that we are connected to others or something bigger, or that the world is much larger than we'd imagined. This was definitely how I felt when I stood at the edge of the Grand Canyon. This sense of awe can also help us feel as if our own concerns are less overwhelming, and it can evoke feelings of curiosity and wonder.

Take a moment to do a quick brainstorm. Where might you immerse yourself in natural beauty, live music, art, or spirituality—somewhere that might summon forth a feeling of awe? List in the space here as many places as you can think of.

These are some of mine:

- Hiking in the redwoods
- Listening to my son play drums
- Reading poetry

Now put a star next to the two that you most want to try. Plan a time to do these things and put it on your calendar. Really. Right now!

---

[1] Stellar, J. E., N. John-Henderson, C. L. Anderson, A. M. Gordon, G. D. McNeil, and D. Keltner. "Positive Affect and Markers of Inflammation: Discrete Positive Emotions Predict Lower Levels of Inflammatory Cytokines." *Emotion*, 2015, *15*(2), 129–133.

From *The Onward Workbook: Daily Activities to Cultivate Your Emotional Resilience and Thrive* by Elena Aguilar. Copyright © 2018 by Elena Aguilar. Reproduced by permission.

Strengthen a Friendship

Perhaps in the course of this chapter, you've found yourself appreciating someone in your life who is an acquaintance or a friend with whom you'd like to be closer. Strong friendships are key to resilience. And they make our life so much richer.

Is there an acquaintance or colleague who could be a close friend? Is there a friend whom you haven't seen much lately or from whom you have become distanced? Identify one or two people with whom you'd like to feel closer.

Now, create a plan. What could you do to strengthen these connections? This will most likely entail taking a risk—reaching out to someone, inviting connection—so be mindful of the feelings that surface. Use the emotional self-awareness you've been cultivating in this book to help you take a risk—to ask someone if he or she wants to get together and do something, to share a personal story, to connect.

Recently, I decided to follow this advice I'm giving you. I decided to be direct (this feels most comfortable to me; I'm a rather direct person), and I said to an acquaintance, "We've known each other for a couple of years. I really like you, and I want to be your friend." Yes, I felt as though I was six years old when I said, "I want to be your friend," but it felt authentic. I was nervous. I was aware that I was afraid of being rejected, but I didn't really care. The huge smile that lit up her face when I said this was the affirmation I needed. She said, "I would *love* that!" And then she jumped out of her chair and hugged me.

What could you do to strengthen or cultivate a friendship? When could you do it?

From *The Onward Workbook: Daily Activities to Cultivate Your Emotional Resilience and Thrive* by Elena Aguilar. Copyright © 2018 by Elena Aguilar. Reproduced by permission.

The Awe Narrative

What experiences in your life have most filled you with a sense of wonder and inspiration? A hike through a misty forest? Your child's first steps? Seeing the stars on a dark night? A celebration? The simple act of writing about awe can be very powerful.

Write about a personal experience of awe in as much detail as possible. Recall the experience in vivid detail and conjure up the feelings you had. This may be especially useful when you're feeling emotionally worn down. Even just a brief recollection of an awe-inducing experience from your past may remind you that the world can be a magical place.

Movie Time!

Even if you're stuck at home, awe can be found on your computer screen: You can find nature videos, recordings of speeches and performances, and so much more that can induce feelings of awe.

My favorite source of digital awe is *Planet Earth,* a TV series produced by the BBC. *Planet Earth* came out in 2006 and was followed by *Planet Earth II* in 2016. Both of these are stunning nature documentaries that you can watch over and over.

If you want a short video to watch about the natural world that might evoke awe in you, look up *Fantastic Fungi—the Forbidden Fruit.*

What kinds of videos stir up feelings of awe in you? Make a list of a few of your favorites. Ask your friends and colleagues to contribute: "What have you watched lately that has evoked in you a feeling of awe?" Save this list and come back to it on one of those days when you need a quick boost of awe.

Live as If You Liked Yourself

Live as if you liked yourself, and it may happen.
MARGE PIERCY

In the morning, reflect:

How would you live as if you liked yourself? What would that mean to you?

What could you do today to reflect self-appreciation?

Write Marge Piercy's quote on a piece of paper or a sticky note and take it to work with you today. Put it somewhere you'll see it.

In the evening, reflect:

Was there a moment during the day when you consciously thought, *I'm going to live as if I liked myself right now*? What happened? What did you do?

How did it feel to hold this notion of self-appreciation in mind today? Did you notice any difference in your thoughts, feelings, or behaviors?

What would it take for you to live as though you liked yourself?

Thank You, Elbows

Your body does so much for you and probably rarely receives appreciation. Lie down, close your eyes, and go from head to toe (or toe to head) thanking your body for what it does for you. Speak directly to it, being specific and kind. For example, say *Thank you, ankles, for connecting my feet to my legs, for moving so smoothly.* Give some love to the parts of your body that you rarely think about—perhaps the ligaments that connect your kneecap to your leg bones or the soles of your feet or your kidneys. At no point are you allowed to be mean to your body or shame it or be critical of it. You can only offer it gratitude and appreciation.

From *The Onward Workbook: Daily Activities to Cultivate Your Emotional Resilience and Thrive* by Elena Aguilar. Copyright © 2018 by Elena Aguilar. Reproduced by permission.

Capture Awe in Nature

Over the next week or two, every time you are outside, photograph images of nature that are awe inspiring. The twist on this activity is to look for tiny things: A new blade of grass coming out of damp soil, a bee on a flower, the streaks of color in the sky at dawn. You don't need a macro lens for this—just apply the concept of looking at little things. Of course, if possible, you could take a field trip to a place of great beauty—a park or a natural body of water—and you'd have even more opportunities.

Each time you notice a natural element of beauty, take a photo. After a period of time, organize your photos into an album and watch a slide show of them. Share your slide show with colleagues.

My Yearbook Page

In some yearbooks, each high school senior gets a page on which to leave a message. Select a quote that captures your feelings about this year; it could be a quote from a poem, movie, song, or anywhere. Then write a message to your friends and colleagues about the year—perhaps what you learned, what you're grateful for, or what you wish for others.

Draw a cartoony headshot of yourself here, in this imaginary yearbook page.

My quote:

My message:

I Would Like to Be More Grateful For . . .

The Chilean poet Pablo Neruda is famous for his collection of odes, many of which were collected in a book called *Odes to Common Things.*

What could you be more grateful for? Which common, mundane things? Write as many things as you can think of—without guilt or shame, but with awareness that perhaps you've never appreciated your elbows very much, or the mail carrier, or your whiteboard markers.

An Awe Walk

Travel can be a great source of awe, but awe can also be found closer to home. Take a walk somewhere that has the potential to inspire you. This could be somewhere in nature, an urban setting, or an indoor location, such as a museum. Approach your surroundings with fresh eyes, as if you were seeing them for the first time. Pay attention to the colors and sounds around you. Imagine you are showing them to a visitor or a very young child who has never seen such things before.

From *The Onward Workbook: Daily Activities to Cultivate Your Emotional Resilience and Thrive* by Elena Aguilar. Copyright © 2018 by Elena Aguilar. Reproduced by permission.

The heart creates an electromagnetic field that expands up to five feet outside of the body. Its electrical field is 60 times stronger in amplitude than that of the brain. Studies show that when people cultivate positive feelings, the heart's electrical frequency changes, and its waves become smoother and more consistent, whereas anxiety waves are shorter and less organized. Though most positive feelings were capable of affecting the heart in this way, researchers found that feelings of gratitude changed the heart's rhythm more easily and quickly than any of the others.

What's more is that this frequency can entrain other hearts and brains. It's likely that the heart with the smoothest, most consistent frequency will be the heart that other people sync up with. This means that if you're cultivating gratitude, it's likely that you're changing the feeling state of those around you.

Even when we aren't aware of it, our heart is communicating with those around us. Intuitively, this makes sense. We talk about having a "heart-to-heart" with someone when we're engaged in a sincere conversation. Researchers have found that hearts between lovers sync even when the people aren't touching or conversing.

What this research suggests is that you can change the world for the better just by having feelings of gratitude. Your body talks to others through its feelings. Of course, there's also an implication here for whom you spend your time with and what their hearts are communicating, but today, focus on your own heart.

As you imagine the day ahead of you, whose heart do you want to connect with? Draw a sketch of that here—of your heart reaching out and connecting with someone else's heart. Drawing will make it more likely that you'll remember to hold this intention when you're near the person.

A Letter to Awe and Wonder

What would you like to say to awe and wonder? Write a letter to awe and wonder and ask whatever you'd like and say what you have to say.

Here's the first line of my letter to awe and wonder: *I am sorry that I haven't recognized you when you showed up so many times in my life because I was distracted, preoccupied, or unfocused. I'm so grateful that you've persistently made appearances in my life. From now on, I pledge to acknowledge your presence more often and to pause and take you in when you're here.*

Artistic Depictions of Awe

Go to your preferred online search engine and look for images of awe—or another term that reflects awe, such as wonder or reverence.

See what comes up, and then search for "depictions of awe in art."

Look closely at a few of those images. Sit with them and spend some time getting to know them. Pay attention to how they make you feel and what thoughts go through your mind.

Reflect

What do you notice in the images that come up?

What have you learned about awe through doing this exploration?

How did this exploration help you understand your own experience of awe?

If you'd like, print out one (or more) of the images that particularly speak to you and stick them in here.

Destination Postcard: Trust

What would it look and sound like if you were a deeply trusting person? Draw a picture of yourself with thought bubbles and labels to depict yourself as a trusting person. If you'd like, draw this you at work, surrounded by kids and colleagues. How might you be in that space?

Chapter Reflection

What were your biggest takeaways from this chapter?

Of the different activities in this chapter, which were most useful?

Which activities would you like to revisit periodically? How might you get that habit going?

What implications do the ideas in this chapter have for the work you do?

From *The Onward Workbook: Daily Activities to Cultivate Your Emotional Resilience and Thrive* by Elena Aguilar. Copyright © 2018 by Elena Aguilar. Reproduced by permission.

Conclusion

The following activities will help you reflect on all your learning this year and identify next steps to fill your resilience reservoir.

Reflecting on a Year of Cultivating Resilience

Take some time to capture a written reflection on this learning.

Which of the activities in this book, or the ideas shared in *Onward,* had the biggest impact on you?

Which activities helped you the most when you were having a difficult moment?

In which habit or disposition do you think you made the greatest growth?

Think of a moment that was challenging during the last year. How did your resilience strategies help you in that moment?

How do you feel your life is different based on the learning you did in this book?

Symbols and Metaphors for Dispositions

Now that you've engaged in some exploration of the 12 dispositions of resilient educators, identify some symbols or metaphors that represent these dispositions for you. Consider the natural world as a resource for symbols—animals, plants, and landforms as well as myths and legends. Draw a sketch of the symbol that resonates most for you, or paste an image into the space here.

Disposition	Symbol or Metaphor
Purposefulness	
Acceptance	

(continued)

Optimism	
Empathy	

Humor	
Positive Self-Perception	

(*continued*)

Empowerment	
Perspective	

From *The Onward Workbook: Daily Activities to Cultivate Your Emotional Resilience and Thrive* by Elena Aguilar. Copyright © 2018 by Elena Aguilar. Reproduced by permission.

Curiosity	
Courage	

(*continued*)

Perseverance	
Trust	

Choosing Dispositions

We can choose how we want to feel and which disposition we want to express—but we often forget that we have this choice. This exercise invites you to state your intentions, which improves the likelihood that you'll make a choice to feel a certain way. Complete the following sentence stems.

I choose to feel purposeful when . . .

I choose to be accepting about . . .

I choose to feel optimistic about . . .

I choose to feel empathy for . . .

I choose to find humor in . . .

I choose to hold a positive self-perception about myself when . . .

I choose to feel empowered about . . .

I choose to find perspective about . . .

I choose to cultivate curiosity about . . .

I choose to have courage when . . .

I choose to persevere when . . .

I choose to feel trusting in . . .

From *The Onward Workbook: Daily Activities to Cultivate Your Emotional Resilience and Thrive* by Elena Aguilar. Copyright © 2018 by Elena Aguilar. Reproduced by permission.

Create a Poster

Create a poster with your top 20 ways to fuel your own resilience. (See http://www .fullcupthirstyspirit.com/includes/50-ways-to-take-a-break-printable.jpg for an example of what this could look like.) You could also do this as a collage and collect images and words that reflect your learning.

Which of the strategies in this workbook had the greatest impact on your resilience? What can you draw to represent those? Which words could you include?

Take a photo of your poster and glue it in here.

Now What?

Our reservoirs of resilience will always need tending to and filling. Life will inevitably bring change, and change can be stressful—so the journey doesn't stop here.

What do you feel is next for you on your journey to cultivate your resilience as an educator?

What learning do you want to do next?

Which changes might you need to make in your life? How might your life be different if you make these changes?

How might you help others cultivate their resilience based on what you've learned?

From *The Onward Workbook: Daily Activities to Cultivate Your Emotional Resilience and Thrive* by Elena Aguilar. Copyright © 2018 by Elena Aguilar. Reproduced by permission.

APPENDIX

Resources for Further Learning

The following is not intended to be an extensive list, but rather a selection of places that you might begin to continue your learning. Please consider buying books from a local independent bookstore. They can usually order anything you want. Local bookstores are essential resources for resilience! Spend a couple hours in one, get to know the sellers, and you'll find out why—if you haven't already made this discovery.

General

Books

Goldstein, Dana. *The Teacher Wars: A History of America's Most Embattled Profession.* New York, NY: Doubleday, 2014.

    Whether you're a new or veteran teacher, this fascinating and thorough book provides a rich historical context for those of us in the field of education.

Intrator, Sam, and Megan Scribner. *Teaching with Fire: Poetry That Sustains the Courage to Teach.* San Francisco, CA: Jossey-Bass, 2003.

    _____. *Leading from Within: Poetry That Sustains the Courage to Lead.* San Francisco, CA: Jossey-Bass, 2007.

    _____. *Teaching with Heart: Poetry That Speaks to the Courage to Teach.* San Francisco, CA: Jossey-Bass, 2014.

    These three books have the best collection of poems that speak to every habit and disposition in *Onward.* They're essential additional resources on the journey to resilience.

Other

- The *On Being* podcast (www.onbeing.org), with Krista Tippet, is an exploration of the "big questions of meaning." This is my favorite podcast, and I always discover new ideas, people, and books through it, as well as a lot of inspiration and hope.
- *Greater Good Magazine* (https://greatergood.berkeley.edu/) is an invaluable resource for information, news, activities, and so much more.

Chapter 1: Know Yourself

Books

Block, Peter. *The Answer to How Is Yes.* San Francisco, CA: Berrett-Koehler, 2002.

Brown, Brené. *Daring Greatly.* New York, NY: Portfolio, 2015.

Buckingham, Marcus, and Donald Clifton. *Now, Discover Your Strengths.* New York, NY: Free Press, 2001.

Cain, Susan. *Quiet.* New York, NY: Random House, 2013.

McKee, Annie, Richard Boyatzis, and Frances Johnston. *Becoming a Resonant Leader: Develop Your Emotional Intelligence, Renew Your Relationships, Sustain Your Effectiveness.* Cambridge, MA: Harvard Business Review, 2008.

Seligman, Martin. *Authentic Happiness.* New York, NY: Atria, 2002.

Other

- CliftonStrengths: www.gallupstrengthscenter.com/home/en-us/strengthsfinder
- Free Myers-Briggs test: www.16personalities.com
- Free Myers-Briggs test: www.humanmetrics.com
- "The Holstee Manifesto." Google it. Read it. Post it somewhere that you can see every day.

Chapter 2: Understand Emotions

Books

Bradberry, Travis, and Jean Greaves. *Emotional Intelligence 2.0.* San Diego, CA: TalentSmart, 2009.

Brown, Brené. *The Gifts of Imperfection.* Center City, MN: Hazelden, 2010.

Foster, Rick, and Greg Hicks. *How We Choose to Be Happy.* New York, NY: Perigree, 2004.

Goleman, Daniel, Richard Boyatzis, and Annie McKee. *Primal Leadership.* Boston, MA: Harvard University Press, 2002.

Lyubomirsky, Sonja. *The How of Happiness.* New York, NY: Penguin, 2007.

———. *The Myths of Happiness: What Should Make You Happy, but Doesn't, What Shouldn't Make You Happy, but Does.* New York, NY: Penguin, 2013.

Olivo, Erin. *Wise Mind Living.* Boulder, CO: Sounds True, 2014.

Rosenberg, Marshall. *Nonviolent Communication.* Encinitas, CA: PuddleDancer Press, 2003.

Seligman, Martin. *Flourish: A Visionary New Understanding of Happiness and Well-Being.* New York, NY: Simon & Schuster, 2012.

Other

- Dr. Martin Seligman's website: www.authentichappiness.sas.upenn.edu, has a number of free quizzes you can take to build self-awareness.
- Here's an emotional Intelligence Quiz that I really like: greatergood.berkeley.edu/quizzes/take_quiz/ei_quiz
- The Yale Center for Emotional Intelligence has created a very useful tool called RULER: http://ei.yale .edu/ruler/ RULER is an acronym that stands for **r**ecognition, **u**nderstanding, **l**abeling, **e**xpressing, and **r**egulating emotions. It is a research-based approach for integrating social and emotional learning in schools.

TED Talks

- Brené Brown, "The Power of Vulnerability"
- Neil Hughes, "Walking on Custard: How Physics Helps Anxious Humans"
- Alison Ledgerwood, "Getting Stuck in the Negatives (and How to Get Unstuck)"
- Kelly McGonigal, "How to Make Stress Your Friend"
- Andrew Solomon, "Depression, the Secret We Share"
- Guy Winch, "How to Practice Emotional First Aid"

Chapter 3: Tell Empowering Stories

Books

Frankl, Viktor. *Man's Search for Meaning.* Boston, MA: Beacon Press, 1959.

Haidt, Jonathan. *The Happiness Hypothesis: Finding Modern Truth in Ancient Wisdom.* New York, NY: Basic Books, 2006.

Hutchens, David. *Circle of the 9 Muses: A Storytelling Field Guide for Innovators and Meaning Makers.* Hoboken, NJ: Wiley, 2015.

Kegan, Robert, and Lisa Lahey. *Immunity to Change.* Cambridge, MA: Harvard Business Press, 2009.

Seligman, Martin. *Learned Optimism.* New York, NY: Vintage Books, 2006.

Solnit, Rebecca. *Hope in the Dark* (2nd ed.). Chicago, IL: Haymarket Books, 2016.

TED Talk

- Chimamanda Ngozi Adichie, "The Danger of a Single Story"

Chapter 4: Build Community

Abrams, Jennifer. *Having Hard Conversations.* Thousand Oaks, CA: Corwin, 2009.

Abrams, Jennifer, and Valerie A. von Frank. *The Multigenerational Workplace.* Thousand Oaks, CA: Corwin, 2014.

Coates, Ta-Nehesi. *Between the World and Me.* New York, NY: Spiegel & Grau, 2015.

Delpit, Lisa. *The Skin That We Speak: Thoughts on Language and Culture in the Classroom*. New York, NY: New Press, 2002.

DiAngelo, Robin. *What Does It Mean to Be White? Developing White Racial Literacy* (rev. ed.). New York, NY: Peter Lang, 2016.

Fleischman, Paul. *Seedfolks*. New York, NY: Harper Trophy, 2004.

> A beautifully written short story that's incredibly inspiring.

Kegan, Robert, and Lisa Lahey. *How the Way We Talk Can Change the Way We Work: Seven Languages for Transformation*. San Francisco, CA: Jossey-Bass, 2001.

Schein, Edgar. *Humble Inquiry: The Gentle Art of Asking Instead of Telling*. San Francisco, CA: Berrett-Koehler, 2013.

Scott, Susan. *Fierce Conversations*. New York, NY: Berkley, 2002.

Showkeir, Jamie, and Maren Showkeir. *Authentic Conversations*. San Francisco, CA: Berrett-Koehler, 2008.

Tatum, Beverly D. *"Why Are All the Black Kids Sitting Together in the Cafeteria?" and Other Conversations About Race* (updated ed.). New York, NY: Basic Books, 2017.

Wheatley, Margaret. *Turning to One Another: Simple Conversations to Restore Hope to the Future*. San Francisco, CA: Berrett-Koehler, 2009.

Wise, Tim. *White Like Me: Reflections on Race from a Privileged Son*. Berkeley, CA: Soft Skull Press, 2008.

Chapter 5: Be Here Now

Books

Baraz, James. *Awakening Joy: Ten Steps to Happiness*. Berkeley, CA: Parallax Press, 2012.

Boorstein, Sylvia. *It's Easier Than You Think: The Buddhist Way to Happiness*. New York, NY: HarperCollins, 1997.

Dalai Lama, Desmond Tutu, and Douglas Abrams. *The Book of Joy*. New York, NY: Penguin Books, 2016.

Gunaratana, B. H. *Mindfulness in Plain English*. Somerville, MA: Wisdom Publications, 2002.

Hanson, Rick. *Hardwiring Happiness: The New Brain Science of Contentment, Calm, and Confidence*. New York, NY: Random House, 2013.

Hanson, Rick, and Richard Mendius. *Buddha's Brain: The Practical Neuroscience of Happiness, Love, and Wisdom*. Oakland, CA: New Harbinger, 2009.

Kornfield, Jack. *No Time Like the Present*. New York, NY: Atria Books, 2017.

Nhat Hanh, Thich. *How to Eat*. Berkeley, CA: Parallax Press, 2014.

———. *How to Walk*. Berkeley, CA: Parallax Press, 2015.

———. *Peace Is Every Step*. New York, NY: Bantam Books, 1992.

hooks, bell. *Teaching to Transgress: Education as the Practice of Freedom*. New York, NY: Routledge, 1994.

Rankine, Claudia. *Citizen*. Minneapolis, MN: Graywolf Press, 2014.

Srinivasan, Meena. *Teach, Breathe, Learn*. Berkeley, CA: Parallax Press, 2014.

Steele, Claude. *Whistling Vivaldi and Other Clues to How Stereotypes Affect Us*. New York, NY: Norton, 2010.

Tolle, Eckhart. *The Power of Now*. Novato, CA: New World Library, 2004.

Audio Recordings

- Rick Hanson, *Meditations for Happiness: Rewire Your Brain for Lasting Contentment and Peace*
- Rick Hanson and Richard Mendius, *Meditations to Change Your Brain: Rewire Your Neural Pathways to Transform Your Life*

Other

- Mindful Schools (www.mindfulschools.org) is a fantastic resource for educators that offers online and in-person courses.
- A wealth of podcasts on mindfulness, meditation, compassion, and more is available at www.beherenownetwork.com
- The Heart Wisdom podcast, with Jack Kornfield, is my favorite podcast on Buddhist philosophy.
- Sounds True, www.soundstrue.com, is a multimedia publishing company that has podcasts, books, audiobooks, and much more.

Mindfulness Apps

- **Insight Timer** is one of the most popular free meditation apps out there. It features more than 4,000 guided meditations—on such topics as self-compassion, nature, and stress—from over 1,000 teachers, plus talks and podcasts. If you don't want to listen to a meditation, you can always set a timer and meditate to intermittent bells or calming ambient noise.
- With the **Aura** meditation app, every day you get a new, personalized, three-minute meditation. To personalize the experience, Aura initially asks about your age and how stressed, optimistic, and interested in mindfulness you are. The daily meditation that appears also depends on your mood. On Aura, you can also listen to relaxing sounds or try its Mindful Breather feature, where you synchronize your breath to an animated circle that gently expands and contracts.
- **Headspace** is a very popular app that is free to download, but to access all the lessons, you'll need to pay for a subscription. The guided meditations are based on Buddhist mindfulness, but are completely secular. Lots of people love this app. If you want guided meditations, this is a good option.

Chapter 6: Take Care of Yourself

Books

Blackburn, Elizabeth and Elissa Epel. *The Telomere Effect: A Revolutionary Approach to Living Younger, Healthier, Longer.* New York, NY: Grand Central Productions, 2017.

Buettner, Dan. *The Blue Zones of Happiness: Lessons from the World's Happiest People.* Washington, DC: National Geographic, 2017.

Medina, John. *Brain Rules: Twelve Principles for Surviving and Thriving at Work, Home, and School* (2nd ed.). Seattle, WA: Pear Press, 2014.

Pick, Marcelle. *Is It Me or My Adrenals?* New York, NY: Hay House, 2013.

Roach, Mary. *Gulp.* New York, NY: Norton, 2013.

Ross, Julia. *The Diet Cure.* New York, NY: Penguin, 2012.

Chapter 7: Focus On the Bright Spots

Books

Cooperrider, David L., and Diana Whitney. *Appreciative Inquiry: A Positive Revolution in Change.* San Francisco, CA: Berrett-Koehler, 2005.

Gottman, John. *The Seven Principles for Making Marriage Work.* New York, NY: Harmony Books, 2015.

> Gottman's research is applicable to making all kinds of relationships better—not just marriages.

Hammond, Sue A. *The Thin Book of Appreciative Inquiry.* Bend, OR: Thin Book, 1998.

Whitney, Diana, and Amananda Trosten-Bloom. *The Power of Appreciative Inquiry: A Practical Guide to Positive Change.* San Francisco, CA: Berrett-Koehler, 2010.

Websites

- For resources on appreciative inquiry: https://appreciativeinquiry.champlain.edu/
- A site that'll just make you feel good: www.1000awesomethings.com

Chapter 8: Cultivate Compassion

Books

Jinpa, Thupten. *A Fearless Heart: How the Courage to Be Compassionate Can Transform Our Lives.* New York, NY: Avery, 2015.

Manson, Mark. *The Subtle Art of Not Giving a F*ck.* New York, NY: HarperOne, 2016.

> If you care too much about what others think and you need compassion for yourself, then you'll find this an amusing read.

Neff, Kristin. *Self-Compassion: The Proven Power of Being Kind to Yourself.* New York, NY: HarperCollins, 2011.

> This is a more serious reflection on self-compassion.

Ricard, Matthieu. *Altruism: The Power of Compassion to Change Yourself and the World.* New York, NY: Little, Brown and Company, 2015.

Salzberg, Sharon. *Lovingkindness: The Revolutionary Art of Happiness.* Boulder, CO: Shambhala Press, 1995.

_____. *Real Happiness at Work: Meditations for Accomplishment, Achievement, and Peace.* New York, NY: Workman, 2014.

Sutton, Robert. *The Asshole Survival Guide: How to Deal with People Who Treat You Like Dirt.* Boston, MA: Houghton Mifflin Harcourt, 2017.

> If you have a hard time drawing boundaries with others, and if you work with difficult people, this is an insightful, wise, and useful resource.

Videos

- Amma and Dr. James Doty, "Conversations on Compassion with Amma"
- Paul Ekman, "The Roots of Empathy and Compassion"
- Thupten Jinpa, "The Science of Compassion: Origins, Measures, and Interventions"
- Dacher Keltner, "The Evolutionary Roots of Compassion"
- Daniel Siegel, "Interpersonal Neurobiology: Why Compassion Is Necessary for Humanity"

Chapter 9: Be a Learner

Books

Heyck-Merlin, Maia. *The Together Teacher*. San Francisco, CA: Jossey-Bass, 2012.

_____. *The Together Leader*. San Francisco, CA: Jossey-Bass, 2016.

Holmes, Jamie. *Nonsense: The Power of Not Knowing*. New York, NY: Crown, 2015.

Hubbard, Ruth, and Brenda Power. *The Art of Classroom Inquiry: A Handbook for Teacher Researchers*. Portsmouth, NH: Heinemann, 2003.

Leslie, Ian. *Curious: The Desire to Know and Why Your Future Depends on It*. New York, NY: Basic Books, 2014.

McGonigal, Jane. *Super Better: A Revolutionary Approach to Getting Stronger, Happier, Braver, and More Resilient*. London, England: HarperCollins, 2015.

It's also worth checking out McGonigal's 2010 TED Talk, "Gaming Can Make a Better World."

Newport, Cal. *Deep Work*. New York, NY: Grand Central Publishing, 2016.

Rock, David. *Your Brain at Work: Strategies for Overcoming Distraction, Regaining Focus, and Working Smarter All Day Long*. New York, NY: HarperCollins, 2009.

Chapter 10: Play and Create

Books

Barry, Lynda. *What Is*. Montreal, Canada: Drawn and Quarterly, 2008.

_____. *Syllabus*. Montreal, Canada: Drawn and Quarterly, 2014.

Brown, Brené. *Braving the Wilderness*. New York, NY: Random House, 2017.

Brown, Stuart. *Play: How It Shapes the Brain, Opens the Imagination, and Invigorates the Soul*. New York, NY: Penguin, 2009.

Cameron, Julia. *The Artist's Way* (25th anniv. ed.). New York, NY: Penguin Random House, 2016.

See also *The Artist's Way Workbook*. New York, NY: Penguin, 2006.

De Botton, Alain, and John Armstrong. *Art as Therapy*. New York, NY: Phaidon, 2013.

Edwards, Betty. *Drawing on the Right Side of the Brain* (4th ed.). New York, NY: Penguin, 2012.

Gilbert, Elizabeth. *Big Magic: Creative Living Beyond Fear.* New York, NY: Penguin Random House, 2016.

Kaufman, Scott, and Carolyn Gregoire. *Wired to Create: Unraveling the Mysteries of the Creative Mind.* New York, NY: Perigee, 2015.

Kleon, Austin. *Steal Like an Artist.* New York, NY: Workman, 2012.

Krahula, Beckah. *One Zentangle a Day: A 6-Week Course in Creative Drawing for Relaxation, Inspiration, and Fun.* Beverly, MA: Quarry Books, 2012.

Palmer, Parker. *The Courage to Teach* (20th anniv. ed.). San Francisco, CA: Jossey-Bass, 2017.

Movies

- *Cave of Dreams,* about prehistoric art
- "Power of Art—Picasso's Guernica": https://www.youtube.com/watch?v=tI4OABAP4Is
- *Waste Land,* about garbage pickers in Brazil
- *A Strong, Clear Vision,* about Maya Lin making the Vietnam Memorial

Other

- Sketchbook Skool (www.sketchbookskool.com) has really fun, engaging online courses; so does Skillshare (www.skillshare.com).
- Look for Neil Gaiman's 2012 commencement speech at Philadelphia's University of the Arts, "Make Good Art," on YouTube: https://youtu.be/plWexCID-kA
- "The Art of Emotional Healing" (https://www.expressiveartworkshops.com/). This site offers an extensive list of therapeutic and reflective art-related courses.

Chapter 11: Ride the Waves of Change

Books

Chödrön, Pema. *Comfortable with Uncertainty.* Boulder, CO: Shambhala Publications, 2002.

_____. *When Things Fall Apart* (20th anniv. ed.). Boulder, CO: Shambhala Publications, 2016.

Day, Laura. *Practical Intuition.* New York, NY: Broadway, 1996.

Duhigg, Charles. *The Power of Habit.* New York, NY: Random House, 2012.

Heath, Chip, and Dan Heath. *Switch: How to Change Things When Change Is Hard.* New York, NY: Broadway Books, 2010.

Horton, Myles, and Paulo Freire. In Brenda Bell, John Gaenta, and John Peters (Eds.), *We Make the Road by Walking: Conversations on Education and Social Change.* Philadelphia, PA: Temple University Press, 1990.

Kegan, Robert, and Lisa Lahey. *Immunity to Change.* Cambridge, MA: Harvard Business Press, 2009.

McGonigal, Kelly. *The Willpower Instinct: How Self-Control Works, Why It Matters, and What You Can Do to Get More of It.* New York, NY: Penguin Books, 2013.

Ryan, M. J. *How to Survive Change You Didn't Ask For.* San Francisco, CA: Red Wheel, 2009.

Sinek, Simon. *Start with Why: How Great Leaders Inspire Everyone to Take Action.* New York, NY: Penguin, 2011.

Thaler, Richard, and Cass Sunstein. *Nudge: Improving Decisions About Health, Wealth and Happiness.* New York, NY: Penguin, 2009.

Wheatley, Margaret. *Perseverance.* San Francisco, CA: Berrett-Koehler, 2010.

Chapter 12: Celebrate and Appreciate

Books

Emmons, Robert. *Thanks! How the New Science of Gratitude Can Make You Happier.* Boston, MA: Houghton Mifflin Harcourt, 2007.

Kaplan, Janice. *The Gratitude Diaries: How a Year Looking on the Bright Side Can Transform Your Life.* New York, NY: Dutton, 2017.

Loeb, Paul Rogat. *The Impossible Will Take a Little While.* New York, NY: Basic Books, 2004.

Pasricha, Neil. *The Book of Awesome.* New York, NY: Putnam, 2011.

Robbins, Mike. *Focus on the Good Stuff: The Power of Appreciation.* San Francisco, CA: Jossey-Bass, 2007.

Tippet, Krista. *Becoming Wise.* New York, NY: Penguin Press, 2016.

Other

- With the free app Gratitude 365 (gratitude365app.com) you can capture a photo a day that reflects what you're grateful for.

ABOUT THE AUTHOR

Elena Aguilar is the author of *The Art of Coaching* and *The Art of Coaching Teams*. She has also been a longtime contributor to *Edutopia* and *EdWeek*. She is the founder and president of Bright Morning Consulting, an educational consulting group that works around the world supporting educators to meet the needs of children. Bright Morning offers dozens of workshops each year where educators dive deep into the ideas presented in Elena's books. You can learn more about Bright Morning at www.brightmorningteam .com. Elena lives in Oakland, California, with her husband and son. When she's not writing, coaching, or teaching, she enjoys being in nature, reading fiction, making art, and traveling abroad.